Creative Management of Small
Public Libraries in the 21st Century

Creative Management of Small Public Libraries in the 21st Century

Edited by Carol Smallwood

ROWMAN & LITTLEFIELD
Lanham • Boulder • New York • London

Published by Rowman & Littlefield
A wholly owned subsidiary of The Rowman & Littlefield Publishing Group, Inc.
4501 Forbes Boulevard, Suite 200, Lanham, Maryland 20706
www.rowman.com

Unit A, Whitacre Mews, 26-34 Stannary Street, London SE11 4AB

British Library Cataloguing in Publication Information Available

Library of Congress Cataloging-in-Publication Data

Creative management of small public libraries in the 21st century / edited by Carol Smallwood.
pages cm
Includes bibliographical references and index.
ISBN 978-1-4422-4355-2 (cloth : alk. paper) — ISBN 978-1-4422-4356-9 (pbk. : alk. paper) — ISBN 978-1-4422-4357-6 (ebook)
1. Public libraries—United States—Administration. 2. Small libraries—United States—Administration. 3. Public libraries—Administration. 4. Small libraries—Administration. I. Smallwood, Carol, 1939–, editor.
Z678.C758 2014
025.1'97473—dc23
2014028355

∞™ The paper used in this publication meets the minimum requirements of American National Standard for Information Sciences Permanence of Paper for Printed Library Materials, ANSI/NISO Z39.48-1992.

Printed in the United States of America

Contents

Part Three: Management

Part Four: Technology

Part Five: Networking

Part Six: Fundraising

Foreword

The public library is a key part of the *global* marketplace of ideas. But ideas start locally and the success of the public library is built upon its recognition of and connection to community. The three pillars of library service—information, education, and entertainment—must reflect a local community's interests and sensibilities if that community is to fully embrace, sustain, and grow public library services.

Libraries have traditionally been valued for the contributions they make to the community; however, we know that the relationship between the community and the library is based more on reciprocity than a one-way transfer of value. Communities contribute to libraries through volunteerism, financial support, advocacy, and, in some cases, sweat equity. It is through those *shared* contributions that the library and the community co-create the most compelling, relevant, and valuable service.

If the library is to truly be embedded in the community, then its director, staff, and board must make customer relationships a number-one priority. Libraries serving populations with fewer than 25,000 residents have a unique opportunity to connect directly with the individuals and groups that comprise the community. These relationships provide the library with powerful insights into the needs and aspirations of the community as a whole and enable the library to develop a resonant strategy.

Creative Management of Small Public Libraries in the 21st Century provides the tools to lead a local public library with relevant and successful services. It shares a commonsense approach to providing a small (in staff size or budget) but mighty (in impact and outcome) public library service. By turning the service delivery team outward to the community with enthusiasm and positive energy, it is possible to achieve significant results. Many chapters summarize best practices that can serve as checklists for the novice library director or as a review for the more seasoned manager working through new responsibilities. Chapters are tactical, focusing on specific issues for managers such as performance evaluations, effective programming, or e-reader services. The content acknowledges the issue of time management in a small or rural public library as well as the challenges associated with managing Friends and volunteers. Readers of this warm and upbeat guide will know that they are not alone.

While most public libraries do not have the resources to satisfy customer expectations for instant gratification, ultra-convenience, and state-of-the-art technologies, the profession has always responded with top-notch customer service. The authors of the many chapters in *Creative Management of Small Public Libraries in the 21st Century* recognize that great public libraries move beyond customer service to meaningful customer relationships. I believe that this volume will make an important contribution to the literature by reminding us that public libraries transform communities of every size. In fact, never before has the role of the public library been a more crucial thread in the fabric of community life.

Sari Feldman,
executive director of Cuyahoga County Public Library in Ohio
and president-elect of the American Library Association, 2014–2015

Preface

Creative Management of Small Public Libraries in the 21st Century is an anthology addressing small public libraries as centers of communities with populations under 25,000, which comprises most of the public library systems in the United States. It contains a wide selection of topics from contributors with varied backgrounds, reflecting the diversity of small public libraries. The thirty-two chapters are arranged into the following parts: Staff, Programming, Management, Technology, Networking, Fundraising, and User Services.

The Library Services Act of 1956 (coming before the Library Services and Technology Act) was enacted in part to improve the role that public library services play in rural areas. Nongovernmental agencies have also recognized the important role they play in their communities; the Bill and Melinda Gates Foundation, for instance, has played an important part in securing public libraries' place as community computing centers.

Despite tight budgets and technological challenges, services in small and rural public libraries continue to serve and reach their communities: through creative management, small libraries prove their resilience and continued relevance. A general observation is the smaller the community, the more important these libraries are to their patrons.

Acknowledgments

My thanks to the thirty-six dedicated librarians who have shared with colleagues. It has been a pleasure working with these professionals dedicated to local community service. A special thanks to Lawrence Grieco, library director of Gilpin County Public Library, Black Hawk, Colorado, for suggesting this anthology and supplying the cover photo, and to Sari Feldman, ALA president-elect, for graciously writing the foreword. Thanks also to:

Linda Bostrom, Public Library Association, American Library Association

Donna Brice, vice president and president-elect of the Association for Rural and Small Libraries, Inc. and library director of the Eastern Lancaster County Library, New Holland, Pennsylvania

Vandella Brown, contributor to *Mentoring in Librarianship*

Lisa Fraser, services implementation coordinator, King County Library System, Washington

Vera Gubnitskaia, youth services manager, Orange County (Florida) Library System

Kerol Harrod, librarian, Denton Public Library, Denton, Texas

Valerie Hawkins, library reference specialist, American Library Association

Part One

Staff

Chapter One

Attitudes

Padma Polepeddi

My supervisory experience in public library branches serving communities with unique needs has taught me that it is important for all leaders to create positive work environments so staff can experience that they are working with you on a team rather than for you. When the leader of the team demonstrates genuine love and enjoyment for the service provided, the excitement catches on and staff begins to understand their value in the overall impact of the service. It is also important to establish open communication lines where everyone feels their voice is heard as that is the next step to building a positive relationship. Another factor that fosters positivity is acknowledging and celebrating staff contributions and treating them as valuable human capital. This is as important as providing direct input and coaching for performance inefficiencies that pave the way for an honest, open professional relationship in a working environment. Finally, humor in the workplace also helps in generating a positive attitude during times of stress and change.

TEAM SPIRIT

Team spirit starts with a sense of trust and shared responsibility where each staff member is contributing to the work at hand by taking responsibility for each of the tasks. Creating a work flow chart where staff members' tasks and responsibilities are outlined is the first step toward establishing expectations for team building. It is important for all staff to be aware of the responsibilities of their supervisor and each of their team members. This awareness builds a sense of importance regarding their role and the roles of each of the team members. It also helps the team not to view their roles as something merely fulfilling the basic expectations outlined for the job, but to see how it all fits into the bigger picture. It helps them to see the value of their contribution on a bigger scale toward the progression of the strategic goals outlined for the success and growth of the organization. It is also important for the leader of a team to demonstrate that he or she can jump in and take on the tasks of a team member in the absence of a team member as it builds trust and sends out a positive message that it is important to take care of each other during times of need. It is a well-known fact that informal fun gatherings build camaraderie and team spirit. Going out for a ball game or having a team picnic or holiday dinner are all easy ways to build relationships with team members and their families.

COMMUNICATION

It is important for leaders to have open communication with their team as it builds trust and an honest and open relationship. It is equally necessary to cultivate the art of listening as that is crucial for the success of effective communication. Listening to merely get your point across is not effective listening. The underlying question, anxiety, or fear can be identified by listening carefully through empathetic questioning and leading toward a proactive solution approach. By taking small steps such as inviting staff to provide input on decisions that impact everyone, checking in on staff when new things are started or old practices have been discontinued, agreeing to disagree amicably and modeling out proactive and nonreactive or defensive approaches in communication, and implementing a constructive feedback approach will all foster a trusting workplace environment. One of the aspects of healthy communication in a work environment that contributes to the overall positive health of an organization is to identify and address inefficiencies. Any inefficiency in team members should be addressed by leaders through one-on-one coaching and support. Additionally, a clear message of consequences if the inefficiency is not corrected should also be outlined. This fosters healthy work styles and practices. Any inefficiency in processes and systems can also be addressed through open communication and all affected teams coming together for effective problem solving.

ENJOYING WHAT YOU DO

It is an uncontested fact that genuine happiness and joy breeds positivity. Given this truth, it is hard not to be drawn into the excitement and happiness of leaders who genuinely love and enjoy their jobs and are able to show their teams the transformative impact of their collective contribution. It is such leaders who go out into the world and draw others into understanding the value of the job or service thereby creating a ripple effect of positivity.

Happiness and positivity are cultivated by making conscious choices on a daily basis to either have a good day or a bad day. No work environment is immune to stress and challenges. However, it is the spirit and strength of the team to make conscious choices to stay away from the blame-game and work toward problem resolution that keeps the positive environment intact. It is also not uncommon for individuals to face stress and challenges in their personal lives. The positive-minded leaders are always able to offer a sense of support and hope to their team members to believe in the best outcome under any given circumstance.

WE VALUE YOU

Leaders who take personal credit for the hard work of their team members will create an environment of distrust and negativity. The acknowledgment of the role and contribution of team members is highly important in a positive work environment. The human capital generated by the combination of staff talents and strengths, their knowledge and experience, is something that is often overlooked by most organizations. When staff talent and potential is tapped and channelized effectively, it results in creating not just a positive workplace, but a progressive workplace too. By celebrating individual team member's contributions and sharing out their best practices in larger forums like conferences builds confidence in staff regarding their individual talents and contributions and its far-reaching impact. In addition to acknowledging staff through financial remunerations like annual raises, sharing the impact of individual team member's contributions at monthly meetings or monthly reporting out to the management do contribute toward building staff members' confidence and sense of self-worth. It is important to encourage staff to share their best practices on bigger and larger platforms like conferences so they are able to experience the response received for their innovative thinking. My leadership experience has taught me that the acknowledgment of talented, innovative thinkers is more than just basic courtesy. It is giving them the professional respect they deserve and inspiring them to reach out to greater things.

INFORMAL GATHERINGS

The advance of technology has resulted in isolationism and reduced opportunities for group interactions in a physical social setting. One of the secrets to cultivating a positive environment and being a successful leader is to find opportunities for the team to have group interactions in a physical, social setting. This allows for healthy relationship building, sharing of common interests outside the workplace, and generally just having fun. There are also online team-building activities like an online bookclub, online gourmet club, online Scrabble game, and so forth, that also result in building a team that has a fun and positive outlook. Such informal relationship building can also lead to future professional collaborations and building a network of positive-thinking individuals. The element of humor also builds friendship and camaraderie as there is a sense of feeling secure and comfortable with a group with whom you can joke around knowing that no offense is taken. It is such humor that often keeps group dynamics strong and vibrant.

BEST PRACTICES

Here are some examples of tried-and-true practices by supervisors that foster positive attitudes among staff:

- Make sure to always greet your staff member with a warm smile and by their first name and with personalized greetings like "Good to see you, Susan" or "Robert, how is it going today?" or "Isn't it a lovely day out there, Tara?"
- If it has been a highly challenging day for your team member, it is best to approach them in person and give them an opportunity to talk about it and acknowledge their role in it with words like "I value your patience" or "It is amazing that you came up with an alternative even when . . ." or "You should consider sharing this experience in your monthly report so others can benefit from how well you handled this situation." If you're not able to acknowledge them in person, do so via email as timing of the acknowledgemnt is very important for staff. This in turn helps them end their day with a feeling of positive attitude rather than feeling worn down by the challenging situation or experience.
- Bringing homemade treats during days when new changes are being implemented and to celebrate staff accomplishments goes a long way in creating nurturing, positive work environments.
- Having various incentives for all sorts of staff accomplishments cultivates achievers going after bigger and better things for the success of the organization.

It is quite fitting to conclude this chapter on positivity with the words of Mahatma Gandhi: "Keep your thoughts positive because your thoughts become your words. Keep your words positive because your words become your behavior. Keep your behavior positive because your behavior becomes your habits. Keep your habits positive because your habits become your values. Keep your values positive because your values become your destiny."

Chapter Two

Employee Energy = Motivate Connect 2 Empower (E=MC²)

Amanda D. McKay Biarkis and Johnna Schultz

Our library, Helen Matthes Library, located in Effingham, Illinois (population 12,300), is in the midst of a building campaign. At $2 million, it's an aggressive fundraising goal for our community, and it will require the support of a wide range of people. The board and the director have contacted various local leaders and are building support and financial commitments for the campaign. However, each staff member plays a part, even if they aren't going on fundraising calls. An example occurred a few weeks before the end of the year. We had a young family visit the library. The family was relatively new to town and made the library one of their first stops. They commented several times on how lovely our library was and how it reminded them of bigger libraries they've visited. The next day, we received a $1,000 donation toward our campaign. They sent the donation, not because we have a state-of-the-art facility (we don't—it was constructed in the 1950s and is bursting at the seams) or have multiple copies of the latest best-selling children's book (we don't—we buy as aggressively as our budget will allow, but it's never enough and it's frequently one in, one out), but because they had an amazing experience, all created by our staff. The family loved that staff were available to them and made them feel special and anticipated their needs.

However, it wasn't always like that. While we have always had wonderful and dedicated staff, they didn't always feel empowered to take their love of books to the next level. Oftentimes, they would stay behind the desk and simply point to what the patron was asking about or they would miss an opportunity to provide stellar customer service. They weren't rude or combative, but they would miss chances to take the patron's experience out of the realm of ordinary into amazing. To combat this, we implemented a range of tools to help foster growth within our staff and to empower them to take charge of the library and the experience of our customers. Our stable of tricks took a number of years to develop over several different administrations—as they say, it didn't happen overnight!

BACKGROUND

The groundwork was laid when the management team undertook the challenge of reading and discussing a variety of management titles during our weekly meeting. Our management team consists of the following positions: director, adult services manager (oversees reference desk, collection development, and adult programming), circulation manager, youth services manager, and evening operations manager (oversees facility and technology). Two books that had the most impact on our development as an organization were *The Energy Bus: 10 Rules to Fuel Your Life, Work, and Team with Positive Energy* (Jon Gordon, Wiley and Sons, 2007) and *The Three Signs of a Miserable Job: A Fable for Managers (And Their Employees)* (Patrick Lencioni, Jossey-Bass, 2007). Though seemingly simple, the process of reading and discussing these books created an opportunity for dialogue that created a shared culture and expectations. This also allowed management to set the tone for growth and direction—where we wanted to lead the other staff members (the circulation assistants, technical services people, youth services assistants, information assistants, and other reference staff).

One of the biggest lessons from this exercise was the role of energy within an organization. Energy can exist as either positive or negative and all organizations have the potential for both. We wanted to create an environment that actively created and harnessed positive energy. Our first step was to get the entire staff on board by creating shared expectations to which we all agreed. This step was so important that we codified it and have all new staff sign the Staff and Management Expectations sheet. This provides management and staff with accountability and a shared sense that we are all in charge of creating a positive environment.

Our staff expectations, which were developed with staff and management input, include the following principles:

- Ask if you don't know.
- Come ready to work.
- Be flexible.
- Respect the privacy of patrons and other staff members.
- Keep disagreements with others between you and that person.
- Regularly communicate with your supervisor.
- Inform your supervisor of positive and negative occurrences.

• Don't dwell on negative situations.

Our management expectations, developed in the same way, include the following assurances to staff from the management team:

• You will be paid.
• We will support you to the public.
• We will listen to you.
• We will provide a safe environment to work in.
• We will inform you of goals and help you work toward them.
• We will provide open and honest feedback.

These shared expectations create the framework from which all staff and management can grow, innovate, and creatively meet the needs of our patrons while providing a positive patron experience. This framework was critical as we not only entered into our ambitious capital campaign but also as we encountered a dramatic increase in the use of our very tiny facility. In one year, our circulation statistics grew by 16 percent and program attendance exploded by 30 percent and has continued to increase by the same percentage or greater each year. Because we had a shared framework of how to create the energy needed to produce positive patron experiences, our staff met the challenge. Along the way, we developed some additional strategies that evolved into the $E=MC^2$ model, or Employee Energy = Motivate Connect 2 Empower. What follows is a breakdown of each element along with some examples of how we use this in our library.

EMPLOYEE ENERGY

We think any library would say this: our employees are our most valuable asset. However, in a small rural library where everyone in the town is trying to keep the focus on the town and encouraging residents to remain invested locally for entertainment and economic opportunities rather than seeking them in another, larger city, our employees become even more valuable. Library employees in small towns in particular often function as a gatekeeper to all of the formal and informal knowledge of the town—we know what book to recommend for your next trip and we know which farmer has the best produce. Keeping our employees engaged and ready to share that information is our challenge as administrators.

We use staff learning experiences cloaked as parties to help keep staff energy high. We hold them after hours and on site and schedule them around key times within the cycle of our library. Typically, we have one prior to our summer reading program as well as one after to wrap up the summer events and prepare for the change in tempo with the start of the school year. These parties are about one hour. We serve food and provide time for socialization, which may include learning games to introduce the concepts we want staff to focus on during that season. We've used Word Bingo, Book Speed Dating, and matching games to make the events more interactive and engaging and also to match the energy that we want our staff to project. Book Speed Dating was especially popular as it allowed staff to talk about their favorite books as well as "meet" other favorites that they could then recommend to patrons. It was a fun way to expand our Readers Advisory efforts without staff feeling pressured into learning about a new genre.

While attendance is not mandatory at these events, we do pay our staff to attend. It's another way to keep the energy up and show our commitment to continuing their education. It also helps reinforce the expectations that staff have of us as management: we'll honor and reward the time and dedication they put into making our library a positive place to work and visit.

Another method we use to engage employee energy and keep things moving in a positive direction is to live by the mantra "We never go backward." Management tries to take into account staff thoughts and ideas once a new tool or concept has been rolled out, but we never revert to the old way of doing things. An example of this is when we transitioned to only one person behind the circulation desk. The goal was to take the staff and put them into the stacks where they would be available to the patrons, allowing them to share their positive energy about the library's materials. This was a huge shift for staff and, even though management rolled it out in stages, there was initial hesitation. However, we stuck to our core belief of not going backward and remained open to staff suggestions for making it work for both them and the patrons. One such suggestion was to invest in a paging system so that staff that was in the stacks would have a better sense of when they were needed back at the desk. It allowed the person at the desk to feel less isolated and encouraged the person in the stacks to return rather than getting lost in the moment. In the end, we were able to navigate the challenges and increase employee energy as they started to see the positive impact they could have on patrons' experiences.

MOTIVATE

The next piece of the $E=MC^2$ formula is "Motivate." For us, motivation starts at the beginning with the interview. Every candidate, regardless of position, is asked a few of the same key questions to ensure that we are screening for employees that are motivated, customer-service oriented, and energetic.

The first question every candidate is asked is "What do you know about the Helen Matthes Library?" We ask this question because we believe it gets to the heart of motivation and customer service—if the candidate cannot be bothered to look up a little bit of information about us ahead of the interview, then he or she is probably not going to go the extra step when working with a patron. While it is rare, we have had interviews start and end with that single question. More commonly, a candidate will provide an answer that shows that they have an antiquated idea of what a modern library in general, and our library in particular, work to achieve every day. That answer becomes an important barometer in determining their future with us.

Another key question in our interview process is judging how someone will respond to a silly and unanticipated question. With this question, we are testing to see if the candidate can think quickly in the moment to come up with a logical path to a solution. One of our favorites in this category is "If you were a giraffe what kind of ice cream would you eat?" Questions like this give candidates a chance to show their personality as well as their deductive reasoning skills. It shows us if they will dig further to find an answer or solution, or if they will just give up in the face of adversity.

Once a candidate is hired, we have other ways that we use to help motivate and inspire staff to greatness. The Genius Cup is one of those tools. This simple coffee mug is now shared throughout the library staff as a way to recognize the hard work and dedication of fellow staff members. Sometimes given anonymously, this mug fills the important role of empowering library staff to recognize the achievements of coworkers without management directing praise or specific appreciation. The Genius Cup moves freely among staff—management doesn't dictate that it move on to another person after a certain amount of time or that staff can only receive it a specified number of times or even that everyone gets a turn with the cup. It has been great to hear why people have received the Genius Cup, because it is usually for something that the recipient deemed small and not worthy of attention. It's been a great tool for staff to show each other that what they do is noticed and appreciated.

CONNECT

We want our staff to feel connected to each other and to the community we serve. As the gatekeepers of the community, we encourage them to find out as much as they can about current events and activities that impact our community. We encourage staff to read the local paper and keep our local radio station's website open and refer to it throughout the day.

Using the experiences shared in titles we had read as well as other places we have worked, the management team brainstormed a simple concept for sharing our customer service priorities with staff. We called it "Navigating the Cs." Basically, we drilled down to the ten most common customer service concerns and found a way to tie them all back to the letter *C*. Then we defined each term by what was priority for our library. Printed on bright paper, these simple business cards (for an example, see figure 2.1) change weekly and are posted at each staff phone, work station, and break area throughout the library. These serve as visual reminders to staff of what is a priority and how we expect them to interact with patrons.

To further ensure that we are connecting within the community, management staff has added the following goal to our action plan: partner with a minimum of six organizations each year to enhance a program. We also make it a personal goal to host these events outside of the walls of the library. A good example of this is our participation in the Effingham Arts and Hearts event. This event highlights local nonprofits and is held the night before our Artisan Fair. Our library hosts a craft table with information about the library on the courthouse square. This gets us outside of the library and exposes us to the community and to new potential patrons.

We also use these community events as another avenue for staff to get involved. Being a part of the Effingham community is so important to us that we have challenged our staff to volunteer as a library staff member at three community events each year. Similar to the staff learning parties, we pay our staff for their time at these type of events as a way to honor our commitment to them and to both thank and encourage their service. We believe that it is important for staff at all levels to get involved and represent the library at community events because their faces are the ones that new patrons will encounter when they enter the library.

customer
*always first
*respond calmly, correctly, and with care
*create convenience, offer choices

Figure 2.1.

EMPOWER

Empower is the last element of our E=MC^2 formula. Ultimately, we believe that the goal of management is to recognize the talents and strengths of individual staff members and as much as possible lead by "getting out of the way." We want to create an environment where staff are free to explore and try new ideas. We want them to always be thinking of creative ways to solve the problems that they might encounter and create a patron experience that sets us above the rest.

We have several tools that we use to encourage empowerment among staff. One of the most powerful tools at our disposal is the "I Have an Idea" sheet. It is a simple paper form, used to capture those daily epiphanies that staff have. All library staff members are encouraged to jot down their ideas and work on the development of the idea with the appropriate staff person or manager to see if the idea can gain traction. Sometimes, the idea is simply common sense, such as changing the placement of a display piece to get greater exposure; other times, it's much more complicated, such as changing how we shelf nonfiction and moving away from the Dewey Decimal System. Each idea is developed by passing the sheet between staff members that are in a position to make the possible change occur. Finally, the sheet is presented to the director for a final look and an approval to move forward with implementing the idea. Sometimes, the sheet's entire life cycle is less than one day, but more commonly, it is a few days to a month.

We use this model for capturing ideas for a variety of reasons, but the main ones are that it saves staff time and helps staff see the life cycle of their ideas. While it might seem cumbersome to stop and write the idea down and seek out the other people that this idea impacts, we have found that it encourages staff to really focus their ideas as well as give the staff that are responding time to digest and process an idea before either dismissing it or moving ahead.

Although this seems simple, the "I Have an Idea" process is a powerful tool that ensures staff that their ideas do matter and that they can make a difference and improve the library for customers as well as themselves and coworkers.

The "I Have an Idea" sheet is great for ideas that are in response to a perceived problem, but we also encourage staff to think on their feet to creatively solve a problem in the moment as well. "I Have an Idea" is meant for long-term problem solving; short-term problem solving happens at the point of interaction with the patron. Management supports whatever solution staff come up with and work with them ahead of time to brainstorm possible solutions to challenges. While the solution to the problem might differ from that of management, as long as it works within the policy and the patron is happy, then it is always the right solution.

CONCLUSION

We've slowly built up our program of $E=MC^2$ over time. We wanted to give staff a chance to adjust to each change and fully embrace each new skill and method before adding the next. This is a constant cycle of evaluation and evolution for management and staff. We make it clear to all new hires that we are an organization that evolves to meet the needs of our community, rather than try to keep things the same. Our goal is to support a staff that is engaged in upselling the library and its resources to the Effingham community. The more tools we can give our staff to encourage this development, the more we gain as a library. When we experience such tangible rewards as a new family becoming a donor, all based on a single, initial experience, we know that the hard work our staff has put into becoming deeply connected within the community is paying off. We also know that this is the key to keeping the library at the center of our community well into the future.

Chapter Three

Staff Evaluations

Padma Polepeddi

There are several staff performance evaluation products on the market that can be customized to every organization's needs. What I choose to focus on in this chapter is the philosophy of staff evaluations and what can make staff evaluations effective. The job delivery and work performance of staff members is assessed through staff evaluations. More importantly, the tapping of every individual's potential to its fullest and taking them to higher levels of achievement and service can also be achieved through well-designed staff evaluations.

COMPETENCIES AND GOALS

Each organization has a specific set of performance evaluation criteria for various job families. In my supervisory experience, I have found that identifying basic competencies for each job category and publishing these competencies in print format and easy-to-access online format for staff to peruse are all good first steps for creating successful staff evaluations. By starting from a common ground of expectations opens up the opportunity for dialog between the team leader and the staff member and nothing comes as a surprise during the evaluation process.

The next step in effective staff evaluations is setting goals and creating action plans for fulfilling the goals within a certain time frame. The goals have to fit in with the larger strategic plan of the organization and the action plans should be realistic and developed through conversations of mutual understanding between the staff member and the leader. The time frame for achieving the goals should also fit into the large time frame of the organization's timeline for achieving the strategic measures. It is not uncommon to provide stretch goals for staff members as some of the high achievers like to extend themselves beyond the normal expectations outline for their job category. The conversation surrounding goals between the staff member and the team leader should also include the reality of having to give up on a goal if and when there are sudden changes that impede its implementation. Factors like a sudden change in budget allocations for a project due to change in revenues, or some other project replacing the one planned for at an earlier time, are all examples of times when goals are changed or replaced.

One of the factors that contribute to effective staff evaluations is to show staff that their performance matters to the overall health and progress of the organization. The key to staff success is to show how vital they are to keeping the organization vibrant and progressive. I have found in my staff evaluation sessions that the staff appreciates examples that the supervisor cites from his or her observations of staff performance that have impacted the team and the organization. It is a powerful motivator not just for personal success but for professional growth too.

CONSISTENCY

It is important to have consistency when it comes to staff evaluations. It conveys the uniform message that everyone is encouraged to explore their capabilities to the fullest extent, and that there is a place for every kind of player in the organization. As individuals have various personality types and various learning styles, it is important for staff to know that everyone is assessed by the same criteria. By having a consistent model in place for rewarding staff that fulfill expectations, and rewarding those who go above and beyond expectations, rules out any possibility for favoritism. This model also helps weed out underperformers who drag down the efficiency of any organization.

MUTUAL INVOLVEMENT

Both staff and supervisors should receive a certain amount of training in regard to staff evaluation. This results in conveying the importance of performance evaluation and more importantly establishes the fact that evaluations are not subjective, and there are guidelines to be followed by the person who is being evaluated as well as the person involved in the evaluation.

Another factor that contributes to the effectiveness of staff evaluations is the involvement of the supervisor in the goal-achieving process of his or her team members. A continuous feedback model is critical for team strength and team success. By showing interest in every staff member's responsibilities at work, brainstorming interesting and innovative ways of fulfilling goals, doing regular informal check-ins, and scheduling formal quarterly one-on-one meetings sends a positive message that the staff member's progress is important to you as the leader. Due to the ongoing nature of the feedback model between the supervisor and staff members, the formal evaluation sessions turn out to be enjoyable and mutual learning interactive sessions. This level of involvement from the supervisor also opens doors to difficult and courageous conversations in cases of underperforming staff. The struggling staff member is coached and offered help to address the inefficiency. If and when underperformance continues in spite of help given, the difficult decision of terminating an employee takes place.

One of the challenges for any leader in staff evaluations is to get staff interested in it and not to view it as a mechanical process. In my experience of staff evaluation sessions, I've seen that treating each of their achievements as something to feel proud of and acknowledging how well they have handled challenging workplace-related situations conveys your genuine sense of in their professional growth. That is what seems to matter to them the most—your joy for their capabilities and achievements. Of course, the acknowledgment from upper management also reiterates the positive staff evaluation process.

The staff's interest in the evaluation process can also be achieved by inviting them to participate in a self-evaluation process. If the staff member and the supervisor are participating in the evaluation of the same criteria, it opens up the opportunity to have a healthy dialogue of how each area was assessed by the staff member and the supervisor. If the supervisor has followed an ongoing feedback model, there should not be too much of a difference between the staff member's self-evaluation and the supervisor's evaluation. If there is a significant difference in how the staff member has assessed his or her performance compared to how the performance has been evaluated by the supervisor, it is time to go back to the basic expectations and start the conversation from that point.

Any evaluation is incomplete without staff evaluation of their supervisor. Once again, there are products out there that organizations use to assess the effectiveness of a team leader by the team. It is important for the supervisor evaluation piece to have specific categories in order for staff to be able to give meaningful feedback. The participation of the human resources department is important as it brings in the level of objectivity required for this exercise. The anonymity of staff providing feedback on a supervisor's performance is also important in the supervisor portion of the evaluation process. In cases of underperforming supervisors, there should be a follow-up action in place so staff can see that their input does matter to the organization. This fosters a healthy checks-and-balances working environment, where everyone feels accountable and involved in fulfilling the vision of the organization.

BEST PRACTICES

Here are some tried-and-true practices that make staff evaluations useful to both the person conducting the evaluations as well as for the group being evaluated:

• Personalize evaluations by sharing observations and examples indicative of the staff member's performance and tying it to the larger strategic goals of the organization.
• Acknowledge staff member's mentoring role toward other team members.
• Acknowledge staff member's assistance to the supervisor.
• Acknowledge staff member's creative ideas and their contribution to the progress of the organization.
• Invite staff members to conduct a self-evaluation of their performance.
• Eliminate possibilities for subjective supervisor evaluations by having the evaluations go through the human resources department; this will bring in an additional layer of objectivity. The role of human resources will come in after the supervisor has submitted the evaluations.
• Foster healthy communication practices through a peer-to-peer constructive feedback model. In a library setting, for example, have staff members observe and critique each other's storytime delivery.
• Call out unethical practices through healthy questioning and courageous conversations.
• Build a healthy and open communication environment through respectful conversations.

In conclusion, the practice of evaluating and assessing is what keeps organizations vibrant and healthy. This cannot be limited to system processes and should extend to the individuals too as staff come and go in every organization. The growth of any organization from good to great results not just from best practices of the organization, but from the people working in it, as it is their collective brain power and innovative thinking that makes it possible for such transformative power.

Chapter Four

Succession Planning Strategies for Small Public Libraries

Karen Harrison Dyck

Succession planning, often seen as a valuable survival strategy for large companies like McDonald's Corporation and General Electric (GE), has recently become a tool used by large public and academic libraries as they cope with the numerous retirements of the baby-boom generation. Businesses began to look at succession planning decades ago. There's a famous story of Jim Cantaupo, chief executive officer (CEO) and chairman of McDonald's, who, in 2004, dropped dead at age sixty of a heart attack. McDonald's shares fell only 2.3 percent that day, while trading at three times their volume. Why? Because the board of McDonald's was able to immediately announce a successor who had the confidence of the markets and investors. The business world took note that this large multinational had a succession plan in place, and succession planning started to become a normal part of business planning strategies (Sellers 2011). Since that time, McDonald's has changed CEOs many times, always with a succession plan in place. Now, large businesses, small family businesses, and libraries, large and small, have started to pay attention to this concept.

The American Library Association (ALA) has a handbook on succession planning developed by Paula Singer and Gail Griffith (2010), and many well-known figures in the library world have given workshops on succession planning at the big library conferences (Singer and Sundberg 2012). However, small libraries have to cope with the departures of their library managers without the resources that large businesses and large libraries have. It is tempting to say that the concept is not relevant to the small public library because the resources to implement a strategy are not ever going to become available. In fact, the small public library can and should take a look at succession planning. The changing demographics of our times, with the baby-boom generation in full retirement mode, dictate that many retirements are occurring among library staff at all levels. Even if your small public library board has a young manager far from retirement age, they too may have to cope with their manager's departure, as the young manager often uses the small library as a stepping-stone to an even greater opportunity or moves to follow a spouse who has a new job in a different location. In fact, small libraries may well have to cope with the departure of their senior manager more often than larger libraries. This fact alone makes succession planning relevant to the small public library.

Succession planning is one way that the library board can exercise its responsibility to strategically position the library to cope with what might be considered a crisis before it happens. A library may lose its manager via a planned departure, with much notice, or it may happen suddenly and sadly out of accident, illness, or termination. This might also include a temporary vacancy precipitated by an illness or maternity/paternity leave. In the event that the library manager's position becomes vacant without prior notice, the library board should have a contingency plan in place to assure the library's smooth operation. This emergency succession planning assures the community and the library's funders that the board has its act together. Library services can continue seamlessly, the staff can continue with less stress, and the board can initiate the search for a new chief librarian, knowing that the rest of their house is in order.

The ideal situation is to have a staff member earmarked as the temporary or permanent successor to the departing head. However, with many small and rural libraries, staffing is such that there is no one who fills this position. The board may want a trained librarian or library technician in its key position. They may not have a person with that training readily available. Many small libraries are staffed with one or two key full-time people and several part-timers. The board may have a staff of dedicated long-term employees, but have no one who wants to step up to the top job. Complicating this, some small libraries offer a less than competitive salary for the chief librarian's position, making it an even more difficult position to fill.

A good beginning point in succession planning is the board's analysis of exactly what it needs in a chief librarian: Do they need an MLS/MLIS or a library technician? Would they be better off finding a local person, with the desire and skills to be their library manager, who will work for the money available and stay for the long term?

While the board is paying attention to the very practical issue of what qualifications their chief librarian should have, they can also address the issue of developing the following "bench strengths" within their staff, as defined by dictionary.com:

Sports. The quality and number of players available to substitute during a game.

Business. The competence and number of employees ready to fill vacant leadership and other positions: *building an organization's bench strength through management training.*

The issue of developing bench strength poses a considerable issue for the small public library board. The problems may include the following:

- Most staff are part-time; sometimes, this problem is compounded by staff who have been with the library for a long time and who are not very flexible with taking on new responsibilities.
- Staff may be organized in "silos" with each person having a distinct job title and set of responsibilities.
- The typical small community may have limited opportunities for the traditional methods of building bench strength: mentoring, secondments, and staff training.
- Time and money may not be available for additional staff training.
- Part-time staff members may or may not have a long-term commitment to and identification with your library.
- Some staff may not be interested in the challenging position at the top.
- There may be no formal way of identifying those employees who do have an interest in management and leadership.

So, another question to ask is this: "Is your library a silo or a haystack?" I say this in all seriousness. In the absence of a library manager, it is important for library staff to pull together to get the job done. In a situation where library staff each has discrete areas of responsibility and no one tramples on anyone else's toes, you may have a problem. It is important that anyone with an area of limited skilled responsibility, such as interlibrary loans or cataloguing, share those skills and job strategies with other similar level employees. Likewise, all library staff should share a common knowledge of basic core responsibilities. For example, when the chief librarian of the (fictitious) Trillium and District Public Library left in May 2012, the library was without a manager for five months. During that time the unionized staff pulled together without any one individual being in charge. The work got done, summer programs took place, and staff even got some summer vacation time. Could your library do that? Or would you be better off placing a senior staff member in charge, or even bringing in an interim library manager? If you have a unionized situation, you need to know what your contract or collective agreement might have to say about this.

How to cope with an emergency vacancy at the top should fit into the context of the board's policy development. It will determine the difference between micromanaging the library and creating a policy solution to the issue. This can be done through the following ways:

- The Strategic Plan
- The board's policy manual, which should include strategic succession planning policies (discussed later)
- Hiring and training policies, which offer direction to the library manager
- Teamwork between the board the library manager and the staff

Since staff (especially the library manager) may be threatened by the suggestion of a succession plan, the board should be careful about how this is presented:

- It's not personal; it's policy.
- It's to ensure teamwork among the staff.
- It will potentially offer staff more access to training and opportunity.

In 1986, I left the position of chief librarian of a small public library in rural Ontario, Canada. I had been there for twelve years, and there was no one on the board who had known anyone but me as the library manager. To replace me, they hired a young MLS grad who was terminated at the end of his first year. The board then turned to Gwen, who had been my assistant (and the only other full-time staff member) for about eight of the twelve years I was there. Gwen was promoted to chief librarian and stayed in that position until she retired. Of course, this was before any of us had given thought to the issue of succession planning. I'm telling this story because it points out that sometimes the solutions to succession planning issues are right under our noses, and there is no reason to overcomplicate them.

In a situation where the library is without a senior manager, managing finances should receive special mention. The board has a major responsibility to make sure that the bills and staff are paid in an efficient way, in the absence of their library manager. They also have a responsibility to the library's funders to be good stewards of public moneys. Both of these are fundamental to the position of the library in the community. The board (or at least the treasurer on the board) should be well informed as to how materials are received and the processes for paying the bills and handling payroll. Periodically it's always a good idea to have your auditor review the library's financial processes. That may be a routine part of his or her job. Or ask the auditor to do an occasional review, spending some time sorting through recommendations emerging from this process.

It is an important part of the bill-paying process to assure that a staff member is verifying that materials have been received, that an invoice should be paid, and that someone else is actually preparing the checks for signature.

In smaller public libraries having two signatures on checks is standard practice. This is usually the library manager, plus one board member, either the chair or treasurer. In the absence of the library manager, two board members or the library's accountant/bookkeeper and a board member might share this responsibility.

Although this is rare, library boards *have* been victimized by library staff who have created dummy suppliers, received fake shipments, and pocketed the revenue. Do not be afraid to question who the suppliers are or what the bills are for, if you are one of the people signing the checks!

Once succession planning for the staff is developed, it's time to turn attention to the succession of members of the board. Does your board reflect

- the diversity of your community,
- the geography of your community,
- the demographic nature of your community (age, language, culture), and
- *people* with a vital interest in your library and *its future*?

It is incumbent upon the existing board or appointing body to have succession and recruitment plans. Most boards are municipally appointed. If the municipality depends on ads (and no other strategies) for board recruitment, it is reasonable that the library board makes efforts to ensure that applications for board members are sought and considered from the various geographic areas of the municipality, the language and cultural groups representing the demographic nature of the municipality, the age distributions representing the demographic nature of the municipality, all the while ensuring that applicants are people who show a clear interest in public libraries and a willingness to advocate and work hard on behalf of the library. There is also a range of expertise in specific areas that board members need, including finance, knowledge of your community, human resources, wise use of technology, fundraising, and government relations. There may be other areas that you consider important.

One thing that we know is that most people who volunteer do so *because they were asked.* What that means is advertising for a board vacancy is not necessarily the best way to attract good members for your board. There is work to be done finding the right people, meeting with them and explaining the board's role in library management, recruiting them for the board, and giving them some training so they will be good board members. There are some excellent board training programs offered by library associations and government library authorities.

If you are well into the succession planning mode now, this would be a good time to put together a Board Recruitment Package, if you don't already have one. This has a place in your strategic planning, too. In addition, take a look at who is on the board now, and how long they are likely to stay. Even if you plan on them serving a couple of terms, they will leave eventually and take their skills with them. But, within reason, you can predict when people are likely to go and you probably know what kind of contribution they have been making to the board in terms of the skills they bring to the table. Note the following example: here we learn the board expects Duffy and Inkster to drop off in 2013.

In table 4.1, we have charted the expected departure dates of board members. We now know who we are losing in 2013: Denise Duffy, young mother and paralegal and Ian Inkster, a retired businessman with an interest in HR. Looking at the characteristics we value in the people who are retiring: we need some bench strength in new board members, including: a young mother or father, a retired person (that is if the board is not already filled with retired people), someone with legal skills, someone with human resources skills—always, of course, searching for those special people who have a definite interest in the library. This is a good time, also, to take inventory of the kinds of skills you might otherwise need, but do not have on the board. The completing jewel in this particular piece would be the development of a board recruitment strategy, followed by a training program for new trustees.

POLICY SUGGESTIONS

As a bare minimum, the board can direct the library manager to develop a succession plan in case the library manager's position was to become vacant. If the board wants to take more initiative, the following more proactive policies (*Houston [BC] Public Library Policy Manual* 2013) might be considered:

Accounting Manual. A comprehensive *Accounting Procedure Manual* is kept in the library director's office. The *Accounting Procedure Manual* contains detailed steps for completing all of the necessary day-to-day bookkeeping and payroll procedures using the library's accounting software.

Name	2013	2014	2015	2016	2017	2018
B. Bailey	X	X				
C. Casey	X	X	X	X		
D. Duffy	X					
G. Garrison	X	X	X			
H. Harrison	X	X	X	X	X	X
I. Inkster	X					
T. Tovey	X	X	X			

Temporary Library Management. In the absence of the library director due to illness, holiday leave, leave of absence, or sudden, unexpected termination of employment, for any reason, the assistant librarian will become acting library director and will be compensated at a rate equal to 90 percent of the library director's current hourly wage until the library director returns to work or is replaced. A budget line under wages contains the amount of the wage budget allotted to the acting library director for holiday and sick leave, education days, suspension, or interim coverage for the library director for any other reason.

Support Staff. Cross training between all support staff positions is a priority and is the responsibility of the library director. Staff members are to be encouraged and supported in skills development, through use of the training budget, and are required to be familiar with all of the procedures as outlined in the *Procedure Manual.*

Of course the development and implementation of policies, such as those in the examples shown above, require the will and leadership of the board. The steps essential to making this happen include the following:

- Working with the library manager and staff to clarify why the board is implementing such a policy, and to solicit their input
- Providing funding for cross training
- Ensuring that the financial management procedures of the library are clearly defined and approved by the library's auditor
- Developing a program to recruit board members who have the skills needed by the board and who reflect the diversity of the community
- Providing an appropriate training program for new trustees
- Reviewing and, if needed, revising the succession plan and its policies on a regular basis to assure that the board is familiar with them, they are still relevant, and they are being followed by the staff

MORE IDEAS TO MAKE SUCCESSION EASIER

Have both the board and the library manager make a list of recurring deadlines. These dates could include such items as (1) when board recruitment needs to start, (2) when an insurance review needs to start, (3) when certain government reports and other forms need to be filed, and (4) when to start planning recurring events, such as volunteer appreciation and perhaps even when to get the furnace checked (or other recurring building maintenance items). Usually every month has a recurring event, and some have several.

Another bit of documentation that will help in a succession emergency, or even an orderly succession, is a library procedure manual. Recording all the commonly performed library tasks—how bills are paid (we've already talked about this), how interlibrary loan works, the cataloguing and processing procedures, and even the trades the library uses to perform routine maintenance tasks—may ensure smooth operations and transitions.

John F. Kennedy said, "The time to repair the roof is when the sun is shining" (Singer and Sundberg 2012). This bit of wisdom captures the essence of succession planning. The library board, however small or large, that tackles the necessity of developing a succession plan is a board that is truly exercising its policy and planning function on behalf of library users, ensuring the library is providing a more efficient service to the community. The succession plan will make the library a better place for the staff to work and will make the transition to a new library manager easier for all staff.

The initial research that resulted in this article was conceived in a series of workshops sponsored by IslandLink Library Federation (Victoria, BC, Canada) in 2013. I thank them for their support.

REFERENCES

Houston (BC) Public Library Policy Manual (unpublished draft, 2013). Houston, BC, Canada: Houston Public Library Board.

Sellers, Patricia. *"How McDonald's Got CEO Succession Right."* CNN Money, August 23, 2011.

Singer, Paula M., and Laura Sundberg. 2012. *"Emergency Succession Planning."* Public Library Association, Philadelphia, March, 15, 2012. Reisterstown, MD: The Singer Group.

Singer, Paula M., and Gail Griffith. *"Succession Planning in the Library: Developing Leaders, Managing Change."* 2010. Chicago: ALA Editions.

"Whitby Public Library Board Succession Plan." Whitby, ON, Canada: Whitby Public Library Board.

Part Two

Programming

Chapter Five

Cultivating Conversation, Memory, and Self-Awareness

Women and Libraries Post-Retirement

Joanna Kluever and Wayne Finley

A common way for public libraries to meet the literacy needs of their patrons is by use of the book club. Though these clubs have become increasingly popular, they are not without their problems and, alone, offer little to fully meet the literacy needs of an aging population of women readers. Julia Hull District Library's (JHDL) original Adult Book Club was no exception to this rule. While it provided opportunities for reading and discussing popular books, it lacked the intellectual inquiry and social interaction integral to providing continuing education opportunities to older women. As a result of these deficiencies, the library director organized a series of extended literature courses that sought to engage women, mostly retired, in discussing some of the great works of literature. The participants were so inspired that the classes transformed from mere reading and discussion, to include writing and scholarly analysis—similar to what one might see in a college classroom. The results have been staggering: the creation of a social network of women readers who have gained knowledge, confidence, and support by their intellectual engagement and vocalization with other women. This chapter examines the programs offered by the JHDL and offers suggestions on how other libraries can incorporate similar programs.

ADULT LITERACY AT JULIA HULL: A BRIEF HISTORY

Prior to August of 2007, the JHDL offered only one adult literacy program: a book club which met one evening per calendar month. At that time, the library purchased copies of a work, usually contemporary fiction or nonfiction, chosen by library staff, which were distributed to participants at each book club meeting. The meetings themselves were fairly traditional: library staff reviewed a biography of the author(s) and followed with direct questions, which were often gathered from free, online reader's guides. In some regards, the program worked, as evidenced by a small group of devout followers and two dedicated library staff members who enjoyed the leadership role given to them. But in many ways, the program never reached its potential. Followers, though dedicated, were few (typically five or less participants at each meeting, including the discussion leaders). And the discussions, though insightful, were less than dynamic. Part of the reason for this being the small number of participants, as well as the selection of books, which tended to be similar in genre and theme, and which also tended to be popular, rather than literary. Aside from posting a list of upcoming book club selections within the library, no marketing was employed to inform or even "sell" patrons on its Adult Book Club.

In August 2007, JHDL's new director sent weekly notices of the book club and other upcoming library programs to two local newspapers. Further, upon redesigning the library's website, a program and events link was added, which included the dates, times, and reading selections for upcoming adult book clubs. The library also began issuing a monthly calendar on paper, which could be picked up at the circulation desk upon checkout or return of materials. In short, the first step to success for revival of the library's then only adult program was to increase awareness of its existence.

The process of building community awareness and enthusiasm for the Adult Book Club took several months before the library noted any differences in the program's attendance. But during that time, the director began to learn more things about community members' wants and needs in regard to literacy. One patron in particular, a retired woman in her mid-sixties who formerly attended the library's adult book club complained that she did so much pleasure reading on her own, she didn't want the commitment of reading another book for a library program, especially if she didn't enjoy the library's selections. Likewise, several patrons commented that they simply didn't have time to read a full-length novel each month.

Such comments led the director to consider the possibility of offering a second adult literacy program that would provide opportunity for reading and discussion, but that would utilize shorter works of fiction (10–20 pages long, on average), rather than novels. Thus, in February 2008, Short & Sweets began: a program named for and adapted from a program offered at the

Davenport Public Library (Davenport, Iowa). Like the Adult Book Club, Short & Sweets would meet monthly for discussion of a selected reading. Unlike the Adult Book Club, the discussion would take place in the morning and would feature a homemade dessert (thus, the word "Sweets"). Aside from providing a catchy title, the dessert part of the program aimed to create a more social atmosphere, and thus a more engaging event. The first program meeting drew nine patrons.

Short & Sweets blossomed into a group of dedicated participants, now averaging fifteen: all women, all retired who grew increasingly hungry to learn. Similarly, they became better readers and better thinkers because of their active engagement with a variety of literatures. The director noticed that many participants in either Short & Sweets or the Adult Book Club began attending *both* literary groups. Further, many of these women began net-working outside of the library as a result of their meetings at the library. One group of Short & Sweets participants, for example, began meeting for lunch immediately following each of their monthly meetings at the library. Further, their conversations outside of the library began to include what they were reading, and what they *thought* about what they were reading. It was common to see women of either group promote these literacy programs to their friends and fellow patrons.

In June 2009, the library piloted a stand-alone literacy program: Life Writing for Older Adults. Similar to the other two groups, Life Writing featured reading accompanied by discussion. But what made this class unique was that it also incorporated writing, including participants' written reactions to readings, as well as more creative writing attempts about their own life experiences. Further, the class would meet three times for two hours each, rather than a single one-hour session like the Adult Book Club and Short & Sweets. The program was so successful that it followed with similar instructional programs over the next year, including How to Read Poetry and How to Read Fiction.

Nearly a year later, in July 2010, the library began its first Great Reads program featuring the novel *Beloved* by Toni Morrison. The premise behind this particular program series was based on the idea that there were many great works of literature that were intellectually intimidating on their own, but which a supportive group of readers and a dedicated group leader could make more accessible. Like the Life Writing course, Great Reads would meet over the course of several meetings, for two hours at a time. Similarly, the programs incorporated written response, as well as reading of some critical analysis by scholars in the field of literature. As one participating woman said of these first courses, "I feel like I've had the opportunity to go back to college!" Since these stand-alone courses began, there have been dozens such programs offered to the patrons of JHDL.

DESIGNING AND SUSTAINING ADULT LITERACY PROGRAMS FOR OLDER WOMEN

Designing and sustaining adult literacy programs are inextricably linked concepts: a library simply cannot sustain any adult literacy program if it lacks clear purpose and guided application. Undoubtedly, some things matter more than others when considering a program's design. To ensure a program's success, one must prioritize the following criteria: book selection, promotion, and instructional approach.

Book Selection

Determining what titles to read with a group of adults often proves a daunting task. For one, groups have varying tastes, no matter what the age group or gender its participants represent. Therefore, it matters that libraries select an array of genres and writing styles. It also helps, in this regard, to vary readings between fiction and nonfiction, since some readers do better when reading informational works (memoirs, biographies, histories, etc.) than they do with creative stories. Adult Book Club members at JHDL thus switch monthly between fiction and nonfiction works, and groups like Short & Sweets and Great Reads are often accompanied by informational texts such as critical responses. Simply put, varying texts breeds varied discussion from a varied group of participants.

Equally important is to select literary works, rather than their popular counterparts. For the purposes of this paper, the term "literary" suggests original, well-written, well-crafted, complex works that raise important questions and foster intelligent discussion. Such works may or may not appear on bestseller lists, and their authors may or may not be recognized by the popular culture. Likewise, since avid readers tend to pick up popular works on their own for pleasure reading, selecting more literary works for program use lessens the risk of selecting books that participants will likely have already read, thus making the experience more challenging. Reading reviews and personally reviewing items (even if only a few pages or chapters) can provide insight into whether a book is "literary" or not.

In selecting a variety of literary works, it's likely that participants will dislike some of the library's choices, despite their being generally regarded as quality works. In the case of reading Toni Morrison's *Beloved*, winner of the Pulitzer Prize for Fiction in 1988, two regular female participants in JHDL's adult literacy programs dropped out of the program because they took offense to some of the book's content. This sort of reaction is natural, even expected, and should never dissuade a library from choosing works that challenge readers. This may be evidenced by the fact that the participants who continued with the course reported a newfound understanding of a work of literature that many of them had previously shied from reading. Likewise, nearly half of the group's participants extended their study of the book beyond the library. In preparation for each session, for example, these women met in a group member's home to read aloud and discuss difficult passages. Thus, besides developing their comprehension of the work, these women also developed their relationships with one another. In this case, while a few participants responded negatively to the task of reading *Beloved*, the majority thrived, given the challenge. (Note that both of the women who chose not to read *Beloved* returned to regularly participate in other adult literacy programs at the library.)

Promotion

As previously noted, adult literacy programs cannot succeed without promotion. Part of the success of any library program is contingent upon the fact that people participate. Previously mentioned mediums included standard newspapers, the library's website, and monthly event calendar. Other mediums might include linking discussion questions on the library's blog, posting announcements and reminders on Facebook and Twitter, or pinning book covers on Pinterest, since a growing number of adults are using these social networking sites. Libraries that have access to a cell phone and the cell phone numbers of their patrons might also send a text message to participating patrons, not merely as a reminder about meeting dates and times, but to foster critical thinking throughout the process. For example, a library might send a difficult question for consideration about a particular book prior to the meeting to give participants the time necessary to process a response.

Even if libraries choose to not utilize such technological methods (JHDL, in fact, used very few of these approaches, at first, since most of the attendees do not actively use social media applications), adult literacy programs will be successful, so long as its participants remain enthusiastic and supportive of the process. In fact, the most important advertisement a library can glean is word-of-mouth promotion from one of its current participants sharing their excitement with a neighbor or friend.

Instructional Approach

Perhaps the main reason the adult literacy programs at JHDL have been so successful is because of the methods utilized to engage the female participants who enroll in them. Unlike traditional book clubs (including JHDL's original Adult Book Club), that rely on direct question and answer, JHDL's discussion leader, in this case the library director, utilizes a variety of strategies to involve all group members.

One of these strategies is active reading. Active reading occurs when a reader engages with the text in a tangible way, including highlighting important passages, making notes on the text itself, keeping a reading journal, and so on. These techniques help readers in the act of reading, as well as later in discussion by providing them something they can reflect back upon. This is why, aside from its Adult Book Club, and in all cases possible, JHDL tries to provide copies of the text for students to keep. Short & Sweets provides the easiest opportunity for this, as most classic short stories are available for free on the Internet, in either PDF or HTML format. In other cases, the library has purchased used copies of books online for only a few dollars per book.

In addition, and as is previously noted in this paper, the discussion leader incorporates information outside of the texts themselves. This includes critical responses, reviews, related readings, and questions or comments to help stimulate discussion. When possible, the leader also attempts to make connections to previous texts or authors, drawing on previously learned information. This sort of recollection can be especially helpful as an aid to memory, a point of particular interest to many older women.

The trickiest part of any literary group, however, is leading the discussion. Anyone who has attempted to lead a literary discussion knows that students can exhibit a variety of responses in a classroom-style setting, including apprehension and uncertainty. It's crucial, therefore, for any leader to make their female participants comfortable and open to respond not only to the discussion leader, but also to their peers. One simple way to do this is by allowing sufficient "wait time" following questions. Individuals often need a moment to process an idea before translating it into words. Thus, effective leaders allow for silence within the discussion. Likewise, probing responders for more information, redirecting questions from one participant to another, and directly responding to participants' comments can help to clarify points of interest. In an informal survey given to the JHDL program participants by the library director, several students observed the effectiveness of this approach. One woman, in particular, responded, "The responses of others are accepted and then tenderly extended or opportunity given for the speaker to modify her response if a misunderstanding is evident." Another noted, "Joanna is . . . never negative about an answer from us, always giving it proper merit." Such comments reflect how certain approaches to leading these sorts of groups can either foster or discourage participation.

MEETING THE NEEDS

When measuring attendance, it's important to consider the number of new patrons participating, but perhaps even more compelling to assess those individuals with repeat program attendance. For example, in the prior mentioned survey of eleven participants at JHDL's literary groups, all of them indicated that they attended more than one type of literary program at the library (Adult Book Club and Short & Sweets, for example), and nine of them reported attending more than two types of programs on a repeat basis. In lieu of such quantitative (albeit vague and unscientific) information, it's fair to surmise that repeat attendance is at least some indication of the success of a program.

However, its participants' qualitative survey responses provide the most insight into how well such programs have met and continue to meet the needs of the post-retired women surveyed. In the survey, women were asked, "For what reasons do you attend literature programs at the library?" and offered five possible answers with the option to circle all answers that applied. A blank space, marked "other," was also provided to allow the opportunity for free response. Eleven out of eleven members surveyed responded, "To interact/engage with others" and "To read new authors/texts." Ten out of eleven responded, "To learn new things" and "To improve reading/writing skills." Seven out of eleven responded, "To increase memory/cognition." Other responses included comments such as "to meet new friends"; "aids in my desire to live a well-balanced life"; "I love the friendly atmosphere at Julia Hull Library; it's very inviting and stimulating."

The previous prompt was followed by the question "What have you gained from attending these programs?" Eleven out of eleven indicated "Interaction/engagement with others," "Read new authors/texts," and "New acquaintances." Ten of eleven reported, "Improved reading/writing skills," "Confidence in talking about literature," and "Learned new ideas." Nine of eleven responded, "Learned something about myself." And at the bottom of the list were "Enhanced memory/cognition" and "Confidence in reading." Other responses included "Pride in our community" and "improved verbal expression." The emphasis that most of these women placed on the idea of engaging with others and meeting new acquaintances seems to stem from their mutual respect for one another. Thus, when asked what words they would use to describe the women they engage with while participating in adult literature programs at the library, the most common responses were "insightful," "interesting," "kind/friendly," and "accepting (of others' opinions)." Such trust and admiration certainly lends itself to fostering an environment that allows openness and honesty between members.

Many of the women expounded upon these points in an optional question at the end of the survey that asked, "What else would you like to share about your experiences with adult literature programs at Julia Hull District Library?" One participant commented, "Our various groups add a rich dimension to my life, for which I am very grateful! I look forward to our groups, with eager anticipation." A similar response expressed, "The literature programs/classes have greatly enriched my life. While I'm a lifelong reader, I've never shared discussions about what has been read. This has taken a bit of courage on my part." Another participant responded, "I would drive many miles and pay a hefty registration fee to participate in the adult literature programs at Julia Hull District Library. But I am privileged to attend free of charge and only two miles from my home. . . . I rearrange my schedule whenever possible to attend. . . . In talking with others—once someone attends, she doesn't want to miss. I wholeheartedly agree."

CONCLUDING THOUGHTS

Although these voices represent a sample of the many women who have been positively impacted by the adult literacy programs at JHDL, the general sentiment of the women who attend is the same. These programs have and continue to help simultaneously foster intellectual and social growth in ways that a traditional book club cannot. Moreover, the literary groups fill a place in the lives of the women who participate, giving them a sense of purpose past retirement. What's more, their stimulation and success in such groups is of benefit not merely on a private level, but also to the community in which they live. That is, by improving the mind of the individual, libraries can grow the mind of the community.

Chapter Six

Patron Facilitated Programming

Shawn D. Walsh and Melanie A. Lyttle

There are so many things to be interested in or passionate about. Where can you go to gather with people who share the same fascination that you do? Your answer, the public library! But how can you make this happen in your community? Your answer, you don't have to. Encourage and allow patron facilitated programs at your library. Your patrons can run programs that interest them, and you can support them where and when they need it.

What is a patron facilitated group, anyway? It is a gathering of people sharing a similar passion who interconnect at the library around this passion. The commonality these people share will most likely be only this one interest. Lead by one patron whose interest in and personal ownership of this particular group energizes all the attendees. The group sees the library as their meeting space.

Who can gather at the library? Each library sets its own guidelines for what kinds of groups can meet there, but it's important to not just look at groups of adults meeting. What about children or tweens or teens? Gatherings of people, regardless of age, are important. Everyone needs a place where they can congregate with like-minded individuals.

Why do people want to meet at the library? This is a neutral space that doesn't require anything from its users. Where else can you go that doesn't require a paid membership or insist that you subscribe to a particular belief system? The public library is the answer. Everyone meets there as equals. The differently abled can come to a place that is completely accessible for them. The person who doesn't want anyone in his home can leave his messy, kid-filled house behind. The library accommodates all these challenges.

What responsibilities does the library have to these groups? That answer will be different for every library. It could be that the library provides a space with tables and chairs only. There may be a space that has an LCD projector and a coffeepot. Maybe there are kitchen facilities for people to bring snacks for their gathering. Ideally, nothing about these groups costs the library money. Perhaps all the library ever hears from these groups is "It's time to schedule next year's/week's/month's meeting."

How do patron facilitated groups come to be? It's a very organic process. No two groups develop the same way. When someone suggests a program to the library, there are three options. One, have the library develop and run the program. Two, have the "suggester" develop and run the program. Three, ignore the whole conversation and pretend it didn't happen. Sometimes when a program suggestion fits within the library's scope of activity or there is a staff person that is truly passionate about the idea, the library can run the program. More than likely the patron will be encouraged to develop the idea himself. Whether the library helps publicize the event or provides various support materials is a library's own decision. If they choose to let a patron organize and run a group, the library has no responsibility for whether the group is formed beyond a germ of an idea. The onus is on the patron who suggested the gathering. In the best case, the library has no risk financial or otherwise.

Is there a time when the library must participate in patron facilitated programs? The best guideline is the age of the participants. If this is a tween- or teen-facilitated group, there may have to be a library staff member that is "the responsible adult in the room" while the tweens or teens actually run the program themselves. The library's mission statement and/or strategic plan will indicate the types of programs the library may choose to get involved in as well. Most libraries have book groups that they sponsor. As an example, a book group focused on Christian fiction may be best left to a motivated patron instead of the library staff.

At this point, you may be wondering who came up with this idea of patron facilitated programs? We definitely didn't. Maybe our wording is newer, but the idea certainly is not. Our library, Madison Public Library (MPL) in Madison, Ohio, uses volunteers to do lots of different things. Many libraries in small towns across the country couldn't survive without their volunteers. We are no different. In our case, not only do we have volunteers doing "normal" stuff like shelving books and helping with clerical jobs, we have people who want to lead programs centered around various interests. We think that's great.

In our current strategic plan, one of our goals is to encourage more groups to use the library as a meeting place. We have a limited amount of staff who can run programs, and it appears our community has almost limitless interests. Even better, there are a bunch of really talented, dedicated patrons who love sharing their expertise with others. Instead of concentrating on what we don't have, we concentrate on what we do have. What we have is space along with the expected library resources like books and other materials to support various interest groups. We feel as a member of the community that we shouldn't charge groups to meet at the library. As such, we are the only place in town where people can meet for free. We also have very few restrictions on who can meet at the library. There can be no selling of merchandise as well as no alcohol or firearms present. As a result we have birthday parties and baby showers and gardening groups and Bible studies here. Sometimes it feels like there are very few groups in town that haven't met at the library at some point in time.

In our Madison community of approximately eighteen thousand people, we have a wide range of patron facilitated programs meeting at the library. There are a number of independent groups that meet at the library but are dying for new members. Those two types of groups get a little different treatment than closed groups or private gatherings that often involve cake like baby showers and birthday parties! Of course, there are also a variety of groups that the library itself sponsors. The following examples are some of our patron facilitated groups. Each has had a slightly different story associated with it. Even if some of them have a staff member involved, the "heavy lifting" for the group is done by the patron leader. Perhaps the descriptions will fire your imagination and give you suggestions of things to try or remind you of patrons who are interested in these same things and might want to lead a group of like-minded individuals at your library.

Yarn N Yak. This weekly knitting group was the brainchild of a handful of Madison residents including a staff member. Since a staff member is involved, this group has a few more freedoms. Their group is listed as a "library activity" because the staff member is there when they meet. She takes more responsibility for building use than we would ordinarily allow a strictly patron-run group. However, when the staff member is not there, the group meets anyway. Instead of staying after the building has officially closed, an option for a group with a staff member involved, they finish their meeting when the library closes, like other groups.

LEGO club. This monthly group for elementary- and middle-school children was the idea of one very determined young fifth-grade boy. He walked up to one of the librarians and said, "I have an idea for a LEGO club at the library, and I will be its president." This young man met with the librarian who handled tween and teen programs on several occasions, and they worked out a plan. This tween now runs the LEGO club each month for between twenty and thirty children and tweens. His unique vision is nothing like other libraries' LEGO clubs. The members of this club don't just sit on the floor and build something for an hour from the library's "vat o' LEGOs." MPL hardly owns any LEGOs at all. Instead this young man wanted his group to be about having a place for participants to show off LEGO creations to others who would appreciate the time and effort involved in building them. Each meeting is called to order by this tween where he starts by asking participants to come to the front of the room, talk about what each brought, and describe how long it took to build it. Then the next forty minutes is about walking throughout the room talking to exhibitors and playing with their creations. At the end of this meeting, he has his group chose new "build off" topics. Each month there is a different topic chosen by the group. Everyone is invited to create their interpretation of the topic and return with it the next month. The adult in the room is really only there to reassure parents there is an adult in the program.

Team 404. This started as a group of high schoolers who sought out an advisor of sorts and a location to gather when they felt their high school no longer offered a club that fit their needs and desires. They came to the library for help. A group of about ten teenagers wanted a place to meet to just talk about technology, the way their high school Tech Club had been. With the addition of a meeting space and the technology librarian, these teens created a new group called Team 404. Meeting weekly, for a few months, it was a popular group. Then real life set in, and the original teens stopped coming. Instead teens not as interested in technology were stopping by to chat with the technology librarian. They complained that high schoolers didn't have the opportunity to help choose library programs like the younger children did, and something should be done about that. So halfway through the school year, Team 404 became less about technology and more about gathering to talk and play board games and advise the library on programs. And there are still five to eight kids who come each week.

The Watercolor Group. Originally this was a similar group to Yarn N Yak. It was supposed to be a group of adults gathering to work on their watercolor paintings together. Up until this point several of the founding members had been going to a gathering offered by the local community college, but these people decided driving twenty-five minutes in each direction once a week, particularly in the snow, wasn't fun. So meeting at the library was closer. Quickly after beginning, this gathering morphed into a teaching group for adults, teens, and tweens. People were coming to get tutored by the attendees who had been painting for a while. Some were coming to the group having never done watercolor before but always wanting to try. Quickly this group outgrew its original meeting space in the library and moved to a different library location.

The Friendly Scrappers. This group of women who both scrapbook and make cards grew out of a somewhat sad experience. There were two different groups from town who met at the library to scrapbook. Several of the now-founding members of the Friendly Scrappers thought they could join these other groups, but they didn't actually want anyone else coming. So the spurned scrapbookers contacted the library. They said they were forming another scrapbooking group where anyone could come and would the library reserve them a space once a month. Additionally, they asked if anyone inquired about an open scrapbooking group, could the library refer those people to this group. Now we have three scrapbooking groups meeting here. Each one of them loves not having to clean their houses, leaving their children with their husbands, and having "girls night out"! Outside of knowing the Friendly Scrappers exist, the library has no real involvement in their group at all.

MPL has long-standing community groups who have met at the library seemingly forever. Organizations like the Madison Garden Club, the Northeast Ohio Rose Society, the Friends of Arcola Creek, the local chapter of the Embroiderers' Guild of America, and the local Toastmasters group who all take new members at any time. These groups have members who are both regular library patrons and those who only enter the building for the meetings. They are an important part of the library and the Madison community.

It's embarrassing to admit, but MPL didn't consciously decide one day to support and encourage patron facilitated programs. It was more like a realization a little more than a year ago that we had a few of these groups going and perhaps we should really try to encourage more to develop. So when we did our strategic plan a few months ago, we specifically wrote into it that we would foster more patron facilitated groups.

If you want to initiate or encourage these types of groups to develop in your library, there are a few things we have learned along the way:

Develop a culture of trust and respect at your library. This is the big element we didn't realize we had already or that perhaps it was a bit unusual amongst libraries. Collectively the MPL staff is interested in so many different things, but we are most interested in the lives of our patrons. We know the name of small children's beloved stuffed animals who attend storytime along with their owners and we know when someone's mother has had hip surgery. Therefore, it's not a big stretch to be interested in and supportive of someone who wants to start a group for people interested in whatever they're interested in. Perhaps a couple of staff members may be interested in it already. If not, the staff probably know someone else in the community to whom they can recommend this new program or idea, because it would be just perfect for him or her.

Be blind to age and ability. Currently MPL has three and soon to be four programs that are facilitated by tween or teen patrons. These groups seem to have a higher than average percentage of youth on the autism spectrum. We seem to be making a name for ourselves in the community as a place that is "spectrum friendly." These tweens and teens don't see labels and limitations in their friends and neither does the library. These groups, particularly the LEGO club, have more people attending each month than many of the adult groups that meet at the library!

Don't limit the groups' development. It was mentioned earlier that these groups develop organically. Groups that are not run by the library can be more specialized and in some ways have more freedoms to grow than a strictly "library program." Let these groups be who they want to be.

Accept the fleeting nature of some gatherings. Some groups may only meet for a short time. Interest wanes. Membership lags. The fad is over. If a group can't or doesn't want to meet anymore, give their space to someone else. There will always be a new group who wants to gather in support of their cause or interest. Let them.

Support self-policing. This is particularly important with groups run by tweens and teens. These groups don't want to lose the meeting space or whatever additional amenities the library provides. If there is some type of concern or problem with a patron group, let them find the answer and fix it themselves.

Relax. This may be the hardest thing to do, particularly if this is a group that occasionally needs to have "an adult presence." Whether a staff member stays there the entire time or just "pops in" unexpectedly from time to time, let the groups be. If this is truly a patron facilitated group then draconian rules and limited creative freedom are not going to make it a successful group.

We really can't stress enough the idea that in order for patron facilitated programs to be successful, your library needs to exude trust and respect for all your patrons. To be brutally honest, without mutual respect, you have very little chance of being successful. No one is going to approach you with their ideas if they think you're going to brush them off or ignore them. This is especially important with tween- and teen-facilitated groups. While it takes the most trust in your patrons to have these types of programs, the rewards are also significantly more. With that said, the cultivation of groups in this age range deserves special mention and extra attention.

Mandatory mutual respect. MPL does not have a monopoly on articulate teens and tweens who see their library as a safe and neutral place to gather with their friends to participate in activities they all enjoy. However, our teens and tweens know that there are multiple staff members that they can approach at any time with their ideas for "cool things to do at the library." These may be programs that need direct librarian involvement, but more often than not, they need a space and the occasional adult to wander through.

The five-person rule. When we have a tween or teen who wants to start a group at the library around a particular interest, he or she has to find five other people who promise to come faithfully to the gatherings. Sometimes this means programs don't go beyond the idea phase because the originator can't find the necessary number of people. Other times, a group has disbanded because after a few meetings, people stop coming.

Pop-up visits. Because teens, particularly, are very zealous in their desire for autonomy, most of the teen groups do not have an adult in their meetings at all times. Instead, they have "pop ups." This makes self-policing, which all groups must do, incredibly important. Teens know that if any library staff member "happens" into their gathering and there is something happening that violates the library's behavior code, that group will instantaneously lose its autonomy and very probably will lose its ability to gather at the library.

Happy parents, happy kids. With programs for people who are not independently mobile, success can be based on whether there is someone in their life that sees the value of the program. We have found that niche-interest groups, like our tween-run LEGO club, make parents very happy. They are more than willing to bring their children to this gathering because the parents don't have a passion for this. At this group their children meet with other children who are similarly crazy for LEGOs and their parents can do something else. Parents of teens are more than happy to drop their children at the library to play Yu-Gi-Oh or Settlers of Catan with other teens instead of having them all crammed in their house being noisy and talking about things that don't make sense. What greater publicity can a library have than happy parents telling their friends how their tween or teen loves to go to the library?

We know that patron facilitated programming may not work for everyone, but consider your community: Are you the only meeting space in town? Are you already the gathering place of the community? How can you leverage what you already have and make it better? Start small; begin a specialized book group. Encourage your staff members to have their card-making parties at the library instead of rotating friends' houses. And of course, do what you do best. Listen to your community, and help find ways to connect people and materials with those of similar interests.

Chapter Seven

Programming—Helping the Community Learn More about Itself

Judith Wines

Programming for small libraries is challenging on two fronts: coming up with the resources to provide programs and providing programs that members of your community find interesting enough to attend. Traditionally, libraries have provided what I'll term "good for you" programs, such as hosting information on health, nutrition, and similar topics. In our experience: the attendance at these programs is often poor. Most adults want to spend their free time doing things that bring pleasure. Libraries, however are drawn to this sort of program because they are often no cost, and because they fit well with our mission to act in an educational capacity.

The need is to find low-cost programs that fall into the category of activities adults elect to do in their spare time. What has worked for our library falls broadly into two categories: programs in which participants learn more about their community and programs where the community members themselves are the substance of the programs (or, as we call them, the events, which just sound more fun than programs).

Our library first ventured down this programming lane by offering library hikes. These outings were billed as family events and featured hiking opportunities within a few miles of the library. We did three hikes per season (fall and spring) and focused on lesser-known walks and hikes. While there are a number of well-known trails at state parks in the area, most patrons who said they enjoyed hiking knew nothing of the less prominent trails that were local. In order to take people to new places, and execute the theme Explore Your Backyard, we had to find new trails. We consulted the website of the Nature Conservancy for trails in the area, and, more fruitfully, the website of the Land Trust Alliance, which links to many local land trusts around the country. Additionally, local hiking enthusiasts are great sources of information and may be willing to lead or co-lead hikes. Because our hikes were billed as family friendly, most were no longer than a couple of miles. Until our suburban library (seventeen miles from the capital of New York) endeavored onto this series, we had no idea that there was a fifty-foot waterfall about a mile from the library and a musical bridge, complete with mallets, five miles away.

The enthusiasm with which these hikes were met prompted us to expand our programming that featured nature in our backyard. We added quarterly bird walks, led by an environmental educator from the community college, and wildflower walks and tree walks. For these naturalist-led programs, we did not go into the woods, but usually walked from the library or drove a few miles away to learn which trees populate front lawns in the village and which wildflowers line the roads on which commuters drove each day.

Not everyone is a nature enthusiast so we applied the same idea about going local to homes in the community. The library organized a house walk in which a staff member from a local historic preservation society came out and pointed out the mansard roofs, eyebrow windows, and widow's walks that were among the architectural features of houses in the village. The walk has prompted an initiative to create QR codes for the homes of willing homeowners that direct smartphone users to a webpage about the history of the house. A garden tour led to a seedling exchange that has connected an avid group of growers.

Another way a library can tap in to community is to crowd-source its programs. An around-the-world potluck series, in which the library provides the space, a sign-up list, and makes cookbooks available for the cuisine in question is a no-cost, low-preparation way to have the community be the program. Potlucks almost guarantee good food, and good food is always a draw. Our around-the-world series always begins with participants introducing themselves, and stating what, if any, connection they have with the country at hand. Each country has had attendees who show up only because it is *their* country, and they want to showcase their family recipes. The events foster a greater awareness of the ethnic and cultural diversity of the community and prompt the regulars to venture into cuisines that may never have otherwise attempted.

In an attempt to give-the-people-what-they-want, our library began a regular trivia night. We were inspired by the popularity of trivia night at area bars and wanted to provide the same experience closer to home. Our policies allow adults to bring their own beverages to designated programs (including potlucks) and we billed our trivia night as bar-style and highlighted the option to bring your own beer. We elected to charge five dollars a person and to allow participants to work in teams of up to four people. The winning team takes half the door, but the cash is usually donated back to the library. The program would work fine without the admission charge, but the heightened stakes and the sense of helping out the library both contribute to the atmosphere of the evening. We have a community member volunteer to compile the questions and emcee the evening. The library provides popcorn for a snack and the space to play.

The third and likely most common way to tap in to your community to improve your programming is to have community members present on areas of expertise. A library in our area holds what they call Friday Morning Free for Alls (FMFFA), in which each Friday morning a member of the community comes in to talk about his or her topic of interest. Recent topics include a Rotary Mission to Africa, a trip to Alaska, Hurricane Katrina relief work in Mississippi, a talk about a collection of historic buttons, and a wood carving demonstration. This library serves a large suburban population (and the timing of the program effectively targets it toward retirees), but the concept could easily be adapted to FFMFFA (First Friday Morning Free for All). At our library we've had excellent results with community member presentations on topics as varied as triathlon training to bread making.

You can also make your program planning community driven. Our library offers two book clubs, one in which the title is selected by the librarian, the other in which titles are nominated and voted on by the members of the group. Libraries have used Pinterest boards to take suggestions for craft and DIY programs. Members of the Pinterest board "like" activities they would like the library to do, and each month the library hosts a program in which participants come in and create that craft. Social media increases the flexibility and responsiveness of your program scheduling. While most of our events are still scheduled far enough in advance to be included in our monthly e-newsletter, our Facebook and Twitter accounts allow us to program spontaneously as well. When we had a week of rain followed by a beautiful Saturday morning, the library posted a hike to a waterfall on Facebook and Twitter on Friday evening and had fifteen hikers show up at the library at eight o'clock the next morning. This versatility allows the library to be more responsive to the needs of its community.

Community member–driven programming dovetails nicely with community outreach efforts. Having a pastry chef teach a class on demonstrating cake decorating techniques gives her new exposure and may bring new customers to her restaurant. Asking the police chief to send an officer to talk about what's real and what's not on *CSI* will help the police department view the library as an effective means of engaging citizens.

The ultimate example of community-centered programming may be libraries that rearrange their purpose in response to the needs of the community. When Hurricane Sandy swept across the East Coast in 2012, libraries in its path accommodated the needs of their community by extending their hours, becoming charging stations for communities without power, providing free coffee, and screening movies to entertain restless kids. When libraries step up in this manner, their communities see them not so much as one of many often bureaucratic services but as a true partner in creating a vibrant community.

REFERENCE

Bayliss, Sarah. "Libraries Respond to Hurricane Sandy, Offering Refuge, WiFi, and Services to Needy Communities." School Library Journal, November 1, 2012. http://www.slj.com/2012/11/featured/libraries-respond-to-hurricane-sandy-offering-refuge-wifi-and-services-to-needy-communities/ (accessed July 5, 2013).

Chapter Eight

Successful Adult Programming Using Local Resources

Diana Stirling

Your library lies at the heart of your small community. And it is not primarily because of the books and videos that you house, or because of your computers and wireless access, although these are important services. Your library is vital because of the relationships you foster with and within the community. And what keeps you vibrant and relevant is excellent programming. Through your programs you can honor your local heritage and resources and expand your horizons.

The first part of the chapter suggests starting points for identifying themes and resources based on the context of your community. Taking the time to answer the questions will provide an abundance of programming options. You may come up with ideas that will serve you long into the future! Keep this list around for times when you need to organize something in a hurry.

Following the context section are ways to identify people and organizations that can present or support adult programs. It's not a bad idea to create a spreadsheet for these contacts. Sometimes it takes several conversations or even several years before a program can be implemented. You won't want to lose important contact information in the interim. The spreadsheet can also hold notes and follow-up questions. A file containing your questions and answers, ideas, and local resources (including people), will be invaluable to your long-term program planning. Setting that up at the outset will help keep all the necessary ingredients for great programming together for future reference.

Here are some suggestions and questions to help jump-start your thinking about the local context. Our answers and some of the resulting programs are offered as examples. Take any useful ideas and adapt and expand them as suits you. Maybe these will set you off in an entirely new direction of your own.

Are there one, two, or more major themes that identify your community in its historical context? What about significant historic events that have taken place in or around your location? Are there historic buildings in your town? Is there a history of industry; are there particular issues related to that industry? What about your town's literary history?

Mining in our town goes back to the late 1800s. Mammoth was established around the stamp mill that served the original Tiger Mine a few miles uphill. Many of the houses from Tiger were moved down to the newly incorporated Mammoth in the 1950s, when BHP bought the mine and established a company town about fifteen miles away. Although the mine itself closed in the late 1990s, it is still a large part of the identity of the area communities.

This historical context provides a wealth of opportunities for library programs. There are families here that have roots going back to the original miners, who were mostly from Mexico. There are photos and stories to be shared. One local author who worked at the big mine for thirty-five years gives engaging presentations with descriptions of the mining process and photos of miners, many of whom are known by community members.

In addition to this large mining operation, there were many smaller mines in the area. Most of these sites are ghost towns or even unmarked ruins now. What a great opportunity for a field trip! Other mining-related programs could include mineral identification and adventures for rock hounds, the future of mining, and mining and the environment. We actually did a program at our library related to possible future mining on Mars.

Ranching and farming have also been important in our area. Programs about historic ranching and farming families would be sure to garner interest. How about a program to explore brands used in the past and those still in use today? What about a program about women and ranching? Why not invite a rancher or farmer to talk about issues and challenges today and the way their practices have changed from those of the past? And we can't talk about ranching without at least mentioning rodeo. Programs about horse training and roping are bound to attract participants.

Significant or dramatic historic events are also a great foundation for a program. If there are different perspectives on historic events, why not design a program to present both sides and spark a discussion? A massacre of Apaches in 1871 in our area had deep political and sociocultural underpinnings and implications for the future of our country. These events can shed light on where we've been and provide lessons for creating a better future.

Who knows better than we do how the power of story moves people? We love not only the stories of the famous but also those of everyday people who overcame difficulties and persevered in troubled times.

Any historical theme is a perfect opportunity to partner with the local historical society. Does your historical society have any special events coming up? Ask how you can support their efforts, maybe by displaying a few relevant resources and hosting author events. A few years ago, the historical society in a neighboring community was chosen to participate in the Key Ingredients traveling exhibition of the Smithsonian Institution. We partnered with them by displaying a few artifacts, gathering submissions for a local cookbook, and then selling some of the cookbooks in the library. We could have extended this program by hosting a potluck of recipes from the cookbook.

What are some of the outstanding characteristics of your natural environment? How has it changed in the past and how is it changing now? What about interesting planned environments in your area? Don't overlook the soundscape. And what about clouds?

Mammoth is in the valley of the San Pedro River. Although the river flows underground most of the year, the mesquite woods along the river are famous as a haven for birds. The library sponsored a bird walk that resulted in the formation of a local birding club. Maybe your library could do something similar or could promote the Great Backyard Bird Count. A program before the bird count could introduce participants to the typical species of your area.

What about ranching and farming? How have these activities impacted the natural environment? Could you invite a local farmer or rancher to discuss this?

Are you near any public lands? Maybe you could have a representative come and talk about specific characteristics of the place, or the library could sponsor a field trip to a local destination.

Is there an arboretum or botanical garden nearby? This is a great opportunity for learning more about plant life and ecosystems. We are fortunate to be near the Biosphere 2 project. Our field trip there was one of the most successful programs we've run.

What about local wildlife? How much do we actually know about the animals we see every day? You might think making casts of animal tracks is an activity only for kids, but adults can really enjoy this, too. Insects and venomous creatures can also make interesting topics for programs.

And in thinking about the environment, look up! Explore the climate and weather. How about a class to learn about different types of clouds or about how to record weather data? The National Weather Service uses citizen scientists for the Cooperative Observer Program to record daily weather data, and for the SKYWARN program, to help provide information about severe weather hazards. Maybe your library could help people get involved in these programs locally.

Another citizen science initiative is the USA National Phenology Network's project called Nature's Notebook, which uses volunteers to observe local plants and animals. You can even set your library up as a shared site for volunteers.

Zooniverse is a site that collects information about a variety of citizen science projects all in one place. A look at these might spark some ideas. A quick Internet search for "citizen science [your state]" could also yield interesting results.

What ethnic groups are represented in your community? How have different ethnicities contributed to your local history (food, traditions, local events, etc.)?

Culture is a terrific place to look for program ideas. Foodways, in particular, have great appeal. What are the traditional foods of your area? Have you explored wild foods and their preparation by early residents? We had a fun program during which we collected cholla cactus buds and then actually prepared (and ate!) several dishes using them. Do you have a variety of ethnic groups in your community? How do their foodways compare? A local cookbook and a potluck to launch it can be fun as well as a great fundraiser.

Do different ethnic or religious groups in your area have traditional ways of dressing that could be the foundation of a program? Why not learn to wrap a sari or tie an obi? How about exploring the culture of work through types of clothing?

What about languages? The library is a wonderful place to offer language classes. Don't forget English (our ESL classes are popular and well appreciated) and American Sign Language as options.

Culture as a foundation for programs overlaps both history and entertainment. Take a look at the variety of stories, dances, music, visual art, and family traditions that could be used for interesting, cross-cultural programming ideas.

What types of entertainment are available in your community? Are there traditional types of entertainment specific to your locale or to ethnic groups within the community?

This category includes performance as well as participatory entertainment. If your library is very small, is there an outdoor space that could be used for performances? We've had a magician who juggled with fire perform outside in the parking lot. (No juggling with fire allowed in the library!) The library could also host music lessons. For example, we have a local volunteer who teaches a weekly guitar class. You could also have demonstrations or classes in different dance styles (depending on the space available). Is there a local square dancing group? How about folklorico?

What about starting a reader's theater group at your library? While most of the resources you'll find are for reader's theater in the classroom, it is an art form that is by no means limited to children. Any scene from literature can be scripted for performance, but scenes with great dialogue are best. And in contrast to regular theater, reader's theater traditionally uses no sets, costumes, or props, and doesn't require memorization.

What kinds of things do adults in your area enjoy learning? Do people mention topics of interest that they want to know more about? What local attractions have you overlooked when planning programs?

People of all ages enjoy learning. The problem with educational programs for adults is that sometimes they're just not fun. Think of hands-on activities where participants are actively engaged. Several of the ideas previously mentioned, such as guitar classes, field trips, and citizen science projects, illustrate the possibilities. Other typical offerings include needlework groups and technology classes. Even topics that require a brief talk can often include a hands-on component.

Don't be afraid to go beyond the book, adding displays, workshops, and field trips related to themes from book club selections.

How does your current programming encourage social interaction? What kinds of hobbies or special interests can you support to help create new social connections and maintain those that already exist in your community?

Social interaction is an important component of small library service. Patrons interact both with library staff and with one another. Many a new friendship has been forged during a library program, while using the computer, or even while browsing for a good movie or book.

Some programs intrinsically invite people to chat. We can all knit at home, but it's fun to get together at the library to relax with other knitters, pick up tips and patterns, and enjoy the company of other people.

A weekly coffeehouse program could be implemented at little expense. Snacks, beverages, and light entertainment are all that is required.

Board and card games also provide an easy way for people to make new friends. How about a weekly or monthly game night? How about a chess, checkers, or backgammon club?

Hobby groups tend to be quite sociable. Model rockets or remote-controlled vehicles, anyone? How about solar projects or an upcycling club? What are people collecting?

Outdoor activities can also contribute to social interaction. Horseshoes? Bocce ball? Croquet?

Small changes to a planned program can make a big difference in supporting social interaction. As previously mentioned, even a lecture/discussion can include a hands-on activity. During the activity, participants will naturally begin to intermingle. Offering light snacks or providing a quick ice breaker can also encourage people to get to know one another better.

Are there local issues that you can help address through education, hands-on workshops, or ongoing projects?

Sometimes the library can become a focal point for addressing community needs. Not only is it a place where people meet who might otherwise not cross paths, but there are also abundant resources for reference and research readily available. Seed exchanges are an example of one program that can address the community need for fresh, wholesome food, in addition to being just plain fun for local gardeners. If you have some outdoor space, why not consider creating a small community garden, as well, where you can experiment with developing and cultivating local varieties?

Other community programs might include home repair and weatherization workshops, DIY solar project workshops (such as how to build a simple window box heater), information about how to start a time bank, a neighbors-helping-neighbors day, or perhaps a walking club.

What kinds of resources are available in your community for job seekers, small business owners, and beginning entrepreneurs? Are there unmet needs in these areas?

Most of our libraries are already offering support to job seekers who use the public computers to apply for work. We can help further by hosting resume and cover letter workshops, and by providing practice in interviewing skills. Adding links to local employers on your library's website or Pinterest site can also be helpful. Some of our local employers don't advertise in our weekly newspaper; they only post openings on their websites. If a job seeker doesn't know to check those regularly, an opportunity could be missed.

Small business owners can also benefit from programs and resources at the library. SCORE is an organization that supports small business with a wealth of information online and with local volunteer mentors. You may be able to get a SCORE volunteer to come to your library to do mentoring or to give a brief presentation. If not, you can have a workshop to orient business owners to all the resources available at their site. The Small Business Administration is also a wonderful online resource. And don't forget local business owners. You could invite those who have successfully run businesses in your area to mentor new entrepreneurs and host a gathering to get the process off the ground.

Check with the economic development organization that serves your area and see what they have to offer. Ours actually has a mobile small business support center.

Even if you know little about running a small business yourself, you can serve the community well by using your expertise at connecting people with resources.

PARTNERING FOR GREATER IMPACT: PEOPLE AND ORGANIZATIONS

You don't have to do everything alone. In addition to your volunteers, there are lots of people and organizations in and around your community that are waiting to help you. When considering your options, don't overlook these possibilities:

- Hobbyists and skilled amateurs
- Retired and currently working experts
- Academics with enthusiasm

Amateurs are people who love what they love, and they typically enjoy nothing more than sharing their enthusiasm with others. Ask patrons and others you meet about their weekends and how they spend their free time. You might be surprised at the knowledge and passion you uncover.

If you're planning a program on a particular theme, try checking to see if there is an amateur club that might help out. An easy example is finding a local astronomer or astronomy club that is willing to come and set up telescopes for a night of stargazing. Rock hounds might enjoy sharing their collections, leading field trips, or even starting a club at your library. Other possibilities are model rocket clubs, robotics clubs, and gardening clubs.

Retirees are another potential source of great program ideas. When you meet a retired person, ask what kind of work they did and consider the possibilities. A retired person may also have skills incidental to their former work, such as computer savvy or business acumen, that could be useful for classes or workshops.

If there is a college or university nearby, check and see what kinds of outreach programs they offer. You might be surprised at the possibilities. Even though the nearest university to us is almost fifty miles away, representatives from the Hi-RISE Mars imaging program have traveled to our library and offered outstanding free programs. Faculty from a nearby community college campus have also provided wonderful programs at no cost. One example was a talk about prehistoric humans—a tie-in to Jean Auel's *Clan of the Cave Bear* series—that included casts of actual bones that could be handled and compared.

Check with your county extension agency and ask about their outreach programs. If you are planning a community garden project or seed savers exchange, programs from your county extension service could fit right in.

At the county level, the attorney general's office may offer programs in protecting one's identity and avoiding scams, while the county health department may provide classes for new parents, senior citizens, and people with specific illnesses such as diabetes. Offering the library as a site for these programs helps provide needed services without straining library staff time and budgets.

And don't forget to check with statewide organizations such as the humanities council, historical society, and state archives. You may find that they have speakers available or ready-made programs that can be had for free or by submitting a simple grant application. In Arizona, the Humanities Council has a wonderful Road Scholar program which provides speakers on a wide variety of topics. The grant application takes just a few minutes to complete and the programs are well worth the effort.

SPECIAL EVENTS

Special events, particularly yearly events, can be a terrific basis for programs. They are appealing not only for their content but also because, from a planning perspective, they can be improved every year but the basic format and materials only require minor alterations after they are in place. They are great for patrons, too, because they grow to anticipate these yearly events.

Most of us are familiar with the yearly events that are promoted by the ALA (American Library Association), but there are many more possibilities. What's stopping you from starting an annual event based on an obscure fact that might appeal to your particular community? A good place to start is *Chase's Calendar of Events*, a book that catalogs special events, festivals, holidays, and birthdays of famous people around the world. You can also look at the history of your community and create a program to commemorate a significant event. Why not start with a birthday party for your library?

Here is a sample of some annual events that we've incorporated into our calendar:

International Games Day—Third Saturday in November

This is sponsored by the ALA and is great fun. Sponsors often provide free board games to participating libraries. Some libraries compete in video game tournaments, but if your technological infrastructure is not up to this, great fun can be had with board games, outdoor games, treasure hunts and geocaching activities, and Global Gossip—a gossip game that travels from library to library around the world. You may think this event is primarily for kids, but we have lots of adult participation.

World Listening Day—July 18

This event marks the birthday of Canadian composer R. Murray Schafer. Schafer was one of the founders of the acoustic ecology movement. The purpose is simple: to raise awareness about the local soundscape. To celebrate the day, we have an annual sound walk. Absolutely nothing is required except the ability to hear and to walk. We start inside the library with a brief explanation of the guidelines. Then we walk to various places nearby and stop and listen silently at each location. We usually provide notebooks so participants can jot down thoughts and observations. Back at the library we discuss what we heard. Either the introduction or the wrap-up can be expanded to include a discussion of the changes in the local soundscape over the years and the potential impact of future changes on the sound environment. Check out the World Listening Project website (www .worldlisteningproject.org) for more information.

National Poetry Month — April

To celebrate National Poetry Month, we mark out a circle on the floor with masking tape. We hang a simple sign above it that designates it as the Poet's Circle. Anyone is welcome to stand or sit in the Poet's Circle and read or recite a favorite poem. The poem can be famous, obscure, or original. We take a photo of each poet and post these on our website. We've found that people of all ages enjoy this activity, which costs nothing and requires very little preparation.

Fall Festival

We set this event up like a carnival with simple, handmade games and activities. We set up tables for crafts and have a bean bag toss indoors. Outside we bob for apples, have relay and three-legged races, do face painting, and have games like bocce ball, horseshoes, or croquet. We use soda cans stacked in a pyramid for a ring toss game (rings made of long, twisted craft pipe cleaners); ring a can and win the soda. We end with a cake walk. This event is popular with people of all ages. It doesn't cost much but it does require a lot of volunteer help.

It doesn't take a lot of money to provide great programs for adults, but it does require careful preparation. If you have staff available or a reliable corps of volunteers, the tasks can be divided and the work shared. Great adult programming will benefit your community and can give you a greater appreciation of the important role you play in the lives of your neighbors.

Part Three

Management

Chapter Nine

Building a Dynamic System for Relevant Statistical Analysis

Joshua K. Johnson

Believe it or not, the most important word in this section's title is "analysis." Why is analysis more important than statistics themselves? Because various researchers over the past decade point out that librarians are good at gathering statistical data, but generally bad at evaluating it. Simply throwing gate counts and circulations at library boards and stakeholders will no longer be enough to compete with other government organizations for tax dollars. The extent to which librarians can prove their value to the public will determine the survival of libraries in the future. Statistics may be evaluated in a wide variety of ways, but the method I elaborate below uses resources commonly available, ties evaluation closely to organizational goals, and advocates leveraging statistics already tracked by many libraries.

UNDERSTANDING THE PROMISES WE MAKE

Often, discussions about statistical analysis will begin by sharing how statistics can show a wide variety of people the value libraries represent to their constituents. That sort of discussion is fruitful, but only if framed in the context of what your library does for the community it serves. I advocate starting your statistical analysis by examining the document that distills what your organization does into a concise paragraph or page: its mission statement. Libraries tend to have some statement of purpose tailored to match their organizational goals. Most importantly, your mission statement contains overt and implied promises made to those who visit and fund your library.

Let's walk through the process of teasing out promises by examining the mission statement of the American Library Association's (ALA) Best Small

Library in America award recipient for 2013: the Southern Area Public Library of West Virginia (SAPL). Using a "real life" example to illustrate will make the process more accessible. Their mission statement reads,

> Southern Area Library strives to create an environment where life-long education flourishes. We are an equal opportunity educational resource for self-directed learning as well as providing research assistance, guided instruction and classroom experiences, and life-enriching activities for the greater community. We work with our patrons to encourage their economic and educational advancement and to enhance their quality of life. (Southern Area Public Library, "About Us," 2010)

Here is a sample list of SAPL promises that library users might reasonably expect after reading the statement:

- We provide life-long learning resources.
- We nurture life-long education.
- Our building's features will emphasize elements that foster lifelong education.
- All library users will receive research assistance.
- All library users will have access to guided instruction.
- Library staff will provide classroom experiences for all library users.
- The library will house or otherwise encourage community activities.
- Library staff will make special effort to advance library users' economic standing.
- Library staff will make special effort to advance library users' educational standing.
- The library will adopt programs and practices that increase quality of life for library users.

You will notice that "all library users" is repeated, but with different promises in several of the listed examples. This is not an accident. It is important, at this stage of analysis, that each listed item contains only one very specific promise because this will aid you later in the evaluation process. It will be nearly impossible to discuss ways to track your ability to do what you say you will if you don't break them down in this way. You may also notice that some of the promises are lifted directly from the wording used in the original mission statement, and some are derived from an implied promise gleaned from what might be reasonably assumed as a library user. I make no distinction because library users, library boards, and others to whom you may need to prove your value are unlikely to make such distinctions. When examining your own mission statement, consider the following:

- Does your mission statement accurately describe what your library does?

- What promises are you making in your mission statement?
- Which of your services, collections, and so on are related to each promise?
- Are you considering adding to your services and unsure if you can handle the change without adding staff?
- Do you make more promises than you can handle with your current staff?

There is nothing particularly magical about your mission statement; it is just a very condensed and commonly available document. Here are some suggestions for other documents that would be equally fruitful from which to extract promises from using the above method:

- Collection Development Plans or Policies
- Public Internet Access Policies or Guidelines
- Employee Handbooks
- Budget/Statistical Documents
- Planning Documents

I think it is important for librarians to start by evaluating how well we deliver on these promises. By doing this, we begin to make ourselves accountable for what we say we do.

INDICATING VALUE

With a clearer understanding of the organizational promises we need to fulfill, now is the time to open up a more traditional discussion of value. When speaking of what libraries have to offer our communities, librarians often use vague phrases like "value added" or "intrinsic value." These phrases are difficult to measure or define. Instead, we need to begin showing solid analyses that give non-librarians, including users and decision makers, a solid understanding of exactly why libraries are important. Recent funding hardships faced by libraries may have increased the urgency we feel to prove our worth, but it will continually be necessary to show the public and those in charge of library funding specific, meaningful, and measurable ways in which we contribute to our communities and society.

Listing your promises also gives you a set of expectations against which you can measure your library's current processes and procedures. To do this, you need a set of criteria for each promise you listed that is concrete enough to be measured, but relatively easy to obtain. It can be difficult to divide out all of the things your library does that relate to a specific goal, so it helps if you ask yourself questions about your goals. To borrow a goal from the SAPL example, you might ask yourself the following:

- What are "lifelong learning resources"?
- How does our staff share such resources with users?
- How often do staff members share such resources?
- How many requests do we get for these materials?
- How do users discover our lifelong learning resources? In what ways do we facilitate this discovery?
- How intuitively are lifelong learning materials shelved? Are they available online?
- How many uses do our lifelong learning materials get in a month? A year? Ten years?
- Are there any success stories from users of these materials?
- Are these resources more/less expensive than other library materials?
- How does our collection of these materials compare with similar collections in other places?
- What options have we given online users? What does this collection have to offer tablet or cell phone users?

There could be many more questions, but answering such questions gives us a start on evaluating ourselves. Sometimes it even helps to have someone who is not a librarian look at your goals and ask questions. This will give you a fresh perspective and may have the side benefit of better understanding public perceptions of your library. You would also do well to take a moment and think about your library. Make an in-depth list of ways users interact with the following:

- Staff
- Website
- Collections
- Buildings and Grounds
- Meeting rooms

This will give you context for your statistics and help you as you evaluate the promises your library makes.

Traditionally, statistical evaluation follows quantitative methods. Generally speaking, a quantitative approach asks "How many?," "How often?," "Is there a pattern?," or "Can we graph it?" However, since analysis is our goal, I advocate evaluating statistical data in light of qualitative methods. A combination of the two types of inquiry is often called a hybrid method. Researchers often favor this method because it paints a more holistic picture of your library than simply reviewing statistics. You will notice that the list we made above is a hybrid list; it has both qualitative and quantitative elements. For example, analyses like this might allow you to evaluate the initial cost of materials while including anecdotal evidence from the community suggesting that these materials led to better education.

As you ask questions like those above for each listed promise, make an organized list of the answers. It can be simple or complex. If you are assembling quantitative data, I suggest using a spreadsheet. This will make it much easier to set up formulas, averages, charts, and other tools that you may wish to use to make the data more meaningful. Consider this suggested format, based on preceding examples:

LIFELONG LEARNING RESOURCES

- 25 checkouts last month, 244 checkouts last year
- Largest collection in state for our service population
- Publication dates for this collection range from 1985–2014
- Distance traveled by user to locate similar items from a bookstore
- Cost to user, if similar items were purchased online

I like to refer to these as "indicators," since they may be used as a guide to indicate how well your library organization does what it says it will.

There are other places to find indicators. The following list is by no means exhaustive, but it may give you ideas you hadn't considered previously.

Quantitative

- Circulation statistics (most commonly "check-outs," but also in-house uses, etc.)
- Website analytics (hits, unique visitors, duration, etc.)
- Subject/date analysis (examining average publication dates in a given subject or collection)
- Cost-per-use analysis
- ILL requests
- Copy machine and printer uses

Qualitative

- Comparison of collections to peer organizations
- User input (questionnaires, interviews)
- Comparison of collection holdings to Collection Development Policies
- Comparison of overall services with peer institutions (print collections, electronic holdings, ebooks/vendors, study space, training/community Outreach, staffing levels)

- Physical examination of collection for evidence of use (wear and tear or dust)
- Anecdotes (patrons' or colleagues' opinions of the library or collection

Also, consider some of the following thoughts from an administrative or organizational standpoint. These may influence how others view your library staff and collections. It may also give perspective to the different cultural or geographical circumstances your library faces. Knowing the context in which your library operates can make a big difference in how you package your statistical analysis when you pass it on to others.

- What factors, practices, and personnel influence your ability to make good on your promises?
- What physical or monetary limitations could impact your organization's ability to fulfill promises?
- Would the organization be better able to fulfill some promises if it changed the promises it made or cut some services in favor of others?

Some things worth examining may require a few from the above list and many more not listed; for example, figuring out why some parts of your website get the most use or deciding if you need to add staff to your library are some good examples. Feel free to mix and match indicators to get the most complete and complex picture of how well your library fulfills its mission.

Be aware: evaluating your ability to follow through on your promises is a double-edged sword. You can use analysis to show you make good on your promises, as an indicator that you deserve more funding or personnel, or to avoid budget cuts. Unfortunately, you are just as likely to discover areas where you do not live up to your commitments. However, your methods of evaluation are likely to give you a good idea where to alter your practices and policies to achieve your goals. In the long run, you will be better off for your analysis, even if you find many places your library can improve. Showing users and library boards that you are aware of the problem and working toward a solution can also be beneficial, even if you haven't solved the problem yet.

LEVERAGING EXISTING STATISTICS

The process above is an excellent way to discover new ways of looking at your library's ideals, practices, and promises. Even so, you should not discount the statistics you already gather. Use the above strategy to interpret them in ways that are meaningful to those who use and fund your library.

It is difficult for me to imagine a librarian or group of library workers that hasn't already begun keeping some form of raw statistical record or rough gate count. Most states, and certainly the national government, require various forms of statistics from libraries; there's no need to completely reinvent the wheel. What becomes important are how you can use the methods suggested above to discover ways to add to your current cache of useful raw data and how you leverage these toward funding and accomplishing other relevant goals for your library.

As you search old physical and computer files for data related to your library's promises, make sure the data you include is relevant. For example, don't toss in gate counts when you are assessing what titles you need to add to your physics section to bring it more in line with what users need unless you have a way to tie them together directly. This is no time to be overly philosophical; the more closely your data is tied to your point, the more credibility it lends your analysis. Make sure you compare like things. For example, if you have raw data that measures your checkouts per month, computer usage per year, and staff hours per two-week pay period, you technically have three separate and different types of information. However, it would be acceptable to compare these if they all had a common factor. So, a comparison between checkouts and computer usage might be easily accomplished by simply dividing computer usage by twelve to give a figure for average usage per month. It would be much more difficult to compare pay periods to any of the others, unless there is a way to figure out the staff hours for a given year, and then multiply checkout figures by twelve so all can be compared because they cover the same amount of time. The process would be the same for any other common factor, for example, number or type of uses per item.

Above all, be logical and thorough. It may be tempting to slant your statistical analysis to paint your organization in a favorable light. If you do it on purpose, it is unethical. If you do it accidentally, it means you need to be more thorough in your examination. Be certain you use common sense as you examine your findings. When a critical look at your findings shows that your analysis does not match your assertions, it is important to review your methods, and possibly change your assertions. If your practical experience does not match your statistical analysis, you likely need to reexamine your findings for flaws or see if colleagues' experiences challenge your analysis. Some types of examination may mean little unless compared with another library of the same type or size as your own. When possible, you may wish to consider duplicating your analysis using statistics from another library.

Take advantage of time and labor saving computer programs when doing statistical analysis. Microsoft Excel, for example, will pull information from other Excel files and update it automatically; this can make pulling raw data for your own projects a relatively painless process. Another helpful tool for statistical analysis is the "find/replace" function found in Excel and many other spreadsheet programs with similar capabilities to Excel. This makes updating monthly spreadsheets less tedious by removing the need to change every formula by hand.

LEAVING ROOM TO ADAPT

Once you have a good working knowledge of the promises your library makes and have finished brainstorming and collating data that tracks your progress toward their fulfillment, you should consider how you wish to organize this information. Ask yourself the following questions:

- How will you lay out your information; is there a way that will make it easier to add or subtract indicators or information later on?
- What ways can you display your findings that will be intuitive to others? Would using graphs or other visual representation make it more approachable?
- How will the layout aid or hinder comparisons between various indicators over and extended time period?
- Will your methods be easily passed to your future successor?
- What will someone who looks at this in five to ten years think?
- How long will it be before we need to reevaluate our system of analysis for relevance? For accuracy?

It may not seem like it day to day, but the tools and elements of libraries have always changed at a relatively fast pace. This pace is increasing; the indicators you use and the ways users interact with staff and information will change in the next five to ten years.

Attempting to build a system of analysis that can withstand such changes may seem daunting. The first step in such a design is to remember that you will not always be in charge of statistical analysis for your library. Whether you roll that assignment off onto a subordinate or you decide to retire, you will eventually need to turn this apparatus over to someone else. If you keep that person in mind as you go, you will save yourself (and the next person) a great deal of work, and you will be better able to describe your methods to library boards and the others to whom you will communicate your library's progress.

A good next step is to leave room to grow in your data sheets. If you are collecting data to represent indicators in a spreadsheet, for example, the simplest way to make sure you have room to add additional data is to leave two to three blank spaces in the dataset. Then, when you, or your replacement, discover another related statistic to add as an indicator, you can simply add the information into the space without redesigning your entire sheet.

At this stage in the process it is also a good idea to create a timeline for reviewing your analysis so that they remain updated. It would be a shame to go to the trouble of creating a truly meaningful set of statistical analyses that match your library's goals only to repeat the process every three to five years. It is the nature of policies to change. Types and numbers of materials shift and move. If you don't do something to counter it from the beginning, your data will become out of date. However, if you make your methods dynamic from the outset, and build reanalysis into your system of analysis, your analyses will remain valuable through any changes your library encounters.

BEYOND SIMPLE ANALYSIS

Once you have gone through the effort described above, you will eventually have a system in place to evaluate your library in terms of how well you do what you say you will do. Then the difficult part begins; you will find places where you do not fulfill your promises. You may even find there are promises you cannot fulfill. Once this happens, you have three choices: change your policies and practices, alter your mission statement or other promises made by your organization, or ignore your findings and continue on your merry way.

Hopefully, once you have made the effort to accurately evaluate your organization, you will discount the last option immediately. That leaves changing what you do or changing what you promise. Either may be an acceptable way to eliminate the discrepancy.

As an example, let's say your library mission statement promises to house and promote community events. Anecdotal evidence and statistical analysis show clearly that the community expects this service. However, you are painfully aware that the current library budget only covers upkeep of the current building and its collections. You may decide to solve this in a variety of ways. One of the simplest would be to alter your library's mission statement, but that would discount community expectations for the library. You may decide to develop a more complex solution by implementing some form of programming in the existing library space. You may select something even more elaborate and attempt to house small programs in the library, while finding ways to support community events with a public bulletin board or part of the library website. All of these are logical responses to the statistical analysis performed in the preceding example.

This example also shows that statistical analysis, while an excellent tool, is only an evaluation. Analysis makes your library's challenges very clear. It may even reveal poor planning, poor implementation, or staffing problems. However, the key to wise use of statistical analysis is remembering that it is one of many decision-making tools.

In sum, the more rigorously you examine the promises your library makes to the public and its funding body, the more likely your library is to continue receiving funding. The process outlined above gives a framework for thoroughly examining what you actually do, so that you can make what you promise and what you do match more closely. Once you've decided on the types of statistics to track and evaluate, be sure to reevaluate frequently, so that your work doesn't become dated when elements of library service change. Organize it in ways that make sense to others; you will eventually pass the task of analysis on to a successor and you will use your results to justify your decisions. Consider using graphs, charts, and spreadsheet programs to increase your effectiveness. Finally, remember that good statistical analysis is not a substitute for good decision making. It simply gives you better information to use when improving your library.

REFERENCE

Southern Area Public Library, "About Us." Last modified 2010. Accessed July 30, 2013. http://southernarea.lib.wv.us/about-home.html.

Chapter Ten

Collection Management in Small Public Libraries

Brady A. Clemens

In a small public library, often the task of collection management falls in part or in whole to the library director, who may only have the training of a single course in collection development as a starting point. The task at first seems overwhelming, especially given the constraints that public libraries currently face. Libraries remain closely linked with books in the mind of the public, and circulation of library materials has increased over the last several years. At the same time, cuts in funding combined with increased costs have led to a gradual decline in spending on library collections. Materials spending once accounted for 25 percent of library budgets in 1942; that figure has steadily decreased to 11.4 percent as of 2011 (Coffman 2013). The small public library faces an even greater challenge as the percentage of the budget marked for library materials represents a far smaller amount of money than it does for a larger public library.

How then does the beginning librarian meet the challenge of providing an excellent collection of library materials for patrons? Collection management consists of three basic components:

- selection of library materials
- maintenance of the collection
- deselection, or weeding

Attention to each of these three components is essential to maintaining a useful and attractive collection of materials for a library's patrons. A final area of concern is the management of specialized small collections, such as a genealogy or local history section in the library. Further, each library must ensure that an updated, clear collection development policy is in place, to assist in the process of managing the collection and as a safeguard in case of challenges to library materials. While the task may seem daunting, the reward is an easy-to-navigate collection of current, high-circulating materials, a collection which helps prove the worth of the library to its community and provides for the needs of the library's patrons.

SELECTION

Selecting appropriate materials for a small public library is already a difficult task; in an era of declining support for libraries the task of selection is made even harder. The beginning public librarian is faced with the need to select materials that both enhance the collection and will be popular with patrons.

The first step, especially for a librarian new to the position, is to assess the current holdings of the library to determine what types of books are popular with the library's patron community. While some libraries will serve similar populations, each library's patron community is unique, with diverse interests and tastes that must be taken into account when selecting new materials for the collection. The beginning assessment of the library's collection needn't be an extensive one, especially given the fact that in a small public library the person responsible for selection likely also has other responsibilities, whether cataloging, manning the circulation desk, or serving as the library's director. A system report showing the highest circulating collections, books, or other library materials can help give a new librarian a sense of what types of materials are popular. Even something as simple as observing what materials patrons are bringing to the front desk, or asking staff and volunteers what types of materials seem to be most popular, can give the selector insight into what materials should be purchased.

Patron material purchase requests and interlibrary loan reports are another useful tool for the selector to make use of. While it is certainly true that not every item requested by a patron for purchase or interlibrary loan should be acquired, taken together the information from patron requests can reveal gaps in the collection that the selector may decide are areas of need. Some libraries are taking this one step further by incorporating various forms of patron driven acquisition (PDA) into their collection management practices. Ward (2014) notes that this model presents a way to not only meet patron needs of the present but also provides the opportunity to select materials that will have a high overall circulation for the life of the item.

Immediate popularity alone, while important, cannot be the sole factor for selection. In order to ensure a current, attractive overall collection, the selector must take the time to add less popular titles that help update library's holdings. This is especially true for topics that may not have a high circulation, but are nonetheless important enough to be represented in the collection. This includes but is not limited to materials containing the following:

- legal information
- tax information
- health and wellness
- test preparation materials (GRE, SAT, etc.)

These are also topics that regularly go out of date and need to be updated. Without taking care to update less-popular sections, over time parts of the collection can easily become stagnant and visibly unattractive to patrons, resulting in fewer circulations and a less useful collection overall.

Standing orders from vendors can assist in the selection process. For materials such as large type books, many vendors offer standing-order programs that allow the library to choose the genre or type book, with the vendor selecting the titles. These can be useful, especially for the beginning selector, in taking some of the pressure of selection away. If the selector knows, for instance, that many patrons enjoy westerns or Christian fiction, but may not be as familiar with the prominent authors, a standing order program can be a great benefit. However, it is essential that the cost of these standing orders is factored into the overall spending budget and that the selector monitors the cost, as the expense of some standing order programs can increase over time.

The format of the material is also a factor in selection of materials. Hardcover books are often the preferred format for print materials, while paperback books offer immediate cost-savings to the library but may not last as long on the shelf. Increasingly libraries may consider choosing e-books as a format for popular or theft-prone titles to allow greater access to their patrons.

It is also important to exercise due caution in dealing with patron donations. Donations of materials from the public should be evaluated with the same criteria as other materials. It is not assured that something donated by a patron, even if it is in new condition, should be added to the library's collection. If it will not be popular with the library's patrons, it has already extracted hidden costs from the library. Simply because it has been donated does not make it "free," and the fact that the library did not spend money to acquire it is not sufficient reason to add it to the collection. The donated book still cost the library money in materials used to process the item and staff time, both of which would be better spent on materials that will circulate.

Once the new materials have arrived and are processed, the work of selection still is not finished. It is the duty of every selector to check to see just how well the new materials have circulated. In this way the librarian can grow as a selector by seeing what works and what doesn't work in their particular library. If an item circulates well, the selector might consider other materials of a similar nature, whether books by the same author or films of a similar genre. If an item does not circulate well, the selector is obliged to determine why that is the case. An item brought into the library that does not circulate represents a waste of library resources, but these mistakes also represent an opportunity for the selector to learn more about the needs and desires of their patrons to avoid non-circulating items in the future.

Beyond the selection of books is the need to stay within budget when making those selections. With luck, your public library is part of a district, system, or consortium that allows for buying at a discount from a vendor. For many public libraries this may not be an option, and those institutions may turn to Amazon.com or other online vendors to purchase their materials, or to supplement their vendor's offerings. In some instances, a selector can choose books from used or bargain-book sellers. The selector should refrain from the temptation to order books simply based on cost; often being willing to spend slightly more money at point of purchase will yield greater benefits in circulation than attempting to cut corners. Titles sold by used or bargain book sellers will not be currently popular titles, but with great care the selector can use these resources to supplement the collection, especially when choosing nonfiction titles.

MAINTENANCE

While selection and acquisition of new library materials is the most visible portion of collection management, continued maintenance of the library's collections is essential to providing your patron community with a collection of useful materials that are easy to navigate. A full, occasional inventory of the library's materials is not only necessary to determine the status of many items that are no longer on the shelves, but it also helps to catch and correct minor errors in the system that build up over the course of years. While a full inventory is a time-consuming task, it need only be done every five to ten years, though inventories of specific, high-use collections such as videogames or DVDs may be conducted more frequently. For a beginning public librarian, inventory is also a good way to become more familiar with the collections of your library as well as the workings, and quirks, of the library's integrated library system. Once a full inventory is completed, your library's catalog, with errors corrected and missing items marked or removed, will more accurately reflect the library's holdings and be more useful to both staff and patrons.

Inventory is only the beginning of the task of maintaining the library's collections. Occasional system reports, such as reports for missing items or items lost by patrons, help keep the catalog updated in between inventories, and the regular use of these reports makes inventory itself a less onerous task.

At least once a year, reports on missing or billed items should be generated from the library's automated system, and, if the items have been billed or lost for several years, a decision should be made whether to replace these items or to remove them entirely from the system. This helps to ensure that the holdings of the library are accurately reflected in the online catalog.

Part of the ongoing maintenance of the collection is the decision about whether or not to replace lost or damaged items. The decision, often in the hands of the librarian in charge of selecting materials, should be made with care. Not every item can or should be replaced when lost or damaged, especially in a time of shrinking materials budgets. The choice as to whether to replace the library material in question should be made using the same selection criteria that the selector uses for choosing new materials. Can the item be repaired? If so, it is often better to make minor repairs to the item rather than going to the expense of finding and acquiring a new one. Other questions that should be asked include the following:

- How well has the item circulated?
- How popular is the author or topic with your patron community?
- Is the material still relevant?

If the answer is in the affirmative, it may be worth replacing as it still serves a purpose in the collection. If the item is low-circulating or outdated, the material should be removed from the collection rather than replaced or repaired.

While the librarian in charge of collection management may find it difficult to find time to engage in collection maintenance, the time spent is worth the effort when it comes to ensuring that the patrons of your library have an accurate, easy to use catalog. The frustration of patrons using a catalog filled with listings for items that are no longer in your library is easily avoided with occasional work by library staff.

DESELECTION

Deselection, or weeding, of the library's collections refers to a systematic, regular effort to remove non-circulating, outdated, or physically ugly materials from the library. Many librarians find weeding a difficult or tedious task, but it is an absolute necessity in order to provide patrons with an attractive collection of useful and interesting materials. As difficult as a librarian may find it to remove books from the shelves, a library's patrons are ill-served by shelves crowded with outdated or non-circulating items.

The art of weeding involves weighing the items on the shelf against a set of criteria. These include the following:

- Is the item dirty or in poor condition?
- Does the work contain outdated information?
- Does the item portray ethnic or religious groups in a politically incorrect fashion?
- Has the item not circulated within a given period of time?

If an item meets one, or several, of these conditions it is a good candidate for removal from the shelves. In many cases books containing outdated information are obvious to anyone. At best an item containing outdated information is an annoyance, of no use to anyone seeking current information on the topic, such as a book about "South Africa Today" that was written before the end of apartheid. At worst the item can pose a danger to patrons, such as a book containing medical information from the 1960s. For the good of the patrons served by our libraries, these items need to be removed as they are found. Different subjects within the nonfiction collection will need to be updated after different intervals; math, for instance, needs to be updated far less frequently than information on job-hunting or pharmaceuticals. Which items qualify as being dirty or otherwise physically unattractive should be similarly obvious. If the librarian in charge of weeding wouldn't consider circulating the item due to its condition, there is a good chance that most patrons will feel likewise. Similarly items that, while once acceptable, contain politically incorrect portrayals of ethnic or religious groups in most cases are excellent candidates for weeding (Kalan 2014). In order to make it easier for patrons to navigate the shelves, and find all the new, attractive materials the selector is adding, these types of items must be removed from circulation.

Another criterion for deselection is the length of time the item has gone without circulating. Different areas of the collection need to be measured against a different circulation standard. High-interest items like DVDs or fiction titles may be subject to more stringent circulation standards; if a fiction title hasn't circulated in two to three years, it may be a good candidate for weeding. For lower-circulating collections like nonfiction, the circulation standard may more lenient, perhaps five to ten years instead. The length of time an item may go without circulating before it is removed will depend on the individual library and collection; it is up to the librarian in charge of weeding, often in collaboration with other members of the staff, to determine this standard.

Two additional complications must be considered. The librarian in charge of deselection may choose to take the approach that each individual material will be evaluated on its own merits. This is a perfectly valid method. Another method is to take a more holistic approach to the process. If, for instance, the works of a given author are still circulating, the librarian might be wise to keep all works by that author, to prevent having to interlibrary loan that author's materials in the future. This is also the case for book series; if a series of six books are still circulating, save two volumes, it might be in the best interests of the library to keep all books in the series to prevent future, unnecessary interlibrary loan expense. This is an area where the librarian has some discretion; each librarian must find what works best for their library.

Increasingly librarians in charge of collection management must also give consideration to a library's e-book collection. While e-book collections do not occupy physical space and do not deteriorate like print materials do, weeding the library's e-book collection is just as important as weeding the books and other library materials that exist within the library building. As Moroni notes, the strength of a library's e-book holdings is best evaluated by the number of circulations rather than the number of e-books in the collection (Moroni 2012). E-books are not exempt from becoming outdated; taking this into consideration, along with circulation statistics, provides a valuable starting point when beginning an evaluation and weeding of the library's e-book collection.

It is important to remember that weeding the library's collections is a process rather than a one-time event. It is unwise to wait until new books won't fit on the shelves to begin the process of weeding; by continuous weeding the process becomes much more manageable, and your patrons are spared having to sort through shelves of unwanted materials to find what they are looking for.

SPECIAL COLLECTIONS

Special collections within the library merit different standards of collection management. Often the most common special collection in a small public library will be a collection of local history or genealogy materials. A collection of local history or genealogy materials may include these items, among other materials:

- works of local history
- microfilmed newspapers
- collections of obituaries
- local family histories
- other items of local interest

It is important that these collections be given clearly defined parameters; local history collections should be, by definition, local. These collections should not contain state histories or national histories save in very specific cases.

The Reference and User Services Association (RUSA) division of the American Library Association provides a useful guide for those libraries interested in establishing and maintaining a local history collection (2012). It is sufficient to say here that selection, maintenance, and weeding of local history collections will take a very different form from the rest of the library's collection. Fewer items will be added to the collection, and each item should be selected with diligence. Very few items, once they have been added to a local history collection, will ever be removed. Clear policies should exist for collection management for the library's local history collection, policies distinct from the general collection development policy. This will help prevent a local history collection from becoming a storage place for library materials that the library simply doesn't know what to do with, keeping the special collection useful for the genealogist or local history enthusiast.

CONCLUSION

Regardless of the state of the collection, the new librarian may feel that the task of maintaining their library's holdings is overwhelming. When broken down into its component parts, collection management isn't overwhelming at all. It is essential to remember patience in working with library collections; the process of collection management is an ongoing one. It is far easier to make these small changes continuously rather than wait until the task of updating the collection is a monumental one. While these duties ensure continuous work, the end result of a librarian's efforts at collection management is an attractive, high-circulating collection of materials for our patrons.

REFERENCES

Coffman, Steve. 2013. "How Low Can Our Book Budgets Go?" *American Libraries* 44, no. 9/10: 48–51. *Library Information Science & Technology Abstracts*, *EBSCOhost* (accessed April 21, 2014).

Kalan, Abby Preschel. 2014. "The Practical Librarian's Guide to Collection Development." *American Libraries* 45, no. 5 (May/June 2014): 42–44. http://www.americanlibrariesmagazine.org/issue/may-2014 (accessed May 14, 2014).

Moroni, Alene E. 2012. "Weeding in a Digital Age." *Library Journal* 137, no. 15 (September 15, 2012): 26–28. *Library Literature & Information Science Full Text (H.W. Wilson). EBSCOhost* (accessed April 17, 2014).

"RUSA Guidelines for Establishing Local History Collections." *Reference & User Services Quarterly* 52, no. 1 (Fall 2012): 59–60. *Library Literature & Information Science Full Text (H.W. Wilson). EBSCOhost* (accessed April 17, 2014).

Ward, Suzanne M. "Patrons: Your New Partners in Collection Development." *American Libraries* 45, no. 3/4 (March/April 2014): 13. http://www.americanlibrariesmagazine.org/issue/marchapril-2014 (accessed April 14, 2014).

Chapter Eleven

Establishing an Inviting Atmosphere through Library Displays

Cynthia Harbeson

In small towns, which have fewer venues and more limited resources, it is even more vital than in larger towns and cities to establish the public library as a community center. The best way to accomplish this task is by creating an inviting atmosphere for all members of the community. Creating that atmosphere hinges upon several factors, but one of the ways it can be developed is through effective and engaging library displays. Librarians have a wealth of opportunities to create these displays in ways that are both timely and cost effective. In this chapter, I will introduce several different types of displays, talk about how they succeed, and offer suggestions and examples for how to make the most of them.

Before proceeding, it is important to establish a working definition for "library displays." For the purposes of this chapter, I have adapted the *Chambers 21st Century Dictionary* definition of the term "displays" to mean any creative arrangement of objects on view for a specific purpose. While exhibits certainly fall under this umbrella term, the focus of this chapter is on library displays rather than exhibits. How are displays different from exhibits? Most of the existing literature on library displays and exhibits focuses on what I would characterize as exhibits. The primary difference is that exhibits are larger-scale projects that require more planning, time, and resources. They are generally topical in nature and often include additional information in the form of labels. Developing exhibits can be a daunting task for smaller libraries with limited staff and resources. On the other hand, displays are much more manageable. In general, displays can stand alone without contextual information, such as labels, artwork, or explanatory text.

SPACE CONSIDERATIONS

Libraries in small towns often have significant space constraints, leaving very limited space for displays. You need to maximize whatever space you have in order to ensure the biggest "bang for your buck." Create displays in whatever space you have available: on top of lower shelves, at the ends of rows, along entranceway walls, near the public computers—these are all great places to develop displays. I have also found displays near the circulation desk to be particularly effective. Anything at the circulation desk can attract attention.

Before you begin creating displays, assess the space you have available. Do you have lower rows of shelving that could be used to display books? What wall space do you have available? If you have multiple floors in your library, are there ways to maximize the wall space in the stairwells? Do you have any counter space at your circulation or reference desks for small displays? Once you have determined what spaces you are going to use, you can customize the displays for those areas.

While some libraries have exhibit cases to create elaborate displays, most small-town libraries do not. Displays integrated into your available space are often more manageable and successful than those behind glass cases because they are more interactive and inviting. Patrons are able to browse through books on display and the materials are available for them to check out. These displays are more accessible to the community and also require less time and resources from library staff. By using whatever space you have available, the displays you create will be a perfect fit for your library and the community it serves.

TYPES AND PURPOSES OF DISPLAYS

Displays can be used for a variety of purposes. They can promote upcoming library events, market services, provide needed information to the community, or highlight collections. When used effectively, displays become more than a collection of books on a single topic. They inform the public about library services. They encourage patrons to explore library collections and invite patrons to discover all the library has to offer.

Most displays will include examples from the library's collection. This is essential when your purpose is highlighting a subject or promoting the use of a material type, but it is not always necessary. For example, your library may have limited information relating to an upcoming community event but a display can still be informative and encourage community involvement. If your library has limited space for full-fledged book displays, there are other kinds you can create. Using bulletin boards, creating posters, or developing vibrant signs are all types of displays that help create an inviting atmosphere. A great example is to use the left or right half of a large bulletin board to create displays highlighting library programs or collections. The other half can be left available for patrons to post information about events or services in the community. Before implementing this idea, be sure to develop policies on what is and is not acceptable to post. Commercial products and services, overtly political messages, and personal messages with limited appeal such as "Happy Birthday, Natalie" may, for example, be things you want to restrict.

There are many types of and formats for displays. They can be as simple or as elaborate as you choose. Some of the easiest displays to create are also the most effective. You can prepare display resources well in advance, such as a variety of signs dealing with subjects like holidays, scheduled events, and local groups. Topical displays are among the most effortless because you can have signs relating to a variety of subjects already on hand and pull one out in a pinch. Gather a few books on the subject together and you're done. You can add additional books to the display to fill in gaps as books are checked out. These easy-to-create displays encourage the use of library materials and invite patrons to explore all the library has to offer.

PROMOTING UPCOMING PROGRAMS AND COMMUNITY EVENTS

Some of the most effective—and inviting—library displays are created to promote upcoming programs. Displays that advertise library events should be built around a flyer or poster that provides basic information about the program. In this case, the simpler is the better. Only include the most important details on the signage. Program title, date, time, and location are essential elements. A one-line description of the program can be included when necessary. If registration is required, make sure instructions on how to register are prominent and clear. Depending on the demographics of your town, you might also consider including a QR code on the display that links to an online registration form. Gather books or other library materials that are topically related to the program and display them around your signage. Provide takeaways as part of the display. Bookmarks with program information are easy and inexpensive to create. Flyers are another option. The most important part of any promotional display is to spark interest in the program. The community needs to feel as though they are invited to take part in whatever program is offered.

Creating displays in support of community events is another way to increase the connection between the library and the public. It is also an opportunity to collaborate with members of the community. In her book *Great*

Displays for Your Library Step by Step, Susan Phillips suggests that you "tap into your community's talent. Find the artists, craftsmen, writers, photographers and collectors who live among you and feature them in a display or program" (Phillips 2008). Featuring local talent in library displays will strengthen relationships among the library and different constituencies in the community. I would suggest creating displays that showcase the work of local artists, but also inviting these talented individuals to help work on other displays. Community events, such as festivals or community theatre performances, are an opportunity to collaborate with interested individuals who may have more subject expertise to contribute to a display.

THEMED DISPLAYS

Themed displays are a popular choice and can be among the most useful for patrons, if done successfully. Create displays based on themes that are of interest or importance to your community. For instance, around tax time you can create a display with tax-related books, helpful tips, and signs listing additional resources. Travel displays during the summer are another great idea. You can even use older maps as the backdrop for your display or encourage patrons to mark the places they visited recently. Highlighting past Best Picture winners is a great display around the time of the Academy Awards. A display of banned or challenged books will coincide nicely with Banned Books Week in September. Some themes will be better received than others, depending on your specific community. Feel free to experiment and explore what kinds of themes work best for your library.

Displays that highlight library collections are also very effective. These types of displays are easy to create and target specific formats. They also have the added benefit of increasing circulation of the featured items. Book displays of staff picks are always a fun and inviting means of highlighting collections. You should not feel limited to using only fiction for these types of displays; staff picks can also include biographies, cookbooks, music, movies, or a combination of genres and formats. Libraries with few employees can still create effective staff picks displays; however, an alternative is available. Get the community involved in these displays by soliciting ideas from patrons. Instead of a staff picks display, create one of community recommendations. This is also a great way to increase community engagement. Patrons will be excited by the opportunity to provide their own opinions and see their choices featured in the display.

THE PLANNING PROCESS

Planning and creating displays need not be an overwhelming experience. In the best of circumstances, the responsibilities are shared among the staff. Even if you are the sole person in charge of displays, the same planning techniques can be applied to make the task more manageable. Planning on the front end will make it easier and less time-consuming in the long run. Here are some things to keep in mind when it is time for you to start the planning process:

Set aside time for planning. Meet regularly either with all staff involved with displays or set an appointment with yourself. Use this time to brainstorm ideas, evaluate the success of past displays, and determine ways to improve the effectiveness of your displays.

Plan ahead. A calendar is your friend. Take a blank calendar and pencil in different display ideas based on the seasons, annual events, and upcoming programs. It is a good idea to plan at least three or four months in advance. When you know what display is going to be installed next, you won't have to scramble to create signs or gather books together. Decide how often you are going to change displays and incorporate that time frame into the planning process.

Be flexible. You want to leave room to incorporate those last-minute opportunities as they come up. Some displays will be time sensitive, but others will be topical. You can easily shift these topical displays to a later time.

Consider your needs carefully. Think about what kinds of supplies or decorations you might want to use in your display well before you are going to install it. Keep an inventory of your supplies and reuse what you can. Knowing your needs for each display ahead of time will save you from scrambling to find supplies during installation.

CREATION AND INSTALLATION

Once you have a plan in place for your displays, you are ready to start creating. Displays allow you to make the most of your innate creativity. Create colorful, eye-catching signage to complement the books you wish to display. You can use a variety of inexpensive materials to spice up these displays. Professional-looking, colorful signs can now be easily created on the computer and printed in-house. Using general arts and crafts supplies, such as construction paper, pre-printed borders, and stickers, is a nice way to create a warmer, more welcoming feel. Visit other libraries and cultural institutions for ideas you can incorporate in your own displays. Remember: imitation is the sincerest form of flattery.

While books and other library materials will usually be the main focus of your displays, you will need some other supplies. Start by keeping a box of supplies and decorations to use in displays. Many of the decorations and signs you use or create can be reused in later displays, especially if the theme is an annual one. Pictures from discarded magazines, maps, party decorations, and old book jackets can all be saved for use in your displays. Most, if not all, of the supplies and materials you will need to create displays can be obtained for little to no money. While your library will have the basic supplies you will need to put together the physical displays, such as scissors, tape, and book cradles, other specialty supplies may need to be ordered. Depending on the kind of backgrounds you will use, you may need to buy some wall mounts or exhibit tape.

When you are ready to create a new display, start by gathering any books or library materials you will use. Next, pull out the decorations and supplies you will add to the display. With these items at hand, you can then create any signage you will need. Because you have already chosen the books and decorations, you can use these materials as a base for the color scheme and overall design of your signs. If you are unsure about designing signs, there are several templates you can download or you can look online for examples to use as inspiration. For instance, the popular website Pinterest has many examples of library displays from which to gather ideas. Once you have all the elements of your display together, you are ready to install it in your chosen space.

Now that you have your signage, examples from the library's collections, and any decorations you will use, you are ready to install your display. If possible, set up displays when the library is closed or at times of low traffic to minimize disruption of library services. Start by placing your signs and any other informational materials to ensure they are given prominence. Books and decorations can then be worked in around these focal points. Once you have your signage in place, decide how many books to include and how you want to display them. The number and placement of books will largely depend on the amount of space you have available. Be sure not to overcrowd the display with too many books. You can always add more materials as people check out the ones in the display. Finally, add any decorative touches to the display. Before finalizing the display, take a few steps back and evaluate your work from a distance. If possible, ask a coworker for his or her opinion. Once you are satisfied with how it looks, take a moment to admire your work and congratulate yourself on the successful completion of your display.

PUBLICIZING YOUR DISPLAYS

Once you have created your display, it is important to promote it. Take advantage of the available avenues for free publicity. Include a brief entry on your latest exhibit in your library newsletter or post an entry to your library's blog or Facebook page. If your town has a community events website, you can include a mention of your display there. Inquire with your local newspaper to see if they will advertise your display in their paper or on their website for free or at a reduced rate. Publicizing your displays beyond your library will encourage some people to visit who may otherwise never have come to the library.

Marketing and promoting your displays is a great way to publicize the library's collections and services. Displays are a form of outreach and actively engage patrons through eye-catching visual elements. Explore many possible options for promoting your displays. In cases where you have created bookmarks to accompany your display, you can ask local businesses to keep some on hand to give away to their customers. This will also strengthen your ties with the community by building relationships with local business owners—who are also potential library users.

TIPS AND TRICKS

Easy does it. The most effective displays are the ones that are simple and encourage exploration. Displays can be as effortless as a handful of books and a sign. Sometimes even the sign is optional, especially with topical displays. These displays are easy to refill. You can even have a stack of additional books on hand to fill gaps as people check out materials from the display.

Keep it moving. Frequently changed displays attract more attention. Rotate displays at least once a month, preferably more often. Because different displays will appeal to different people, you create a more inviting atmosphere by changing displays often.

Be as inclusive as possible. Think broadly about your community and their interests. Incorporate some displays that have wide appeal and others that are more targeted. By getting to know your patrons, you will be in a better position to create more meaningful displays.

Record new ideas. Keep track of ideas for new displays. When you see displays you like at other places, take pictures of them to use as references (you might want to ask permission first). If you have access to a mobile device, you can use Apps such as Evernote, Pinterest, or Popplet, to keep track of all of your design ideas.

Collaboration is key. Trying to develop displays on your own can be a daunting and overwhelming task. Form a display committee in your library to share responsibilities. If you are the sole person in charge of displays at your library, collaborate with librarians at area libraries. You can meet every few months to share ideas, discuss strategies for improving displays, and trade supplies.

Have fun. Creating displays should be fun and rewarding. It is an opportunity to unleash your creativity. Be playful. Experiment and try new ideas. The most welcoming displays are the ones that reflect the joy in their creation.

FINAL THOUGHTS

The library can continue to be a vital part of its community by developing itself as a gathering place for community members. In order to become a center of the community, the library must be a welcoming and inviting place. Displays are some of the first things newcomers see when they enter the library. For this reason, they are an important part of making people feel welcome.

REFERENCE

Phillips, Susan P. 2008. *Great Displays for Your Library Step by Step*. Jefferson, NC: McFarland & Co.

Chapter Twelve

The Helping Hands of Boomers in Friends of the Library Groups

Kim Becnel and LouAnn Morehouse

LIBRARY FRIENDS GROUPS AND BABY BOOMERS: A NATURAL FIT

Educated, healthy, and committed to their communities, baby boomers are proving themselves to be dedicated and determined volunteers. According to the Corporation for National and Community Service, 23.4 million people age 45 to 64 volunteered in 2012. These citizens have developed considerable skills and expertise in their lifetimes, and many want to keep using them even after they have left the work force. In an article on volunteerism, Richard Eisenberg (2013) reports that groups who recruit older volunteers have come to understand that this new breed of retiree expects to help in a meaningful way by making unique and purposeful contributions to causes they care about. Eisenberg interviews Wendy Spencer, CEO of the Corporation for National and Community Service, who adds, "The thing I love about boomer volunteers is that they offer seasoned experience and lifelong lessons they've learned. Young people have great skills in technology and social media, but they don't have the lessons to share that boomers and seniors do" (quoted in Eisenberg 2013, 2).

In the search for meaningful work that will enable them to draw on their considerable skills and expertise, many boomers zero in on the public library as an organization worthy of their time and energy, approaching their local branches in search of quality volunteer opportunities. Often, these prospective volunteers are steered toward Library Friends groups, nonprofit organizations that support the library by having their members perform key volunteer tasks and conduct fundraising activities. In fact, as budgets have tightened over the past decade, many libraries find themselves increasingly dependent on the money raised by their local Friends groups through various creative fundraising activities, including the ubiquitously popular Friends of the Library book sale. In some cases, special projects are funded by Friends' monies and in others, entire library services, such as programming, are contingent upon the funds brought in by the Friends. While library administrators certainly appreciate the volunteer work and the financial boost provided by the Friends, they also depend on these organizations to advocate for the library and its services, giving it increased credibility in the community and with local government officials.

A vibrant Friends group not only helps the library financially and politically, it provides an essential connection to the community, ensuring an exchange of support and ideas between librarians and citizens, an exchange which is vitally important to maintaining effective library services. Volunteers who join Friends groups are involving themselves in a considerable and important mission. Thus, in a thriving Friends group, volunteers can be expected to take on serious leadership roles, accept responsibility for complex tasks, and devote a significant amount of time and energy to the cause. This makes the work an especially good fit for baby boomers, who are not only searching for meaningful causes with which to become involved, but who are also looking for volunteer positions that require a significant commitment and that place them in professional or managerial roles. In brief, Friends groups are good for libraries, and boomers are good for the Friends.

CASE IN POINT: FRIENDS OF THE WATAUGA PUBLIC LIBRARY THRIVES WITH BOOMER LEADERSHIP

A 2012 study of the Friends of the Watauga County Public Library in Boone, North Carolina, reinforces those findings. The 380-plus member organization is led by a board of directors who collectively embody the boomer generation. Of the fifteen directors, the youngest is fifty-five years old, and most are sixty-five or older. All have acquired at least some postsecondary education. Among the experiences garnered from their careers are those from the banking, accounting, engineering, publishing, and university teaching professions. The group also includes a retired county commissioner, a former regional library director, and several business owners. A couple of the directors have earned public regard as a result of their charitable efforts on behalf of social services organizations.

Founded in 1974, the organization has an impressive record of service. According to a retired regional library director, the Friends' community activism was responsible in large part for the construction of the present day 16,000-square-foot facility, which was built in 1998 (personal communication, Feb. 3, 2012). In 2011, the Watauga Library Friends won statewide recognition as an outstanding organization The Friends website contains a lengthy account of activities they annually support. Programs and services range from producing the annual book sale to providing $7,000 in matching funds for a RFID grant.

In 2012, the board of directors inaugurated a two-day book festival with free admission to more than two dozen literary events for all ages. The event, which necessarily required intensive planning and cooperation, was deemed a success. More than three hundred audience seats were filled. Sponsorships by book publishers and area businesses were sufficient to both cover expenses and add to the Friends revenues. The book festival has subsequently been added to the schedule as a recurring event.

POTENTIAL PITFALLS AND STRATEGIES TO AVOID THEM

Given their accomplishments, the board of directors of the Watauga Friends could have been satisfied with resting on their laurels. Instead, they discovered a major flaw in their organization. Producing the book festival required a huge effort. It revealed the fact that the fifteen people who comprised the board were also the fifteen people who looked after every Friends program and service. Where were the other volunteers? There were some members who could be counted on to staff a table or tote a book box, but who was prepared to take over the leadership?

The board of directors realized that they had become disconnected from their members. They commissioned a survey, and for the first time in its thirty-eight-year history, members were asked how they felt about being a part of the Watauga Friends. A strong 40 percent response rate revealed that, by and large, members believed in the value of their organization and trusted the board to carry out the mission. However, three areas of concern stood out. Respondents repeatedly asked for more communication from the board, more notice of volunteer needs and activities, and more turnover in board leadership.

Some valuable lessons can be learned from the Watauga group's experience and the feedback it received from its members. First, to sustain a successful Friends group, it is necessary for the group to keep itself fresh by constantly welcoming new ideas and people. Second, it is critically important that all members of the group feel like significant contributors and are provided with plenty of opportunities to use their strengths and skills in major group initiatives. By following some relatively simple guidelines and suggestions, Friends groups can retain their strong boomer membership without falling prey to stagnation or member dissatisfaction.

OPENNESS TO NEW MEMBERS AND NEW IDEAS

Any group or organization runs the risk of becoming stale and irrelevant if it does not welcome fresh perspectives, yet it is widely known that change in institutions often encounters some level of resistance. This resistance is a natural response that often stems from deeply rooted fears and anxieties related to the disruption of routine and grief over the loss of the status quo (Firoozmand 2014, 31). Although it can be a daunting challenge, Friends groups that have become static must find a way to move past resistance to change in order to remain the flexible, responsive organizations needed by public libraries, which are themselves constantly evolving to meet the needs of their communities. The following are some tips designed to help Friends groups cultivate a culture that embraces necessary change.

Create clear lines of communication both ways—from leaders to membership and membership to leaders. Groups should provide members with some type of forum to share ideas with each other and with group leaders. Friends groups may want to include time for open discussion in their regular meetings and consider creating an email group or listserv for between-meeting conversations. Open communication will help to build trust in leadership, ensure that members understand changes or new projects that are underway, and encourage members to feel invested in the work of the organization.

Hold an open, well-advertised membership drive, targeting people of all ages. If the organization is predominantly made up of boomers and seniors, try to purposefully recruit younger folks, particularly those of the millennial generation. This generation, like the boomers, is characterized by its drive to volunteer and great passion for the causes it believes in. Unlike most boomers, millennials are used to working collaboratively in nonhierarchical situations. They will bring fresh perspectives and a willingness to voice those perspectives. Adept at information sharing and networking through a variety of technologies, they can also help to grow membership and promote the Friends' agenda in the larger community (Kaifi et al. 2012, 89).

Be willing to work past initial emotional responses and rejection to proposed changes. If we understand that fear and insecurity are normal first reactions to proposed change, we can be better prepared to allow for negative reactions and emotions to be aired and articulated. When these sentiments surface, leaders should listen without reacting defensively, keeping in mind that "these emotional responses may not be pleasant but they cannot be forbidden" (Firoozmand 2014, 31). Each member of the organization will experience some type of emotional reaction to change; some will be minor while others will be more dramatic and will take longer to work through. To assist in the process, leaders should not punish reluctant members, but instead continue to engage them, asking for their ideas and input, allowing time for building consensus first and then momentum. With patience and persistence on the part of those initiating the change, the group will likely coalesce around the new mission or project. Keep in mind that in the case of Friends organizations, which are volunteer run and typically meet only once a month or less, the time needed to adapt can be lengthy and might require a change in leadership to become fully established.

Make it standard operating procedure for board members to join the Friends listserv maintained by the ALA (American Library Association). This free conversation thread is an ongoing source of discussions and sharing of best practices on a wide range of Friends issues.

Enlist the support of librarians as promoters of the Friends to other library patrons. According to the survey conducted on the Watauga Library Friends, a majority of members were introduced to the organization by librarians. Patrons often develop friendships with their librarians, and respect and trust their recommendations.

SPREADING THE WEALTH—AND THE WORK

It is worth mentioning again that when the Watauga Friends members were surveyed, they largely approved wholeheartedly of the Friend's mission and major projects, yet many of them made comments which indicated that they felt underutilized by the group. These eager members wanted to offer more of their time and talents, but they felt there was a dearth of opportunities being offered to them. If volunteers—especially baby boomers—are not regularly engaged in the work of an organization such as the Friends, they may become disaffected or disinterested and look for a group in which they feel more useful and valuable. A vibrant and healthy Friends group will find ways to capitalize on all members' strengths, skills, and willingness to work. Here are some ways to start:

Change leadership roles often. Putting a term limit on how long officers can serve will ensure that many members get a chance to hold the reins for a while.

Form subcommittees or workgroups. This will facilitate division of labor and give those members who might not be ready to take on leadership of the entire group a chance to lead efforts on a single project by serving as a committee chair.

Divvy up the work. It can be tempting for leaders or officers to do the bulk of the organization's work, but if other members are given the chance to take on responsibility and execute important tasks, they will be happier and the organization will benefit from a diversity of perspectives and work styles.

Keep all members updated. One way to do this is to enlist a tech savvy member to create an e-blast system utilizing a social media service such as

Constant Contact or Mail Chimp. E-blasts can be formatted as the Friends newsletter, with the added advantage of being deliverable on members' Facebook, Twitter, and LinkedIn accounts with one click. Easy to create and cheap to send, e-blasts assure that members stay updated on news from their Friends. Millennials, who rely heavily on social media as their news source, are the ideal members to develop this communication service. Both Constant Contact and Mail Chimp offer low cost rates to nonprofits and have a wealth of support guides and workshops as well as related applications such as membership campaigns and registration formats. Keeping the information flowing is crucial; informed members are active members.

NO FRIENDS GROUP YET? START ONE TODAY!

A library looking to start a Friends group would do well to begin by locating some local boomer volunteers. If the library is already providing some kind of adult programming, such as a regular book club, this would be an ideal avenue through which to recruit some interested parties. Also, since many baby boomers who volunteer are involved in more than one group, it would probably be worth calling or visiting some local charities or volunteer organizations to see if any of the regular volunteers might have an interest in devoting some of their time to creating a Friends group for their local library. The library may even have some boomers already working there in a volunteer capacity or a list of patrons who have expressed an interest in becoming more involved.

A useful example to consider is the Avery County Public Library in Newland, North Carolina, which has recently undertaken a revival of their long-inactive Friends group. The original Friends ceased meeting years ago as leadership failed to make room for transition and the organization ran out of steam. Now, some of the boomers retiring to this scenic region have recognized the potential in this small-town library to become a vibrant community center, and they are beginning to mobilize. The head librarian wisely hung onto a list of patrons who had at one time or another inquired about a Friends group. With her encouragement, and with the approval of the regional director, one willing boomer volunteer started calling the patrons on the list.

A handful of people were interested enough to meet to discuss the next step. The agenda was simple: what kind of library program did the new Friends want to sponsor? It was decided that a book discussion group was a good activity to offer. The library did not offer this amenity, and several of the new Friends felt that it would get the ball rolling. Library staff made a flyer and one of the Friends wrote a simple announcement for the local newspaper. Dues were set at very modest levels to assure that no one need be excluded for monetary reasons. Thus begun, no one was overwhelmed by the burden of big responsibilities, and the prospect of a reward—a stimulating hour of friendly discussion—was immediate. Library staff are maintaining a supportive role in this fledgling organization, sharing news of the new book club, keeping a stack of membership forms at the desk, and taking dues. In time, the Friends anticipate a more formal structure, with a board of directors and regular meetings. At this point they are focused on raising community awareness of the benefits of having a library. As this example makes clear, starting a Friends group doesn't have to be complicated; groups can, and often do, evolve from humble, informal beginnings into independent organizations with their own mission, policies, and leadership.

CONCLUSION

Many public libraries are leveraging the commitment and talent of their local baby boomer populations into effective and indispensable Friends of the Library organizations. The Friends of the Watauga Public Library is one such group which has become an essential asset to the library and the community of Boone, North Carolina. Always eager to improve its service, this group was willing to take a hard a look at itself by asking its members for candid feedback, and it learned some vital lessons in the process. Members of the group, it turns out, want to be right in the thick of things; they want to be kept in the loop, they want more opportunities to use their time and talents for the good of the organization, and they want the chance to lead. This feedback is helpful not only to the Watauga group, but to the many other boomer-led Friends group out there supporting public libraries every day. Any steps they can take to ensure that the culture of the group is forward-looking and thinking, democratic, creative, and open to new ideas, the more likely it is to thrive. Another important lesson to take away from Watauga Public Library's experience is this one: public libraries without Friends groups would do well to recruit some boomer library lovers to get one going; they won't be sorry they did.

REFERENCES

Corporation for National and Community Service. 2012. *Volunteering and Civic Engagement among Baby Boomers*. http://www.volunteeringinamerica.gov/special/Baby-Boomers.

Eisenberg, Richard. 2013. "Why So Few Baby Boomers Are Volunteering." *Forbes*, January 4. http://www.forbes.com/sites/nextavenue/2013/04/01/can-we-get-some-volunteers-please/.

Firoozmand, Naysan. March 2014. "Managing Resistance to Change." *Training Journal*: 27–31.

Kaifi, Belal A., Wageeh A. Nafei, Nile M. Khanfar, and Maryam M. Kaifi. 2012. "A Multi-Generational Workforce: Managing and Understanding Millennials." *International Journal of Business & Management* 7, no. 24: 88–93.

Chapter Thirteen

Making an Inviting Library Atmosphere

Jan Burns

Making the library a place people want to come can be a challenge. The community will always have those individuals that naturally gravitate to the library but pulling in non-library users takes planning.

THE LIBRARY BUILDING

Find some volunteers to look at the library building who do not see the library on a daily basis and would be willing to offer constructive feedback. Have the individuals walk around the outside and inside of the building and make notes of what they find. Get the group together to share findings and then put a plan in action to address the issues found.

Does your library building look like a fun place to be or does it look dull and boring? Make sure that trash is picked up, that sidewalks are swept, and that items are not stored haphazardly outside. Some libraries are maintained by city departments; some libraries have to provide services on their own. Look to the community for assistance. Homeschooling groups can help sweep and pull weeds. Master gardeners can help with landscapes and flower boxes. Divide the library up into areas and assign library staff to monitor them for possible improvements. Rotate these areas several times a year to get a new perspective on issues.

Bring some color to the building. Banners can be hung on the outside of buildings or posted in the yard to advertise events, programs, or resources. Library themed posters can be hung in the outside windows to attract patrons walking and or driving by. Sidewalk signs can be changed to promote weekly activities. Outside seating and statuary in a reading garden can provide attractive areas for groups to congregate while providing an inviting natural atmosphere.

What about the inside of the library? Does it look outdated or in disrepair? A coat of paint will do wonders to the look of a room. Adding artwork or rotating displays will help add color and interest to an area. The local furniture store may be willing to donate some items for display in the library that could be made into comfortable quiet reading areas. Books can be front-faced on the shelves to add more color and possibly attract more readers.

Over time things will be stored behind doors or under counters and then be forgotten about. Once a year do a spring cleaning of the library and throw away old brochures, torn posters, dusty knickknacks. Take a look at the circulation area and remove items that clutter the surface area and make it difficult to interact with the patrons. Have an ongoing plan for deep cleaning the shelves of dust and dirt. Find volunteers that would be willing to take responsibility for an area in the library to keep it straightened and inviting.

Evaluate the collection space of the library. Which collections are being used the most, which ones are basically inactive? There may be times when a collection is no longer needed and needs to be removed in favor of newer items or formats. For example, a collection of older educational computer games that are no longer compatible with newer computer formats should be removed from the collection. An oversized, under-used reference collection could be reduced in favor of adding or expanding a teen area.

Evaluate the location of collections to make sure they meet patron needs. Are the large print books close to the front of the library for the senior patrons who have trouble walking? Are the bookshelves in the children's area at a level where the children can reach them? Is the quiet reading room away from the noisy traffic areas of the library?

MEETING COMMUNITY NEEDS

The library serves the whole community and as such should have something for all age groups and interests. By studying the community, the library can adjust its collection, resources, and services to better serve its patrons. Needs assessments can help gather information from library patrons and the community. There will be times when the results of needs assessments will vary differently from what the library staff perceived as needed services.

The library should keep up with new technologies and evaluate their value to library services. One of the biggest trends in recent years has been the availability of downloadable books to personal devices. Having services that match community requests will ensure that patrons keep coming back to the library.

Making the library a fun destination will bring more people into the library. The days of librarians shushing patrons are less frequent. The library is a lively place with programs and daily activities. The library acts as a social hub where friends can meet. Letting organizations and groups meet in library spaces brings in individuals that may have never entered the library before.

Libraries can be scary places for those unfamiliar with them. Have a greeter program in place using staff and volunteers that welcome people into the library, answer their questions, and help them find what they need. Have policies and procedures in place that are in favor of the patron helping them to keep access to library services and resources. Whenever possible allow cell phones (except at the circulation desk) and allow food and covered beverages in designated areas of the library. Invite a local coffee shop to sponsor a coffee hour where individuals share what they are reading.

The library should take part in community fairs and activities whenever possible. This gives the library an opportunity to market the library to an audience outside of the library. Rotate the members of the booth to include staff members, library board members, and volunteers. Highlight different collections and services in the library. Bring in displays of library resources and have a computer available to show the library's webpage and demonstrate the databases and downloadable services.

Hold events in the parking lot or in areas surrounding the library. The aspects of people having fun might bring in first-time users or reluctant members of the community. Simple events like having the fire truck on site, hosting a classic car show, sponsoring a Dutch-oven cooking class, or having the local humane society bring out the animals may entice someone to stop by and see what is going on.

TWO OBSTACLES EASILY FIXED

In some communities the library has to overcome the old stereotypes of dusty buildings filled with books and stern librarians requiring absolute silence. There also may be some individuals who had bad experiences in a library environment and may hesitate to return to the library. Make sure all the staff are trained in customer service and know how to greet patrons and solve problems. All improvement efforts are in vain if the person does not feel comfortable and welcomed into the library.

Make sure all staff know and abide by the written and approved library policies. The library may have the most friendly staff possible; however, if a patron gets inconsistent service with each visit it could produce an uninviting place to visit. Hold staff accountable to the policies and evaluate staff and policies on an ongoing basis to make sure that they are providing the patrons with a positive library experience.

Below are some examples that might work for your library and community:

The Library Looks Like a Bank

An old bank building is given to the city to be used for the library. The building is in good shape but is all in brown and beige colors making it still look like a bank on the inside and the outside. There are large windows in the front of the library, which faces the main street. Posters and displays were created to go in these areas to add color and attract people into the building. High walls at both entrances were used for huge 3D displays that changed each year for the Summer Reading Program and could be seen from both inside and outside the building. Planter boxes were added to the front of the library and the master gardeners took on the responsibility of planting and maintaining decorative plants. The inside of the library was given a few new paint jobs to add splashes of color throughout the library. Furniture was rearranged into small areas to allow for comfortable reading or meeting areas for friends. Local artists were approached about displaying pieces of art in the library on a rotating basis. The addition of color and art seemed to make the place a livelier environment for both patrons and staff.

Quiet Reading Space

The library had a designated area at the back of the building for quiet reading. In addition to housing the newspapers and magazines, it also had plush seating as well as WiFi computer stations. The area was in constant use. Several times a day the library staff would receive complaints about the noise in the quiet area. The new library director started an evaluation of the situation and found the noise was coming from the audiovisuals section that was next to the quiet reading area. Families would gather in the audiovisual area to pick out movies and then talk with other patrons making enough noise to disturb those reading. It was decided that the audiovisuals would be moved closer to the circulation desk, which was normally a busy and noisy section of the library. This arrangement allowed the quiet area more isolation and brought a high-use collection closer to the circulation desk.

Every School Child Needs a Library Card

A small rural library strongly supports the idea that every child in school needs a public library card. The library director and children's librarian work with the school system to send home library applications for each child in first grade. The school system then arranged field trips for every first-grade class to go to the public library for a tour of the children's department, participate in a craft, and to receive their new library card. As students enter the eighth grade, they are brought back through the public library. Any fines and fees on previous cards are discharged and the individuals start with new, fresh cards. The eighth graders get a tour of the teen, adult, reference, and computer sections of the library. Any fines that are accumulated on the new card can be worked off by providing a public library service under the supervision of a volunteer program.

Update the Classics

The school system has a list of books that are required reading. The public library also has a copy of this list to make sure that a copy is available in the library. While helping a patron find a copy of the classic *The Red Badge of Courage* the new library director notes that the only copy that is on the shelf is a very old copy published in the 1950s, the pages are yellowing and loose, and the binding has book tape around it to hold it together. The library director is embarrassed to offer this copy to the young patron, but the young man needs it to complete the reading assignment. The library director asks the library staff to pull any old copies of classics that they come across and soon there is a cart load of titles in the director's office in varies stages of disrepair. The library director finds inexpensive copies of the titles and is able to purchase multiple copies of each classic title for the shelf. The new copies are placed on display with other new books in the library. It is soon noticed that many adults are checking out the new copies of the old classics in addition to the copies being used for school assignments.

Baby Corner

During the weekly storytime hour, mothers and children too young for storytime wander the children's room and the lobby of the library. The children's librarian and the library director decide to move some work tables to another area of the library and create a small baby area with soft toys and board books. The area is surrounded by existing plush chairs gathered around the library. Now the young mothers have a place to gather during the children's storytime while the babies discover the toys and books in the library.

The Travel Collection

While weeding the history and geography section, the library director discovers that the travel area is very outdated. To help decide what countries should be purchased, a simple survey is created to gather patron input. A slip of paper is placed in checkouts and/or handed to individuals as they interact with staff. The paper explains that new travel books are being added to the collection and asks the simple question, What is your favorite vacation spot? As the slips are returned to the library a list is created. The top-ten places are purchased for the collection. A small display is created with the new titles along with posters gathered from the local travel agency. The books are a big hit not only with potential travelers, but armchair travelers and schoolkids working on country reports. The books are being checked out on a regular basis so the library expands the collection by purchasing the next ten suggestions on the list.

Fishing for Comments

The library staff has noticed that the last hour of the day—from 7:00 p.m.–8:00 p.m.—has very few patrons. The library staff has also noted that patrons are waiting outside of the door at 10:00 a.m. to get into the library. The library director approaches the library board with the recommendation that the library hours shift to open an hour earlier and close an hour earlier to align more with patron needs. The library board wants more information before making a decision. A fish-shaped comment jar is placed at the circulation desk along with slips of paper asking for input on the proposed hour changes. Among the comments on library hours are other comments by patrons making requests or suggestions. All items are tallied and shared with the library board at monthly meetings. The support for the change in hours is overwhelmingly positive and the library board approves the change. All other issues from the comment jar are addressed by the library director and board as well. It was decided to keep the comment jar a little longer and a sign was added: "Fishing for Comments." The comment jar has become a regular fixture at the circulation desk and a wonderful way for patrons to communicate to the staff and the library board about issues.

Recreational Needs

A small library has a low circulation of the nonfiction adult titles except for cookbooks, gardening, crafts, and interior design. The adult fiction and biographies are highly used and the numbers show growing usage in the audio books collection. By looking at the community the librarian finds the town is changing into a retirement community where less research is done and more recreational materials are needed. To serve this need, the educational sections (science, math, technology, literature) were reevaluated and reduced to smaller collections with solid titles. The space created by heavily weeding the educational, nonfiction sections were used to expand the recreational and fiction collections. The circulation statistics showed a vast increase in usage because the library was providing what the community wanted. The library also began offering programs on recreational topics that brought in new patrons therefore increasing the number of people using the library.

Christian Fiction

A small, isolated town is very religious minded. It is estimated that 75 percent of the library's circulation comes from Christian fiction titles and another 5 percent of its circulation from the religious section. Should the public library spend the majority of its budget on these Christian-based titles? The librarian evaluated the collection and found the majority of Christian fiction titles were checked out an average of seventy times where even the best-sellers like John Grisham or Nora Roberts were at about fifty circulations. On further inspection, the older Christian fiction titles remained on waiting lists while older best-sellers were available but rarely circulated. The library board supported the decision to continue purchasing large quantities of Christian fiction and religious titles as long as the other patron requests were met.

Audio CDs versus MP3-CD

The library has a collection of audio CDs (compact discs) that are very popular. The majority of titles come from recorded books that provide high quality recordings of popular titles. The average cost of a title from recorded books is $100. The library received a catalog from the company Blackstone Audio that sells audio books in MP3-CD format for an average of $20 a title. The reduced cost would allow the library to purchase more titles. An added bonus is the majority of books are available on one disc compared to eight-plus CD discs for recorded books titles. The condensed discs allow for less shelf space needed to house the collection. There were two drawbacks to the MP3-CD format: (1) it requires the listener to have newer technology, and (2) it does not provide all the titles needed especially in the Christian fiction genre. The librarian purchased a few of the titles and asked a few of the regular audio book patrons to use the new format and provide an evaluation. Overall the results were great leading the library to split the audio books budget between the two companies. To make room for the newer MP3-CD collection, the underused audio cassette book collection was weeded down to a small core collection.

Purchasing Patron Requests

The library had printed up small yellow cards that asked for author, title, and requestor. These were kept at the circulation desk and filled out whenever someone requested a title that was not owned by the library. The cards would serve as a collection development tool when ordering new books. There were always the best sellers listed, but also the titles of books that may have never been purchased without someone asking about it. Every Friday morning, the cards were reviewed by the library director and a book order was placed. If the title was out of print or was outside of the collection policy, the library would try to borrow the title through interlibrary loan (ILL). Books ordered on Friday would usually arrive by Tuesday. Requested titles were processed first and made available by the next Friday to the first patron that requested it. The system was a wonderful way of providing needed books and wisely using limited funding for resources. Patrons were impressed with the great customer service.

No Room for Teen Section

A library had come to the conclusion that it needed to create a teen area in the library. There were some teen titles available in the collection but they were scattered among the adult resources. The library was going to postpone the project because there was no space available to start a new collection. The library was encouraged to evaluate its overextensive, under-used reference collection and the large floor space that it occupied. By realistically evaluating the reference collection based on actual use, two-thirds of the collection was weeded, 90 percent of the standing orders for new materials were cancelled, and the collection was compressed into a small area making room for a teen area. The teen area became a popular area with the high school–aged patrons and the weeded reference materials were not even missed.

Consortium Deal for Downloads

Several small libraries wanted to start a download collection but the cost of $18,000 for an individual library to start a collection was beyond their financial resources. Sixteen individual libraries came together through a consortium agreement and based on their population were able to contribute between $1,000 and $5,000 to join the consortium to share one download system. An oversight committee was established with representatives from across the consortium and, as a group, monitored the usage and maintenance of the system. The results were well received by the members of the sixteen communities who now had access to this popular new technology.

Programming for Adults

A new library director is a strong supporter for library programs designed for adults. The library board is unsupportive stating that programs in the past were not well attended. The library director makes the point that programs will help bring new patrons into the library, and if done correctly they will be well attended. The library board agrees to give the library director a chance to prove her case. A series of programs are offered over the next couple of months including local author signings, a book club discussion group, a historical lecture on southern foods, a tasting party, an art exhibit, and a journaling workshop. Attendance starts slow but picks up due to word of mouth from satisfied patrons. The programs are successful enough that the library board agrees to continue the programs for adults and agrees to approve a small allocation in next year's budget for adult programming.

Display Cases

There were three small empty spaces in the library where there was heavy foot traffic. Three locked display cases were purchased from a used furniture store in town. A library staff member volunteered to oversee the display cases and be in charge of changing them every month. She started by asking the library staff if they had collections to display. Staff displays led to patron displays and then community participation in bringing in display items. In addition to the items in the case, the library asked the owner of the collection to help identify books on the subject for the library's collection, which were then displayed near the case. Whenever possible a program was designed around the theme of the displayed items. The owners of the items on display would bring in friends and family members to see the items neatly arranged in the cases (some who were not library users). The displays became so popular the library had to design a sign-up sheet to cover all the offers made by patrons and the community for possible displays. The most successful display was the one for Veterans Day. When individuals were asked to bring in family military items, the items filled up all three cases, and there were uniforms posed around the cases. It was so popular that it stayed until New Year's when reluctantly it was taken down for a new theme.

Chapter Fourteen

When Small Means Really Small

Joy Worland

MLS programs, library science literature, and professional development workshops rarely address the management challenges experienced in very small libraries with no full-time employees, yet these libraries exist in many rural areas. They are often bursting with potential; invested community members; and committed staff, trustees, and volunteers eager to grow and try new things. Their success depends on formidable time management and multitasking skills on the part of staff, a strong pool of volunteers and management techniques unique to working with non-paid workers, good communication skills, and collaboration with other libraries of similar size.

TIME MANAGEMENT

Key to getting all the necessary things accomplished is prioritizing the importance of tasks, when they need to be completed, and which can be delegated. This isn't unique to small libraries, but the librarian's relatively small number of paid hours means great efficiency and multitasking become necessary, as does possibly fitting in another job in order to make a living. In libraries with only one or a few paid staff members, work gets delegated to volunteers, some of whom have limited computer skills, and all of whom only work a few hours a week, which makes training retention a challenge. Here are some specific things that help:

- Figure out what things can be done when the library isn't open. The lack of distractions makes for great efficiency, and also allows for more patience and focused attention to patrons when the library is open. An added perk is getting to have the library all to yourself!

- Plan time away from the library for meetings, conferences, other work, and vacation when the most qualified volunteers are at the desk. Leave at the wrong time and even a quick trip to the post office can mean misplaced holds, interlibrary loans gone awry, patrons told we don't own a book that we really do, and so on.
- Do technology trainings when they're offered in the state or through webinars. Every time the platform for downloading books does an upgrade, patrons are going to come in distressed because it's changed, so it's good to be prepared.
- More generally with technology, be realistic about your abilities. There are times when even if you could eventually figure something out, the most efficient tactic is to enlist help from a seasoned tech person.
- The above holds true for other areas, too, whether it's designing brochures and posters or building a graphic novels collection. Someone nearby is a specialist, and perhaps you can barter your knowledge of YA (young adult) historical fiction, for example, in exchange for their cataloging expertise.
- Designate a specific time by appointment or outside of regular hours to help patrons with technology, such as downloading books or using the library catalog. This takes time, patience, and concentration, and if there are other things going on simultaneously, it's hard to give the patron the attention they deserve.
- Delegate to volunteers, but only if they're completely competent with the task. It doesn't save time to have something done wrong and then have to redo it. Sometimes it's more efficient just to knock something out, rather than to repeatedly train someone or fix mistakes.
- Try not to be a control freak. For example, getting publicity out for a program is more important than making the poster for it a work of art. Let people who offer to help do it their way (sometimes, anyway).

VOLUNTEERS

Recruitment, training, and management of volunteers, without whom small libraries could not survive, requires a different approach from working with paid employees. Volunteers are often retired. This can sometimes go hand in hand with limited experience with technology, or physical issues like not hearing the phone when it rings. Retirement might also mean large chunks of time when they aren't available because they travel. Most are great about finding subs, but if they aren't or can't find someone, one of the paid employees has to spend time either working the desk or finding someone else to do it. Some of our volunteers are seasonal residents, so when the seasons change, so does the volunteer roster. And even when they work consistently, they work only a few hours a week so it's hard for them to remember skills they don't use often. Updates to the system that change things only slightly can throw off a volunteer who was just getting accustomed to the previous method.

Step-by-step written instructions at the circulation desk, even for seemingly simple, everyday tasks, are a must because the volunteers don't work enough for tasks to become routine. Be practical. If there's a task that only comes up every so often, not everyone needs to try to remember it or risk doing it wrong. For example, in a library that doesn't see enormous numbers of checkouts per hour, if the Internet goes down, it's a lot easier to keep a handwritten list of checkouts than it is to teach offline circulation. Remind volunteers to promote technology like downloading books even if they're not comfortable instructing patrons on using these offerings. Textbox 14.1 lists useful information to store at the circulation desk so volunteers always have access to it.

Textbox 14.1

Items for the circulation desk:

- Circulation instruction handbook
- List of opening and closing tasks
- List of emergency contacts, including people nearby who can help quickly
- Volunteer schedule with phone numbers
- Instructions for what to do if the Internet goes down
- Instructions on how to circulate anything unusual, like reading group books or electronic devices
- Hours for libraries in neighboring towns

Volunteers might not have much experience with technology, which would be a requirement for a paid staff person. On the other hand, maybe they know everyone in town and what books they like to read, or have tips for tourists on how to have a great local experience. That compensates somewhat for being awkward with a computer, but might determine when the best time is for that person to work.

People volunteer for all sorts of reasons. It can be a problem if they're doing it mostly for the benefits it brings to them, because it gives them something to do, gets them time in a pretty place once a week, or makes them feel important. If their altruistic buzz weakens and they stop applying themselves, there's no recourse like docking their (nonexistent) pay. Try to get a feel for their motivation before they start volunteering. Ask current volunteers for suggestions on new people. Nothing works as well as word of mouth in a small town. Putting expectations for volunteer work in writing makes it clear for everyone and is useful to fall back on if things start to sour. But the fact is, there is gray area here. I would have liked a class in school that covered how to respond when someone says in effect, "Seriously? I'm not qualified to donate my time at this little library? Really?"

The upside of this is that most people don't volunteer unless they really want to, so they are often more enthusiastic than someone working a similar job for pay because of financial necessity. The mix of personalities is something that can give a unique, local character to the library. This is an area where a small library might outshine a big library, and having the right personalities in the volunteer pool is a huge part of this. Some people enthusiastically embrace learning new things their whole lives. These are your people! One pretty reliable recruitment tool is to imagine coming into the library as a visitor or a newcomer to town. If you think you'd be delighted by the intelligence, humor, book knowledge, or quirkiness of the volunteer, chances are other library lovers will be, too, and will want to come back if they're local, or go home remembering the wonderful spirit of the library if they're visitors. And so you've made connections and witnessed the power of the library to build community, even if the volunteer doesn't know the difference between a MARC record and an item type.

Utilizing the unique skills of each volunteer is essential, even skills that might not be immediately obvious just from seeing them work the circulation desk. Maybe someone can make posters, publish a newsletter, or build a website. For sure there's someone who bakes really well, which adds greatly to the ambiance of programs. Get the more tech-savvy volunteers to help train the others. Identifying these people is the first step, followed by capitalizing on their close relationships forged over many years. I dubbed one of our volunteers "The Queen of Trouble Shooting When Joy Isn't Around." Having a reliable one (or a few) of these alleviates a lot of stress and is a valuable survival technique.

Alternatively, it's important to know if someone thinks their tech comfort level is higher than it is, being mindful once again of the time drain of fixing mistakes. Be aware of who is at the desk. Take advantage of proximity and eavesdrop just enough to be ready to swoop in and prevent or fix mishaps.

Maintain a healthy sense of humor. If someone says something like, "The scanner hates me," rather than tearing out your hair at the absurdity of this negative anthropomorphizing of an electronic device, breathe deeply, help with the scanner, but store away that comment in order to revisit it with a hearty laugh later. Just remember to be respectful about this and in every other way you treat volunteers. For the library to run smoothly, the volunteers should get the same respect paid employees would, with some extra gratitude, because they're helping run the library for free. They are also the people you'll spend the most time at work with, and the more they understand your world and your responsibilities inside and away from the library, the more supportive they can be. So be nice to them.

A subset of the volunteers is the Friends of the Library. The right group will be comprised of creative, energetic, and dedicated people who are receptive to new ideas and are a font of programming ideas, local resources, and funding. If you ask them for help with something, it will most definitely get done. If your Friends aren't like this, recruit different people, because they are integral to your job success and satisfaction.

COMMUNICATION

While communicating well is important in any work setting, there are some challenges unique to small libraries. It's important to communicate to the trustees how much time it really takes to run the library. This may not match up at all with the number of paid hours for the employees, but the trustees may not realize that if all they see is the library running smoothly. The budget may need to be updated to reflect the work style of the current staff. For example, my first year I blew through the mileage budgeted in half a year, because as a new librarian, I went to every training and workshop I could. I also got involved with the American Library Association (ALA) and joined a committee that required conference attendance, which cost way more than my part-time salary could support. Articulating the benefits of this for the library and asking for help was the only way this could have worked.

Crucial to a strong relationship with trustees is regularly articulating what it means to be an involved, twenty-first-century librarian. The makeup of the board may range from avid library patrons to people who never enter the building except for board meetings. Which doesn't mean they aren't dedicated and contributing to the library, but does create a need for a different kind of communication about the library's mission. Technology priorities in particular need to be articulated to the board by the librarian, whether this means a projector for programs, a laptop for public use, or for the librarian to use at home. No one else has the level of awareness of these issues as the librarian has, so being vocal about them is essential. Textbox 14.2 lists information to share with new trustees.

In my previous job I was in a union. Pay raises, benefits, and working conditions were covered by a collective bargaining agreement negotiated by labor-relations professionals. Now it's up to me to advocate for myself and the other employees. Exert as much influence as you can on the makeup of the people around you. In a small library, you've probably met the people who love the library the most, so try to get them into the circles that improve your professional quality of life. You might know that a patron is a retired librarian or educator who would bring a unique understanding of the library's mission and your needs to the board. Or maybe someone has finance skills that make them able to organize the budget and champion it to the town when necessary. Encourage people whom you know have special skills or backgrounds, particularly relevant to the library, to get involved as trustees, volunteers, or Friends of the Library.

Textbox 14.2

Checklist for new trustees:

- Library policy and long range plan
- Most recent annual report
- Most recent budget
- List of staff and responsibilities
- Library brochure
- Recent newsletter
- Tour of the library

Written policies and procedures are a helpful organization tool that aid staff or subs who occasionally do tasks regularly done by the librarian, and can be passed onto future librarians to ensure continuity. The following are helpful to include:

- Task list broken down to daily, weekly, monthly, annually, as needed
- Template for board reports
- Example of Town Reports from previous year
- List of volunteer responsibilities
- List of current volunteers and their strengths and weaknesses
- List of current board members and their terms
- Instructions for doing annual reports
- How to update the website
- Vendors for supplies, with account usernames and passwords
- Tax-exempt number
- List of service people—cleaning, lawn mowing, snow removal, plumber, information technology
- Contact information for former librarians
- Contact information for other public and school librarians in the area
- State library contacts and who does what at the state library
- Contact information for local newspaper, radio, and TV stations
- List of where and how to promote programs
- List of nearby libraries and bookstores that take used book donations

COLLABORATION

Collaborating with other small libraries and their librarians is vital. In Vermont there are strong formal and informal networks for this. There is the state library association, of course, and many libraries are also members of consortia. These memberships allow us to offer much more sophisticated technology than we could on our own, helping with tech setup, support, and cost. Less formally, the public library listserv is often filled with questions and answers about all sorts of aspects of running a small library. Because of the diverse responsibilities librarians have in small towns, listserv topics range from questions about RDA records to buying popcorn makers for library movie night.

Many different stages of library evolution are represented within small libraries. Some still use card catalogs or have only recently transitioned from one. Making this shift is a huge project, and again, definitely not something I was taught how to do in my degree program that assumed that we'd be working in libraries automated long ago. It would be much more arduous if we couldn't all communicate with others having similar experiences. When my library automated, our neighboring town's library director talked me through many steps of the process, answered countless questions, and invited our volunteers to sit at their circulation desk for hands-on training.

In my region there are three independent libraries in separate towns, but they are as close geographically as branch libraries often are. We try, as much as possible, to operate as branches would. These are examples of ways we collaborate:

- Shared patrons who can borrow materials from all three libraries with the same card
- Co-presentation of programs, and fee sharing for guest speakers, publicity, and program materials
- Capitalizing on the different attributes of each library when planning programs. For example, one library has much more space including a kitchen, another has a nice outdoor area and is more centrally located.
- Coordinating summer reading programs so the local kids have the possibility of three times as many activities
- Shared professional resources like journal subscriptions and equipment, such as a CD cleaning machine
- Discussion and collaboration on collection development. We are experimenting with doing this in a more organized way, such as alternating purchase areas monthly. We also deal with space issues by discussing who will buy what, so we don't all take up precious shelf space with a large book that only one "local" library needs to own.
- Collaboration on periodicals collection to prevent duplication

- Problem solving, especially with big projects, like new technology offerings
- Shared PR, for example joint presentations on the local TV station, alternating writing articles for the local paper
- Shared strategic planning, which more formally aligns our shared goals and the way the communities often operate as a cohesive area, rather than separate towns
- Informal Interlibrary Loan—it's quicker and easier to hand-deliver something sometimes than it is to go through the regular process. Checking the book out to the neighboring library rather than to an individual makes an electronic record for collecting interlibrary loan statistics, but the whole arrangement consists of just a quick phone call or e-mail and a short stop on someone's way home to deliver the book rather than the multiple steps of the formal system.
- Swapping audio book collections for a few weeks to offer local patrons different choices
- Lots of communication, from information on recalcitrant patrons to letting each other know if someone's had a baby and needs to get a baby book gift from whichever town they live in

See textbox 14.3 for examples of how to maximize collaboration efforts both with other libraries and beyond the library network.

Textbox 14.3

Coping with a *really small library* through collaboration:

- Co-present programs with other libraries.
- Explain to presenters that your library is small but filled with passionate patrons who will make a good audience. So maybe they could consider reducing their fee.
- Collaborate with the local bookstore for promoting programs, book donations, and discounts.
- Look for local authors or experts on topics especially interesting to locals. Local talent is more likely to reduce or eliminate their speaking fee.
- Book as many free programs as possible.
- Get people to bring homemade food to programs so you can offer good food for free!

CONCLUSION

The character of a very small library is created by a synergy of attributes universal to all libraries. Yet the atmosphere in these libraries is unique. Patrons benefit from the fact that the person buying the books knows their reading tastes, or that one of the volunteers knows if someone is housebound and needs books delivered. Patrons can enjoy sitting and reading in a cozy building where they are likely to run into friends, or to find out what's going to be discussed at the next select-board meeting. There might be coffee or cookies at the desk, and on a really good day, the library dog might greet them at the door. For staff, the feeling of autonomy and the opportunity to make a personal impact on a community is rewarding and empowering. Spending time in the heart of a vibrant community space, and to be in charge but not in a back office isolated from patrons, makes for quite a joyful work environment. The personalities who associate themselves with small libraries provide laughter, empathy, inspiration, and a microcosm of humanity. While these qualities do exist sometimes in larger workplaces, the village library offers these opportunities every day.

Part Four

Technology

Chapter Fifteen

E-Reading in Rural Libraries

A Guide to Effective Support

David Robinson

With the increasing popularity and affordability of e-readers and tablet computers, librarians are encountering more and more patron questions about these devices. What are the differences between them, and how does one use them to download e-books or audiobooks, browse the Internet, and watch movies or play games? Though considered by some even now as beyond the scope of real library work, these questions are a natural fit for rural libraries. Historically, rural libraries have played important social and informational roles in their communities, given the distances and disparities that have often separated rural residents from available resources. Drawing upon the same community spirit that characterizes so much of country life, rural library staff are well versed in how to accommodate patron needs in the absence of external support. "Where there's a will, there's a way" indeed could serve as the rallying cry of rural libraries everywhere. However, given the challenges posed by these new forms of technology, developing a sustainable approach to staff and patron training can seem an overwhelming task, despite one's good intentions.

As is the case with most rural libraries, the Shenandoah County Library in Edinburg, Virginia, does not have the luxury of a large staff or budget that might be dedicated to "catching up" with patron interest in e-readers and tablets. Nevertheless, through trial and error, we have developed a strategy for incorporating e-reader and tablet support into our daily routine. What follows is a summary of our collective thought process, the specific concerns we began with as well as those we wish now we had emphasized. By thinking about our technology programming as a continuing series of questions to ask and answer—rather than a set of Web 2.0 edicts we think we should follow—we have given ourselves flexibility to respond directly and immediately to patron needs.

Our initial set of questions distilled concerns over motivations and goals. Heretofore, responsibility for technology fell firmly within the purview of specific staff members-primarily, our technology coordinator. However, anyone could assist patrons with navigating our online public access catalog, and if the problems were straightforward enough, assistance could also be provided as needed to users of our Internet stations. To our minds, e-readers and tablets were different. They occupied a strange middle ground between real computers and real books. Moreover, these devices came in many flavors. The prospect of patrons bringing Apples, Androids, Nooks, and Kindles into the library for help in using them was disconcerting, to say the least. Unlike with problems printing documents or conducting Web searches, most of us would have no immediate experience to draw upon in supporting these devices.

Developed and refined over a series of staff meetings and informal conversations, the questions listed below helped us to articulate assumptions about the "purpose" of library work, to establish expectations about what each of us could and could not do, and to create a realistic timeline for staff development:

- Why should we learn about e-readers and tablet computers?
- What do we need to know about e-readers and tablet computers?
- How will we learn and teach about these devices?

Although these questions are presented here in a rough kind of sequential order, they have proven for us even now to be more recursive in nature. With each new update to a device or new question brought to us by a patron, it seems, we find ourselves weaving back and forth between "why," "what," and "how."

WHY SHOULD WE LEARN ABOUT E-READERS AND TABLET COMPUTERS?

This question may seem to be an obvious one, especially in terms of the answers it implies. At a time when the library profession is faced with demonstrating its relevance to a world increasingly enamored of all-things-Internet, remaining uninformed about emerging technologies is not an option. Besides, as more and more libraries broaden their services to include downloadable media, it only makes sense to support the devices that patrons use to checkout e-books and audiobooks. However obvious these answers may be, they pose a dilemma: Should libraries guide users toward the future of technology—and thereby work toward ensuring their long-term survival by serving as pioneers of development—or should libraries focus on addressing patron needs and interests as they arise, regardless of broader cultural trends? How far ahead of the technological curve should libraries situate themselves, if at all?

At the Shenandoah County Library, we found ourselves in the crosshairs of this dilemma at an especially inconvenient point in time. Just as the popularity of e-readers and tablets hit a critical mass in the marketplace, so did we begin offering downloads of e-books and audiobooks via OverDrive. Bluntly stated, we found ourselves in the position of learning and promoting a service that represented a marked departure from our print-oriented collections, while realizing that staff had varying comfort levels with the devices that would be used to access this service.

The first order of business was to alleviate some of the anxiety surrounding the devices themselves, which we felt would impede any training that might take place. Here, an analogy with our more "traditional" responsibilities as library workers helped us to put this anxiety in perspective. We reminded ourselves that librarians have always instructed patrons in how to use the means of accessing information, in addition to providing such information directly. In the days of card catalogs and extensive print reference collections, librarians could be expected to explain the nuances of the data included on individual cards or illustrate the organizational principles of such works as *The Readers' Guide to Periodical Literature*. What has changed is what has to be taught. In days past, no one needed instruction in how to pull out a card catalog drawer or open a book and turn its pages. As technology progressed, not only did accessing information involve understanding the new layouts of Web pages and databases, it assumed a basic facility with a keyboard and mouse. Add the emergence of touch-based devices, incompatible formats, and Digital Rights Management issues, and it is only to be expected that staff feel overwhelmed at the thought of expanding library services to include e-reader support. Knowing that we were right to feel nervous about the work that lay before us, we could begin to develop a realistic approach to it.

WHAT DO WE NEED TO KNOW ABOUT E-READERS AND TABLET COMPUTERS?

The actual process of training and learning began with a division of responsibilities. Rather than expect each staff member to possess a complete mastery of available devices and their downloading requirements, we established a baseline of knowledge that we all could draw from, with the expectation that patrons who required in-depth assistance could be referred to those of us more at ease with technology. What follows is a summary of information that we felt (and feel) every staff person should know, or know how to locate:

- The name(s) of the download service(s) available to patrons, and the basic "rules" of their use (e.g., the number of checkouts allowed at one time)
- The names of supported devices, both in terms of particular products (Nook and Kindle, for instance) and platforms (iOS and Android)
- The location of online tutorials and instructional guides

To aid both our colleagues and patrons in accessing such information, several of us developed a special section of the Shenandoah County Library's Web site that collects important links and "how-to" guides developed in-house. For most staff, most of the time, fielding questions about e-readers or tablets only involves consulting this section and/or assisting patrons in using it.

The importance of these self-developed "How-To" guides for us cannot be overstated. Created to provide comprehensive, step-by-step instructions on accessing the library's downloadable materials, these guides build upon (and perhaps even improve upon) the interactive tutorials available on vendor Web sites in several ways. Firstly, and most importantly, we developed printable documents rather than Web-optimized directions, using a free PDF converter to ensure that our guides would maintain a consistent appearance every time they were viewed or reproduced. Particularly in the case of patrons for whom e-readers or tablets represent initiations into the world of computing, we have found that printing out instructions serves to ease the transition.

Secondly, rather than present all information on a given device in a single document, we have created guides focused on individual elements in the downloading process, such as library policies governing checkouts, the transfer requirements of specific e-readers or tablets, and troubleshooting steps to take in case a download fails. Separating topics in this way has allowed both staff members and patrons to avoid information overload and has made the revision of these documents much easier, especially important in an age of constant updates and upgrades. Lastly, where feasible and appropriate, we have punctuated our guides with images of the screen displays that patrons can expect to see while following a particular step. Nothing helps one explain a complex action better than being able to show what it looks like.

Despite the value of creating these guides, for training ourselves and our patrons, we have found that one aspect of e-reader and tablet support does not lend itself well to being documented in this way: helping patrons learn to interact with the devices themselves, apart from using them to download and read library materials. An anecdote shared by a patron proves telling of this point. As an early adopter of the Amazon Kindle, and with no comparable past experience to draw upon, she found herself at a loss in interpreting the minimal printed instructions included in the box and could not access the more extensive help available as an e-book on the device itself. Hers was a "Catch-22" worthy of Joseph Heller himself. Without knowing how to operate the Kindle, she could not access the e-book that would help her learn how to operate the Kindle. In similar fashion, no amount of printed description or illustration can introduce a novice user to a device that is fundamentally unfamiliar to him or her. On the contrary, there are many ways to misunderstand a new piece of technology and no easy strategy for anticipating and guarding against them in advance. With respect to such situations, the pre-Internet techniques of the reference interview have often saved the day for us. By approaching the more basic dimensions of e-reader and tablet instruction as we would any complex patron question—by paraphrasing the request, clarifying the need, and providing assistance as appropriate—we have developed a model that allows us to perform this work without exceeding our responsibilities as library personnel.

HOW WILL WE LEARN AND TEACH ABOUT THESE DEVICES?

In first getting ready to undertake this level of technological support, we were faced immediately with the conundrum of resources. In creating the initial drafts of our "How-To" guides, we drew heavily upon available tutorials for guidance, replicating steps as much as we could without having actual devices in hand. However, such an approach would not go far in helping us learn enough about the devices to be able to help others in turn. Until such time as we could secure devices of our own, we relied on rural library ingenuity to see us through.

We borrowed devices from colleagues, friends, volunteers, and patrons. We visited local stores to "test drive" products, learning as much as we could in the time available to us. Most helpfully, we prioritized what we needed to learn about the e-readers and tablets while we had access to them. Rather than dive headfirst into the inner workings of these devices, and thereby overwhelm ourselves with too much information too soon, we focused on turning them on and off, accessing their "settings" menu options, and navigating between screens. If the devices before us were touch-based, we made sure we knew what kinds of gestures resulted in what kinds of actions. With at least this basic knowledge under our belts, we felt confident that we could learn the rest along with our patrons when the time arose.

As we should have expected, providing effective technology support is much more art than science. Had we all the time and devices in the world to prepare ourselves with, we still would have discovered more to learn. In fact, were we able to travel back in time, we would offer the following precepts to our younger selves as they busied themselves with various gadgets, thinking at last that they had figured them out:

- Offer tutorials, not classes.
- Distinguish between assisting and repairing.
- Don't forget to empathize with the people you help.

In retrospect, it seems obvious to us that a topic as involved and potentially fraught with anxiety as technology would not benefit from being discussed in a group setting at our library. Admittedly, each of us designated as technology trainers had participated in such classes elsewhere that were presented effectively and were well received. Moreover, given our small staff and the premium on our time, offering classes seemed the wisest choice to make in order to maximize our resources. As we discovered, however, most patrons as well as staff are hesitant to learn or use an absolutely new technology in front of a group. Despite the care with which we developed our PowerPoint slides, we found that students in our classes (when they did show up) became very passive learners, awash in information that bore no direct relationship to them. From the instructor's perspective, these classes were a nightmare to prepare for and conduct, due to the sheer variety of devices, requirements, and challenges that needed to be addressed. In our eagerness to begin, we lost sight of an enduring principle: so much of learning about technology is tied to using it and receiving direct feedback from someone who already knows how to use it. Well-planned though they might have been, our classes could not by definition engage users in this focused and immediate way.

Our solution? To redesignate the block of time set aside for technology classes as a walk-in computer lab, of sorts, where patrons could bring in their e-readers, tablets, and computers and expect to receive individualized assistance. While establishing a weekly lab has improved patron attendance and satisfaction greatly, our balancing of the demands of training and our broader library responsibilities remains a work in progress. More often than not, interest exceeds staff availability, and even though we attempt to provide help when and where it is requested, we have also asked patrons to make appointments with us when staff shortages become an issue.

With respect to the individualized tutorials themselves, the lessons were harder and took longer for us to learn. Wanting to help patrons in any way we could, we found it difficult at first to turn away appeals to repair items, as opposed to merely instructing in their use. Keeping in mind the precedent of tax information—libraries provide tax resources, not tax advice—we concluded that maintaining our focus as library workers compelled us to refer complicated computer questions elsewhere. For us, it is one thing to diagnose a failed e-book transfer, and quite another to diagnose the presence of malware on a computer. Even so, in the spirit of community that brings together the library and its neighbors, we tend to err on the side of saying "Yes" to patron requests, approaching them as "teaching moments" when and where we can.

Indeed, the most important lesson we have learned from our e-reader initiative derives from this very same spirit. Confronting that which is confusing and unfamiliar is not an especially pleasant experience, nor is it always easy to ask for clarification. Nevertheless, our patrons take up these difficult tasks each time they stop by for help. As representatives of a long and honorable tradition, librarians are obligated to approach such moments with the respect and sensitivity they deserve. For us at the Shenandoah County Library, this obligation manifests itself in our attempts to identify with those we assist, to remember what it was like to learn that which is difficult. In this regard, we strive to keep in mind the following as we sit down with our patrons, devices in hand:

- Be polite and nonjudgmental, no matter how basic the request or frustrated the user. A tutorial is not an interrogation.
- Don't jump to conclusions or solutions without fully understanding the patron's questions. Remember the key principle of the reference interview: sometimes a query does not communicate accurately the information truly needed.
- Try not to assume too much about what someone knows or doesn't know. Be a listener first, then a questioner, then a tutor.
- Explain steps while you demonstrate them. Write them down or print them out. Ask the patron to check your work by following the steps as you have recorded them.
- Don't be afraid to make mistakes. Having a patron correct you places the student in the role of teacher, which is a good thing to have happen.
- Help the patron take responsibility for his or her learning by being specific in the wording of your questions. The answer to "Do you have any questions?" will usually be "No."
- When all else fails, be of good humor. Where appropriate, share your own technological shortcomings. Respond to protestations of inadequacy by noting, "If I can learn it, anyone can!"

These days, it is easy to feel despondent about the future of libraries. Much has been written about their apparent decline, attributed by some to the rise of the very devices we have spent so much time and effort to supporting. In truth, the work being done at libraries relative to technology really does belie this sense of decline. Particularly in rural areas, libraries not only provide technological access and training, but they also restore the element of human connection to the process. As worthwhile as using e-readers and tablet computers may be, of more lasting value is the continuing belief in libraries as a means of unconditional and unimpeded learning.

Chapter Sixteen

Facebook Classes for Older Patrons

Sarah Kaufman

Tempe Public Library in Tempe, Arizona, is a small library that likes to program big. Unlike neighboring city library systems in the Greater Phoenix area, the Tempe Public Library has just one physical location, no branches. To compensate for this, the library has a creative outreach model. For over a decade, Tempe Public Library has partnered with Tempe's local community centers to host programs, provide computer labs, circulate print materials, and offer library card registration services. As an outreach librarian, I spend several days a week working at these community centers, frequently with aging adult populations, age 50+. Interestingly enough, although Tempe's population is over 166,842 people, only 8.4% are persons 65 years and over (U.S. Census Bureau 2014). By comparison, this is approximately 40% lower than the percentage of aging adults 65+ living in Maricopa County. Although a much smaller segment of Tempe's population, these aging adults constitute the majority of attendees at my outreach programs. They continue to express a high demand for computer classes and learning about new technologies. In this chapter, I will share my practical tips for engaging this demographic in technology programming, with emphasis on social media programming.

According to the 2012 Pew Internet and American Life Project report, 53% of American adults ages 65 and older use the Internet or have access to e-mail. One in three use social networking websites such as Facebook. Between April 2009 and May 2011 the use of social networking sites by users age 65 and older increased by 150% compared to previous years (Pew 2012). So what does this all mean for libraries serving smaller or targeted populations? While basic computer classes continue to be popular in public libraries, many users age 50+ are looking for more. They want to use technology to stay connected with others, to explore the world around them, and to learn more about current technology trends and news. They are interested in e-readers and tablets, Wi-Fi, and also online safety. Offering these kinds of nontraditional computer classes attracts new library users, repeat programming attendees, and increases the community's awareness and appreciation of the library.

WHY TEACH SOCIAL MEDIA?

Social media provides current events, trends, incentives from businesses, and other potential networking opportunities. Over time, many aging adults have been recruited into using social media, especially in order to stay in touch with family. In a social networking use study conducted by the Pew Institute, as of May 2013, 72% of online adults use social networking sites. Adults ages 18–29 constitute the highest percentage of social media users at 89%, followed by users age 30–49 at 78%. Populations age 50–65+ constitute approximately 38% of the total social networking user population. An additional point of interest from this study was that 74% of women were users of social networking sites, compared with 62% of men (Pew 2012). Viewing pictures, especially family pictures, is particularly enticing to Facebook users. Many aging adults who enroll in Facebook classes want to quickly learn how to post photos and view photos posted by others.

DESIGNING A FACEBOOK CLASS FOR AGING ADULTS

There are many considerations when designing a Facebook class. When working with age 50+ populations, there are certain factors to consider:

When will the class be offered and how often will it meet? Offering a single-time-only Facebook class for this age group is unrealistic. Facebook is a complex product. While there is much to enjoy from the variety of tools and resources available from Facebook, there is too much ground to condense into just a single one-hour or 90-minute class. If your objective is to create confident, proficient Facebook users, plan on several classes with plenty of hands-on lab time. Also, even after class is dismissed, you might plan some extra time to remain in the classroom to answer questions that students may have. This will be greatly appreciated by your students and help you build rapport with them.

Who will teach the class? Facebook classes, if taught correctly, are demanding on an instructor. Aging adults will have lots of questions and want answers to specific scenarios. Some may want to know how to add friends, while some are deeply interested in jumping directly to photo albums. Despite keeping the class on a set lesson plan, sooner or later, you will need to provide one-on-one attention to each student. For this reason, consider co-teaching with a second instructor or enlist a helper. This will ensure students get the help and attention they need when setting up their account and trying new features. It is also important that instructors have adequate preparation time for creating class curriculum, handouts, and researching/re-learning topics. Please do not feel you need to be a Facebook expert to teach a Facebook class. Stick with basics that a beginning Facebook user would need to know. Should you feel comfortable offering a more advanced Facebook class at a future date, you can. Overwhelming students with too much information is not conducive to learning.

What level of student experience is required? Be clear in your class description as to what prerequisites or prior experience is required for the class. If you plan on signing students up for Facebook during class time, it can be a huge time saver to require they have an active e-mail address. Trying to help students sign up for Facebook, while guiding others through e-mail registration or password recovery can take up a large chunk of class time. E-mail sign-up is not a quick process and students may have difficulty completing online forms without one-on-one help. Meanwhile, those students eager to start learning about their new Facebook account will be frustrated that you are using class time and their time to set up e-mail accounts for others.

What topics will be covered? Start with basics and work your way up. Aging adults should be properly educated on what Facebook is and how it is used before being rushed into creating an account. Why? Many people are very concerned about online privacy. Some may not understand that Facebook is about sharing information between themselves and others. Educate them on what to expect and privacy setting options before showing them how to sign up for an account. Prior to learning this, I worked with several aging adults to create Facebook accounts, then subsequently was asked that I help them delete their accounts. After using the site for a few days, they realized they were not comfortable sharing information online and/or that social media was not the right tool for them.

What size class should you have? You may have a high demand for a Facebook class; however, setting class size limits is crucial. Consider making registration a requirement for students who are interested. While you may not be charging a fee for the class, registration will help ensure that you do not end up with more students than computers/seats—it is never a pleasant experience to have to turn folks away. Remember that Facebook classes require more one-on-one attention than most computer classes. Each attendee should have a computer available to practice on. With two instructors you might be able to accommodate 6–8, perhaps even 10 attendees. Remember that more attendees will mean less one-on-one time, which is what beginning Facebook learners need most. If your class is at capacity, students might ask if they can still attend but bring their own laptop. Be careful. Even though they may not occupy a library computer, you will still need to give these students help and provide a handout for them. While it may seem like a reasonable compromise, I would caution against this. Do not be tempted to relax your class size limits; let them know more classes will be offered at a future date and to please check back.

What technology do I need? A computer lab, or adequate number of computers for students to practice on is important. While you might offer lecture material, at some point students will need to practice. We learn by doing. If a screen and projector are available to you, consider using these to demonstrate techniques and steps. Visual learners will appreciate being able to watch and practice along with you.

What day/time for class? As a general observation, most aging adults are early risers and enjoy attending morning classes. Late-afternoon or early evening classes may also work well if your students are working or have busy day schedules. The best way to find out what works is to dive in and try some classes at different times. Ask your students for feedback on what days/times work best for them and adjust future class schedules as needed.

Are handouts necessary? Absolutely. Aging adults greatly appreciate handouts. While Facebook does have an online "help" section, it is no substitute for handouts you create so your students can follow the specific topics and steps you cover in class. Also, students will want to practice what they've learned when they return home. A handout can be very useful for them in case they forget some of the techniques you have shown them during class time. Students will also enjoy writing their own notes on the handouts and sometimes even rewrite your steps in a way that makes more sense to them. Keep in mind that we all learn differently. Handouts help support visual learners who learn best by seeing. Be mindful that Facebook's website design changes often. Make sure your handouts are current. Students can get easily confused trying to match screenshots from an outdated handout to what they are currently seeing on their computer screen.

FACEBOOK TOPICS

Since Facebook is complex, consider grouping topics to make teaching manageable. Each of the following topics could easily fill a 90-minute class.

- What is Facebook and how is it used? Product overview and home screen layout/buttons
- In-class Facebook sign-up and registration
- Facebook privacy settings and security
- Uploading photos and organizing a photo album
- How to post status updates vs. private messages
- How friend requests work / adding friends / blocking friends

- Searching for friends, businesses, organizations, and "liking" pages

RECRUITING AND RETAINING AGING ADULTS FOR CLASS

Popular methods for advertising library programs often include flyers, newsletters, websites, and even social media. When the goal is to reach aging adults, consider using these methods as well as more face-to-face and outreach-oriented ones. For example, try partnering with local senior centers to meet and promote classes to potential students. Local churches and community centers may also help market your programs. Once you have built a substantial base of aging adults, they will usually tell their friends and family. Before you know it you will have wait lists for your classes.

Providing quality programs with excellent customer service to your aging adults takes some work. Executing an informative class with well-designed handouts is important, however, there is more. The positive attitude you bring to the classroom, patience, and willingness to answer questions, and repeat, repeat, repeat is very important to aging adults. The majority of your students age 50+ will need to be taught at a slower pace. That means you need to be selective about what you spend time teaching and pick up on cues to adjust your lesson or review concepts. If you have a room of confused looks, resist springing into the next topic. Take a step back and try re-explaining the current topic in a different way. Encourage questions and do not give the impression that questions are not important. Answering questions leads to teachable moments. Although only one person in the class may be "brave" enough to ask a question, chances are several students have similar questions. Unless you plan to cover a question through a subsequent topic, take a moment and address questions as they are asked. Allocate adequate class time to ensure questions get answered. Remember, there is no shame in slightly deviating from a lesson plan as long as students are engaged and learning. When teaching a new group of students, take some time during the first class to introduce yourself and let students share their names and why they are taking the class. Not only will this help you learn names, and make sure you are meeting the needs of the class, but it helps build new friendships and rapport between fellow classmates.

TEACHING STRATEGIES AND ASSESSMENT

There are two main ways you can approach assessment: formal and informal feedback. Surveys are often used to gather written formal feedback. They may be given at the beginning or end of a class or both (pre- and post-survey). Informal feedback, however, can be obtained in more casual instances and at any time during the class. Walking around the classroom and asking students how they are doing is gathering informal feedback. Noticing if students are keeping up during a class exercise or struggling is also informal feedback. You can tell by body language and facial expression if a student is actually understanding your lesson. Watch for subtle signs, such as crossed arms, yawning, and furled brows. This is all feedback. Become skilled at using informal feedback to modify your teaching. Perhaps you can try re-explaining a topic in a different way, or give a practical example or analogy for a topic. Maybe there is a way to make what you are explaining more visual by using a diagram. With the proper equipment you might consider projecting the actual website or application on the wall as you navigate and explain. Show students how and where you are clicking to navigate. Keep in mind as you teach that your personality, teaching pace, knowledge, and patience for answering questions are being observed by your students. Staying upbeat and pleasant will impact your students. They will feel more upbeat and happy to be in the class with you.

Knowledge of material, explanation of material, and answering of questions are core criteria that a good instructor should welcome feedback on. Build these kinds of instructor feedback questions into surveys when formally assessing your class. Taking the time to design and collect surveys from your students can benefit you in many ways. Below are some general survey questions you might use to collect information about your students. You might want to use a pre- and post-survey to measure the overall effectiveness of your class. The following questions are examples of Yes/No, circle all that apply, and open-ended questions you might consider using. Open-ended (write-in) responses are typically the most valuable as students can explain their needs most accurately and leave comments for improvement and praise. Possible pre-survey questions:

- Have you previously taken a computer/technology class from our library before?
- How would you describe your current computer skills? (Check all that apply.) No previous experience/skill; Some computer skill; I use the Internet; I have downloaded e-books/e-audio before; I use a tablet/iPad/or e-reader; Familiar with social media (Facebook, twitter, etc.); Very comfortable using computers
- Please tell us why you registered for this class. (Check all that apply.) To feel more comfortable using the computer; To learn about the latest technology trends; To feel better connected with others; To improve my skills at work/volunteering; To learn about/find out: (fill in the blank)
- How did you hear about this class?

Possible post-survey questions:

- After taking this class I am now: (check all that apply) More comfortable using the computer/current technology; More informed about the latest technology trends; Able to apply what I've learned to work/volunteering/ leisure; More informed of the library's resources; Other: (please specify)
- Please rate your instructor: (scale of 1 to 5; 5=Excellent, 4=Very Good, 3=Good, 2=Fair, 1=Poor) Knowledge of material; Explanation of material; Answering of questions
- What did you like most about the class?
- How would you improve the class? Please share suggestions for future library programs.

REFLECTIONS ON PERSONAL SURVEY FINDINGS

I first began teaching adults age 50+ in May 2013. I collected survey data from students that participated in Tempe Public Library's "Senior Techs" Computer Classes between August and November 2013. These surveys have helped me customize the kinds of social media classes I teach. The feedback has also advised me on other types of technology classes desired by students. Results from students ages 50+ indicated that 44% of them had no previous computer experience prior to taking a class from the library. Eighty-two percent of respondents did have some computer experience. Percentages for students who use e-mail and the Internet were 75% and 81%, respectively. When asked to indicate whether they were familiar with Facebook (pre-survey), the percentages dropped to 20%. Only 19% of students surveyed indicated that they felt very comfortable using computers. The data collected revealed that aging adults in my classes had prior computer experience and could use the Internet and e-mail. Analyzing this data helped me meet students at their current skill levels and then work on weaknesses or gaps to increase their knowledge and overall skill. In my teaching experience, I have found that aging adults might not always understand many foundational tasks of computer use. They might only know one way of performing a task or computer command, when in fact there are several. They may also not have a home computer on which to practice and rely on the library for computer access.

The highest-ranked reason why aging adults registered for my computer classes was to "feel more comfortable using the computer." The second-highest-ranked reason was "to learn about the latest technology trends." In talking to my students, many have different reasons and motivations for taking a technology class. Some are pressured into it by family while others are self-motivated. Many have a passion for lifelong learning. Whatever the students' motivation, it is the instructor's job to motivate students to continue learning and attend classes. It is not uncommon for my students to repeat classes. This is not because they did not learn anything the first time, but rather, their desire to reinforce and practice what they have learned. This practice leads to long-term retention. Currently, 8% of students who attended a previous class enroll in subsequent classes. I have also observed aging adults "follow" instructors they like into different class offerings and recruit peers to attend as well. Survey responses indicated that 11% of students found out about the library's computer classes from a friend or neighbor. The two ways most aging adults discovered my classes were through the City of Tempe Parks and Recreation brochure and the library newsletter. These percentages were 35% and 32%, respectfully. Class instructors should provide their contact info, along with class descriptions, in brochures and newsletters. This way, potential students can contact them directly with questions. I have had several students call me and ask questions about classes. They might also want to share information about their computer skill level to see if a class fits their needs. Several of the aging adults who call me have questions about registration. Online registration can be especially daunting for those with limited or no computer experience. Consider offering an alternative way for these students to register so they are not deterred from enrolling.

FINAL THOUGHTS

While Facebook and Twitter are currently among the most popular social media sites, library staff must continue to watch and be at the ready. There are always new technologies emerging; however, social media is not going anywhere soon. For many libraries, instituting a website was a major milestone. Now libraries are expected to not only maintain a website but also have a social media presence. Libraries of all sizes across the country are using Facebook and Twitter to reach out to patrons. Through social media, libraries are not only marketing their services and programs, but encouraging dialogue between readers and staff. Whether you are serving or targeting a smaller population or have a single library location, you can have a big impact with the right technology programs. Offering social media and current technology classes to aging adults not only reinforces a library's commitment to educating and enriching the community, but empowers the community to take part in the fun.

REFERENCES

Pew Internet and American Life Project. 2012. "Older Adults and Internet Use." http://www. pewInternet.org/Reports/2012/Older-adults-and-Internet-use/Summary-of-findings.aspx (accessed November 11).
Pew Internet and American Life Project. 2012. "Social Networking Fact Sheet."

http://pewInternet.org/Commentary/2012/March/Pew-Internet-Social-Networking-full-detail.
    aspx (accessed November 11).
U.S. Census Bureau. 2014. "State and County QuickFacts"
http://quickfacts.census.gov/qfd/states/04/0473000.html (accessed May 20).

Chapter Seventeen

Preserving Your Community's Memories

Developing Librarians for Digital Preservation

Vanessa Neblett and Shane Roopnarine

As people reach retirement, they consider their legacies and how they will be remembered. The Orange County Library System (Florida) began a community-based online collection titled Orlando Memory to capture those unique, personal memories and images of our community's past and our residents' experiences in 2008. By developing simple, digital preservation methods, training for librarians and staff on these techniques, and strategies for connecting with the community, the Orange County Library System (OCLS) has been able to expand our local history initiatives into a searchable digital collection of community memories.

GETTING STARTED

Orlando Memory is the story of Orlando, Florida, told by its people. When OCLS began the development of the Orlando Memory website, there were a number of factors that had to be considered. The main areas of consideration for this digital, local history project included the intended audience and who would participate in the project (both behind the scenes and in the community), equipment needed, developing easy digitization methods, staff training, how to store and share this information, and finally, how to market and promote this new venture.

For the Orlando Memory project, OCLS designated the community at large as the audience and that any memory (text, audio, video, or photo) of

Orlando and Orange County would be the objects desirable to capture. This project was initially developed using Kete, an open-source software platform developed by the Horowhenua Library Trust in New Zealand. As additional open-source options became available, Orlando Memory was relaunched in July 2013 using a Drupal platform.

PARTICIPATION

Orlando Memory is open to anyone who would like to upload content such as pictures, video, and audio clips, in addition to creating topics where contributors can share text concerning particular events, people, and/or places that relate to Orlando and Orange County. The immediate audience is the residents of Orange County, Florida, both past and present, but the site is accessible to everyone to comment and share memories. This is especially important in an area such as Orlando that has such a lively tourist community. Many people throughout the world have created a memory in Orlando! All of the content is required to go through a moderator before it is posted to the live site. This allows for quality control and ensures questionable material is not posted to the site.

Once the audience and participation base was determined, OCLS reviewed its archives. Items were digitized and posted as a platform for the community to build upon the library's participation. Exploring the library's own archives is a great foundation for local digital history. This gives staff the opportunity to not only seek and share the valuable pieces of history already collected about the community, but it also gives them practice with digitization techniques. Digitizing the library's own collection is a great marketing tool that illustrates the types of memories appropriate for the project.

While building the online collection, the library system reached out to community contacts, especially those most likely to participate in sharing local memories. The most frequent participants were the boomers in Central Florida. Boomers are frequent users of the library, and it was (and continues to be) up to the library staff to encourage them to share their memories of the development and changes that have transformed the community in their lifetime. They also typically possess photographs of their parents and grandparents who may have been members of the same community in which the boomer is now living. They can share these memories on Orlando Memory for future generations to experience and enjoy.

For instance, think about your Friends of the Library group. Typically, these are established, participating members of the community who have already decided to share their time with the library and the greater community. These members are a great resource. Consider asking them to share their memories and participate in strengthening the online content and stories. Some other people or groups to consider may include the following:

- The library board
- Groups who use your meeting rooms
- Recipients of your publications concerning library events and programs
- Local history societies
- Local genealogy groups

OCLS encouraged participants to spread the word to friends, neighbors, and colleagues about OCLS's new local history initiative. Orlando Memory has its own website, e-mail address, and logo, which are easy items to share with members of the community.

While we had some community participation, it became clear that we needed to facilitate events and to be immersed in areas of the community to encourage the sharing of memories. When we looked within, we saw that we had a valuable resource to facilitate the sharing and documentation of community memories: our librarians. These librarians have worked with and within the community; they have made contacts and have presented information on various library topics to groups in the community. They had made connections and our branch locations are already integral parts of the community.

It became clear that the library needed to establish easy, basic digitization methods for the project that could be shared with both staff and participants on Orlando Memory. These methods would be included on the site to help those who wanted to use the site directly, in addition to becoming the foundation for developing training for librarians and other staff who would be directly involved in recording audio and/or video interviews and scanning items for our digital collection. Here are some tips and strategies for developing standards and trainings.

BASIC DIGITIZATION TOOLS AND STRATEGIES

Photographs, Documents, and Print Media

When preserving items like photographs, documents (letters, certificates, or similar), and other kinds of print media through digitization, there are several basic tools that can be used for this process: flatbed scanners, digital cameras and copy stands, or specialized equipment for certain tasks. Recommendations are based on staff experiences with digitizing print media for Orlando Memory.

Flatbed scanners

The simplest method for converting most types of print media is to use a flatbed scanner. These devices are most commonly available as single-purpose devices or as part of a multi-function unit. Many libraries already own flatbed scanners, so this kind of equipment can easily be repurposed for use with a local history program. Some scanners come with attachments that can be used to scan film negatives or slides. Flatbed scanners are useful for flat media: photographs, documents, certificates, postcards, letters, or similar items. Scans produce high-quality results with minimal customization, and entry-level scanners cost between $100 and $200. While this type of equipment is versatile and easy to use, it is not a good tool for digitizing books or any item that is not perfectly flat. The scanning area of typical flatbed scanners is about 8.5 inches wide and at most 14 inches in length, so it may not easily accommodate larger items. Also, most scanners of this type are not portable, which limits where scanning can take place.

Digital cameras and copy stands

Another method for digitizing print media is to use a digital camera combined with a copy stand. This method usually requires more customization and components than using a flatbed scanner, but it offers more flexibility when digitizing large format items or media that is not completely flat. Most digital cameras with a tripod mount will work for this application and selecting a digital camera for use with a copy stand is primarily dependent on the project's budget. Good results can be achieved with a simple point-and-shoot camera, though a DSLR camera with interchangeable lenses will produce better images. Generally, DSLR cameras have better image sensors and lenses than basic point-and-shoot models. Copy stands are available in a variety of sizes. Smaller copy stands are available for under $100 without a lighting kit, but professional equipment with added accessories may exceed $1,000. Lighting the copy stand area is an important factor because poor lighting can impair results. The simplest method is to use reading lamps with bright, white bulbs to illuminate the area. Larger copy stands are available with lighting kits that include mounted arms and attached copy lights. Avoid using the camera's built-in flash because it may create uneven lighting. Despite the flexibility of this method, there are some limitations to consider. Many library staff members have some existing experience with flatbed scanners, but it is likely that few have used a copy stand. Staff will require some training to use this equipment. However, with practice, most library staff will become proficient using this method.

Specialized equipment

Other more specialized equipment for digitizing print media include book scanners and slide scanners. Basic book scanners are available as flatbed models that can scan to the edge of the device. This method helps to preserve the book's spine while producing a uniform, flat image. More complex models are used by organizations with dedicated digitizing projects or special collections. Slide scanners are useful for scanning film negatives or photo slides, and options range from basic models for simple digitization to more advanced models typically used by commercial conversion services.

ORAL HISTORY INTERVIEWS

Recording audio and video interviews is another important aspect of collecting and preserving stories and memories. Library staff working with Orlando Memory have developed their interviewing skills by recording both audio and video interviews.

Audio Interviews

Audio interviews are better suited for longer interviews that exceed fifteen minutes. Most listeners are willing to listen to a longer audio interview than view a video interview that is more than a few minutes. Audio interviews are typically easier to prepare and managing the equipment is often less complicated. This format lends to fewer distractions for its audience and emphasizes the impact of the speaker. For library staff and the person being interviewed, it is usually less intimidating than conducting a video interview.

Equipment for audio interviews

When selecting equipment for audio recording, most external microphones generate better sound than the built-in microphone in most devices. If available, using a smartphone is one of the easiest tools for audio recording. For better sound, external microphones are available for these devices.

Another simple solution is to use a digital voice recorder, typically used for recording lectures or interviews. The microphones in these devices are usually good for recording but an external microphone is preferable. Recorders start around $50 and should include a 3.5 millimeter jack for an external microphone and the ability to transfer recorded audio files to a computer using a USB connection. External microphones for either a smartphone or voice recorder may cost between $20 and $100.

Recording with a laptop is also possible when using audio recording and editing software combined with an external microphone. When using this option, choose an external microphone designed for podcasts or "home-studio" recording, which usually costs between $50 and $200. After the interview recording is finished, it will be necessary to edit the raw audio. The open source software Audacity is a popular and simple option for this process. This software can record and edit audio, plus it will convert finished projects to common formats, like MP3.

Video Interviews

Video interviews require some extra planning and skill, more so than audio recording, but it can have a bigger impact on its audience. Video interviews create a more personal connection with the viewer and provide additional visual cues about the subject through body language and other aspects of the video. When conducting a video interview, setting the space for an interview is an important factor for having a successful session. The space should be clear of any items that will distract the viewer from the subject. Use a solid background that is neither very light nor too dark. Simple blue backgrounds work best for most skin tones and work well with most video recorders.

Framing the subject is another important aspect of creating the interview space. Simply, framing is deciding how the subjects and other elements fit into the space that the video camera will record. The basic technique is to frame the subject in a medium shot that focuses on the person from the waist or chest to above his or her head. When framing the shot, point the camera just slightly off-center instead of directly at the subject. During the interview, sit facing the subject and ask them to look at the interviewer instead of the camera.

Equipment for video interviews

As with audio recording, the most readily available piece of equipment for video recording is a smartphone. Most current smartphones can record video, and, when combined with a small or simple tripod, will work well for recording video.

For more advanced recording, there are many kinds of single-purpose video cameras available and basic models are relatively inexpensive, usually under $200. Video cameras should include the ability to record high-definition video and connect an external microphone. It should also include external storage capacity using a flash memory card or include high-capacity internal storage (16GBs or more). Many current digital cameras designed for photography now include the ability to record high-definition video and can serve as a multi-function device. Whichever device is selected, a tripod is recommended. Mini tripods with flexible legs work well on tabletops and standard-size tripods are better for heavier cameras or for filming in varying settings.

Whatever the project budget, there is equipment available to match its requirements. Choose equipment that is appropriate for the skill level of the staff who will use it. If project staff have limited experience with recording video, choose simpler devices without advanced features designed for professionals. Consumer-oriented video cameras that are pocket-sized or hand-held are compatible choices.

STAFF TRAINING

Develop a Plan

For any digitization or local history initiative to be successful, library staff working on the project should receive training for conducting interviews and digitization methods.

Learning how to conduct and manage an interview will require practice and experience, but these are important skills to develop. There are many resources available online that will help staff with crafting interview questions and learning interviewing techniques. Two resources that were used with Orlando Memory are the "The Smithsonian Folklife and Oral History Interviewing Guide" (Hunt 2003) and the StoryCorps "Do-It-Yourself" guide (2013). If training several staff for the project, schedule a session to review and practice interviewing skills. Training sessions should include peer-to-peer practice where staff can interview each other. Staff should also use all equipment that will be available for the project. This will increase their comfort level with the tools and techniques they will use throughout the oral history collection process.

Establish a Place for Documentation

The Orlando Memory project uses a wiki to host project documents and training materials. For institutions that do not have an internal wiki or staff-only website, use Google Drive or another free or low-cost service to host and share project materials. This will be especially useful if there are several library staff working on the project because it will help promote consistency and establish a central knowledge base.

One of the most helpful tools used by OCLS staff working on oral history interviews is the "Interview Guide." This guide, developed by staff, is two pages long and includes a pre-interview checklist, tips for a good interview, sample interview questions, and a post-interview closing checklist. The guide is most helpful for staff who have limited experience with interviewing and provides a template for the recording session. The project knowledge base should also include guides for using equipment, guidelines for editing, and instructions for uploading or sharing content. It may also include any specific standards for the desired outcomes of interviews.

Choosing an Online Preservation Solution

As library staff members gather new content, it will be important to store this material in a central location where it can viewed by other staff, members of the public who contributed content, and by those who will discover these memories. Institutions should plan for an online preservation solution early in the project. Any solution that is given consideration should emphasize online sharing and should be easy to use by both internal and external users. While the process for collecting memories is important, it is of equal importance to share these memories with the community at large. It is through the digital sharing of these memories that boomers, and all participants, can readily see and access their legacy, contribute to other people's memories, and promote the online collection as a place to share memories.

Here are three recommended options for online preservation and sharing: use an existing website to host content, create a dedicated website using an existing content management solution, or use a more advanced and specialized solution designed for digital libraries or repositories.

Existing website

For institutions with limited resources, using an existing website to store and share content will be the simplest solution. Consider dedicating a page in the local history or genealogy section of the website for photo or document collections and audio interviews. For larger photo or image collections, consider using an online photo service, like Flickr or Picasa Web Albums, to share photos with the community.

For video interviews, online video sharing sites are a reasonable solution. The Orlando Memory website does not store video interviews. Instead, it stores links to individual videos uploaded by library staff to a shared You-Tube account. This reduces the need for dedicated local storage for large videos. However, it is strongly recommended to keep copies of video interviews on local storage as a backup.

Dedicated content management system

Larger projects with more resources should consider using a dedicated content management systems (CMS). Two popular options are Drupal and WordPress. Both feature collaborative content creation tools and the ability to expand a website's functionality through modules and plugins. These systems are open source and free to use, and support can be found online through software documentation or forums. Using a dedicated content management system will allow an institution to showcase its content online and create a unique identity for its collection. Most library staff will not need knowledge of HTML or advanced technical skills to successfully upload content. While these systems include extensive online documentation and can be easily installed and configured, it is recommended to include library information technology and website staff in deploying a content management system.

Specialized solutions for digital libraries or repositories

Advanced projects or special collections with significant preservation initiatives should consider one of the specialized solutions for creating and preserving digital collections. There are several open source choices available, but Omeka is recommended because it is easy to deploy and popular with museums and libraries (Roy Rosenzweig Center for History and New Media 2013b). Compared to more sophisticated open source digital repositories, like Fedora and DSpace, Omeka is a strong candidate for libraries that are interested in a specialized online collection management tool. Digital libraries using Omeka include Florida Memory (part of the State Archives of Florida) and Treasures of the New York Public Library, which include items from the NYPL's extensive collections. Omeka is specifically designed for "library, museum, archives, and scholarly collections and exhibitions" and is meant to be easy to use (Roy Rosenzweig Center for History and New Media 2013a). For more advanced customization, website themes and plugins are available. The technical skills required by library staff to successfully create and upload content using Omeka are similar to those needed for Drupal or WordPress, so extensive training and specialized knowledge will not be required.

MARKETING AND PROMOTION

Once OCLS completed its website, conducted staff training, and began to upload content, the next step was to develop a marketing strategy. Employees have been trained and provided content that increased their understanding of Orlando Memory and enhanced their abilities to talk about and encourage others to participate in the project. Now it was time to capitalize on our community connections.

The library system looked at the type of outreaches it was currently conducting, and tried to find ways to tie the local history project into these presentations about library activities. Effective promotion can be relatively inexpensive, especially when participants are engaged at an individual/personal level. OCLS created flyers with the website address, succinct information about what the site is all about, and how people can participate. OCLS also promoted Orlando Memory on the website and in library marketing materials.

The Orange County Library System contacted local groups whose members are likely candidates for participation such as veterans' groups, churches, and senior centers. Staff asked to make a presentation at a meeting or participate in a group activity. OCLS also shared flyers containing information about the project with groups already using library meeting rooms.

At OCLS, the public service departments crafted "themed" programs for Orlando Memory including a week-long event around Veterans Day. Flyers were sent to local groups to schedule times for area veterans to share their memories of the community. Participants were encouraged to bring photos and documents for library staff to scan so these items can be shared with the rest of the community on the Orlando Memory website. OCLS also made sure to have staff time dedicated to assisting community members in scanning these objects and in recording the interviews.

In addition, the library contacted local leaders and politicians by sending letters, e-mails and/or making phone calls seeking their participation in sharing their community memories while detailing the importance of participating in this local history initiative. At OCLS, the library has been successful in recording a number of local politicians simply by sending letters detailing the project and providing the questions we will be asking. It is beneficial to come up with simple, consistent questions for interviewing local leaders. Providing these questions beforehand gives them an opportunity to develop their answers in addition to showcasing what the project is all about. When interviewing community politicians, the library poses the following questions:

- Why did your family choose the Orlando area as a home?
- What is the biggest change you have seen in Orlando since your arrival?
- What did you do for fun when you were in high school? (If you did not attend high school here, what did you do for fun when you first got here, or ten years ago?)
- What are your two favorite places to go today?
- What is one place that you wish was still around and why?
- Please give us a six-word memoir about your life in Orlando.

Another effective, easy-to-use marketing tool is social media, especially Facebook. OCLS has used social media to find other people who may be interested in contributing or who may have family members who can contribute memories to the site. When content is uploaded to Orlando Memory, participants are able to share this content with their own followers on Facebook and/or Twitter. This type of virtual sharing reinforces the Orlando Memory brand and may attract a new set of participants who may not be active in community groups but who have a number of friends in the community, past or present.

CONCLUSION

As you can see, engaging with the boomers in your community to create a successful local history preservation program is possible with some preparation and communication. Their legacies are important to them and their community, and the library is a perfect place for this type of partnership. Your staff will learn new skills while engaging in this important project as a gatekeeper for the community's memories and history.

REFERENCES

Hunt, Marjorie. 2003. "The Smithsonian Folklife and Oral History Interviewing Guide." Smithsonian Center for Folklife and Cultural Heritage. http://www.folklife.si.edu/education_exhibits/resources/guide/introduction.aspx.

Roy Rosenzweig Center for History and New Media. 2013a. "Project." Omeka. Accessed July 19. http://omeka.org/about/.

———. 2013b. "Sites Using Omeka." Omeka. Accessed July 19. http://omeka.org/codex/View_Sites_Powered_by_Omeka.

StoryCorps. 2013. "Do-It-Yourself Instruction Guide." StoryCorps DIY. Accessed July 19. http://nationaldayoflistening.org/downloads/DIY-Instruction-Guide.pdf.

Chapter Eighteen

Search Engine Optimization (SEO) and Library Web Content

Lauren Magnuson

As libraries are embracing and transforming access to digital materials for their patrons, the content that patrons can access through a library's website has become increasingly rich. Library websites include everything from blogs, program information, tutorials, subject guides, and more. However, rich content and diverse digital services aren't useful if they cannot be found, and most researchers and library patrons are beginning their searches utilizing a search engine like Google (Georgas 2013). Recognizing the importance of search engines in marketing, in recent years a small industry has emerged devoted to improving a website's findability on commercial search engines. Search Engine Optimization (SEO) is a process of strategically designing web pages and information architecture so that certain pages appear more prominently in search engine results.

WHY SHOULD LIBRARIES CARE ABOUT SEARCH ENGINE OPTIMIZATION?

While the topic of search engine optimization is highly complex, and certain SEO practices can be somewhat controversial, this chapter will focus on three primary strategies: (1) creating and organizing unique and interesting content, (2) behind-the-scenes best practices, and (3) leveraging the power of linking via social media and other digital spaces your users frequent. The strategies discussed will focus on solutions that do not require paid advertising campaigns and can be implemented without an extensive marketing budget.

Information seekers often start with Google and other search engines. When using library resources, users often search commercial search engines in addition to library catalogs and discovery systems (Georgas 2013). When a user ultimately intends to utilize library resources for their research, they may rely on Google to find your library website or other information on your library web pages. If information on your Web pages is not easily findable, users may return to Google to execute more searches rather than browse extensively to find information.

SEO is an iterative process; it is not a one-time project. SEO involves a toolset of technologies and strategies to understand user needs and design content that responds to those needs. Regardless of technical expertise, an understanding of the general principles of SEO is essential for anyone creating library web content or marketing library services online. Search engines help bring our patrons to our information and services—let's help our patrons find us!

UNDERSTANDING USERS AND DETERMINING SEO GOALS

The first step to any search engine optimization strategy is to understand how your users are currently finding and accessing information about services your library provides. If you are not already using a website traffic monitoring service such as Google Analytics, this should be configured before making any decisions regarding SEO. If your library website uses a content management system (CMS) such as Wordpress, you may already have visitor tracking built-in, though you could use Google Analytics in addition to your site's built-in tracking. The richness of Google Analytics and Google Webmaster tools can add considerable data to inform your library's SEO strategy.

Once you have signed up for a Google Analytics account and defined a domain or website you wish to track (Google refers to each domain or site as a "property" or "view"), place the provided tracking code in all web pages you wish to track. For the richest possible data, this code should be placed in all public-facing Web pages. Once the tracking code is in place, it may take up to forty-eight hours for traffic data to start being returned. When the data begins appearing in your Google Analytics dashboard, it is wise to gather data for several weeks to gather a snapshot of how the library's website is being used and what kind of traffic the website is currently experiencing. Establishing a benchmark before making any changes will help determine whether the strategies used are successful.

The elements of Google Analytics data that are important to analyze for a library's website will depend on the specific library and the services provided. However, some key elements to examine in your Google Analytics reports include the following:

Audience demographics/audience interests. Who are your current users? Google draws information about audience demographics from its extensive tracking of user browsing behavior through browser cookies (Google, "Overview of Demographics and Interests Reports"). For libraries, one of the most important aspects of your audience demographics report from an SEO standpoint is what types of users are *not* accessing your library's Web page, especially compared to the demographics you are serving. For example, are the traffic sources from users eighteen to twenty-four dramatically lower than the proportion of those users in your constituency? The absence of particular types of users can be just as crucial as the presence of users when developing an SEO strategy.

Behavior flow and exit pages. When users navigate your site, what are they clicking on? What content are they seeking? What page is the most common "exit page" (the page that users last see before leaving your site)? While this is not always the case, the "exit page" can sometimes be thought of as the page at which users decide to give up and look elsewhere for the information they need.

"Bounce rate" metrics. A "bounce" is counted when users access your site and then immediately leave for another domain. Bounce rates are often high for library websites, because a user may access your home page and then execute a catalog or discovery system search. If the catalog search loads a page on a different domain (which may be the case if your catalog is hosted by a third-party or hosted in the cloud), this type of usage will count as a "bounce." If your bounce rate is high, consider it in light of third-party services accessible through your pages. It is not clear the extent bounce rate is utilized by Google's ranking algorithm, but reducing bounce rate is generally considered a good practice for search engine optimization (Killoran 2013).

Site Search. If your library website has a built-in site search (provided by Google Custom Search or another method) you can use Google Analytics to view what terms users are searching for on your site. To set this up in Google Analytics, conduct a search using your library's site search and observe how the URL is constructed for the result page on your website. Look carefully at how the URL passes the search term you entered. For example, when searching for hours, you may see a string in the URL that looks like *&query=hours*. In this example, *query* is the parameter you can use in Google Analytics to configure site searching. It is possible that the site search uses multiple query parameters, and Google Analytics can track up to five query parameters. Set up Site Searching in Google Analytics under Account Administration > Settings (Google, "Set Up and Configure Site Search").

Once your Google Analytics account is active and retrieving data, you will also want to enable Webmaster Tools (Google, "Webmaster Tools"). You can do this by visiting the Webmaster Tools website and adding the

URL(s) of the sites you manage. When you enter the URL of your website, be sure to clarify whether your domain uses "www" in its URL. To Webmaster Tools, *http://www.example.com* and *http://example.com* may be viewed as two separate websites, but this can be adjusted by specifying the "preferred domain" (Google, "Set Your Preferred Domain [www or non-www]"). Webmaster Tools provides helpful insight into how Google's index has crawled and indexed your web pages, and is a key way to utilize your Google Analytics account for SEO purposes.

Once you have verified your site with Webmaster Tools, link the library website's Google Analytics property to the verified Webmaster Tools website under Standard Reports > Search Engine Optimization. This will allow you to view certain Webmaster Tools data through Google Analytics. The key goal of the data you are gathering in analytics is to understand what users have searched for that led them to your website. The terms that users are searching for can provide a starting point for enhancing and promoting your site's content.

Developing SEO goals can be a daunting prospect when confronted with the variety of dimensions of analytics data available. Focusing on improving just one metric can be helpful. SEO strategists often refer to "conversion rate" as a key indicator of success in an SEO campaign or project. A conversion rate refers to how often a user completes a desired task (Nielsen 2013). For libraries, conversion might refer to each time a user signs up for a library card, RSVPs to a library event, downloads an e-book, or subscribes to the library's e-newsletter. While conversion rate is most often discussed in the context of SEO campaigns involving paid Web advertising (as opposed to "organic search" traffic generated through actual user searches), it can be helpful to identify one "conversion" task that could be improved through search engine optimization of your library's Web content. Identify a task that you know patrons have trouble finding on your website, and focus on improving the visibility and conversion rate of that task.

UNIQUE, RELEVANT, AND FRESH CONTENT

When considering enhancing your website's content to increase SEO, it is first essential to understand what your current users are looking for when they access your site. A key point to remember is that "pages should be designed for users, not search engines" ("How People Interact with Search Engines" 2012). As it happens, both human users and search engines prefer content that is unique and addresses specific user needs. After reviewing your analytics data, are your users finding your website's unique and relevant content?

One common barrier to users successfully finding library services online is the misalignment of user keywords and library jargon (Becker and Yannotta 2013). Libraries often use terminology that is not widely used by users: databases, catalog, e-media, and so on. Your users might be searching for words like "e-book borrowing" or "free e-books." Your library may offer these services, but do these keywords appear anywhere on your website? The process of discovering what kinds of words people use when searching is referred to as "keyword research."

Using Google's Webmaster Tools, you can retrieve extensive data about user "queries." Queries are keywords that currently return pages from your website on a search engine result page. Webmaster Tools features a "query list," which is a list of user search terms that retrieved your Web page in the results (Google, "Search Queries"). Data about queries, as well as the number of times users clicked on your Web page after entering a particular query, is available in Webmaster Tools under Search Traffic > Search Queries. This data is only stored in Webmaster Tools for ninety days, but can provide a useful glimpse into the kinds of keywords that users are entering into Google to retrieve your website.

A useful tool to determine what kinds of keywords users associate with your library's services can be found using Google's Keyword Planner (formerly known as Google Keyword Tool) (Google, "Google Adwords Keyword Planner"). Google Keyword Planner is a service now offered through a free Google Adwords account. This service enables identifying related searches for particular terms. For example, using Keyword Planner, you can enter a product or service (such as e-books) and retrieve a list of keyword ideas along with the frequency with which those words are used. The tool also enables drilling down to discover keywords used by a particular location, such as your city or county. For example, at the time of writing, Keyword Planner can tell me that users in Los Angeles use Google to search for the term "e-books" over 74,000 times a month, and also that related search terms include "read books online free."

Another key consideration when enhancing your library's website for SEO is what services your library offers that users cannot get anywhere else. What is happening at your library of local interest? Do you have events, story hours, special exhibits, or other services that your users may be looking for? The way you organize this type of content has important implications for SEO. The presence of unique content is considered to be highly important factor in how pages are ranked by Google, so it is important to promote the unique and interesting services, events, and material your library provides.

Finally, freshness of Web content is crucial. Websites with frequently updated content consistently rank higher in search results than static websites (Demers 2013). A growing online presence and pages that are revisited and updated is a sign to search engines that your website is alive and continually producing relevant, new information for users. However, updating pages solely for the sake of freshness is not a worthwhile strategy; updates should be meaningful and add value. Updating important page content (such as updating the text in the body of a page) is more valuable from an SEO perspective than updates to peripheral page content like ads and news feeds (Demers 2013). The landscape of library services is changing constantly and rapidly; updating content is a good practice both for meeting user needs and for improving the findability of library web services.

BEHIND THE SCENES: PAGE TITLES, SITEMAPS, AND META TAGS

Google uses automated programs (called bots or spiders) to "crawl" across Web pages via links. When a bot encounters a page, it sends information about the page to Google's index. This bot-discovered information is used to rank pages according to Google's patented PageRank algorithm. The criterion used by the algorithm is not explicitly known, and the algorithm is modified regularly. Fundamentally, Google is thought to evaluate websites on these two factors:

- The intrinsic qualities of the website, including its structure and content
- Extrinsic factors such as links to the website from other sites on the Internet (referred to as "inbound links") (Killoran 2013)

Some behind-the-scenes best practices include the following:

Unique, accurate page titles. Page titles appear at the top of your browser and are generated by the <title> tag of each web page. For example, if you have a page that lists your hours and contact information, avoid using generic page titles such as "About" or "Home." Instead, a descriptive page title could be "Great County Public Library Hours" or "Great University Event Calendar." Also, consider your OPAC or library discovery system. When performing a search, the title that appears in the browser should be something unique to your library such as "Find Books at Great County Public Library." Consider titling Web pages with the kinds of phrases users might enter to search for the content, such as "When is the library open" or "How do I download an e-book."

Human-readable URLs with keywords. Wherever possible, it is preferable to construct URLs for web pages that are human-readable and contain keywords users might be searching for. For example, http://example.org/how-to-download-ebooks is a better URL for search engine retrieval than http://example.org/page/230840 (Fishkin 2014).

Sitemaps. Google bots are better at indexing highly structured information. A key way to deliver this information to the Google index is through a sitemap. The more information that's discoverable through a sitemap, the better Google's index will understand your site's content. A sitemap is a file, usually generated in XML format, that provides information about the pages on your website: when it was last updated, how often it changes, and how important each page is relative to the others on your site. There are several ways to create a sitemap including RSS feeds, simple text files, or third-party services (Google, "Sitemap Formats and Guidelines"). If your Web pages already generate RSS feeds (for example, if your library uses a WordPress or blogger platform) you can utilize the URL of the existing RSS feed. You can submit your sitemap to Google using the Google Webmaster Tools interface.

Meta tags. The <meta> tag is an HTML element that includes descriptive metadata and keywords for a Web page. You can think of meta descriptions as advertising copy for your Web pages (Moz 2014). These descriptions are used by search engines to identify the core keywords associated with a page and display a brief summary of page contents in search engine results. It is important to note that meta tag descriptions and keywords are not included in the Google PageRank algorithm to determine the ranking level of a page (Miller 2012). Google does recommend that meta tags be included on Web pages to improve display of the pages on search results, as meta tag descriptions are often displayed underneath search result links. When defining a meta tag description, Google recommends keeping the description under 160 characters, and it's wise to avoid any non-alphanumeric characters in the meta description tag.

Inbound linking. Google considers both the content of the page itself and certain elements on the page that indicate how it might be relevant to a search. Google also looks for links to the page from other domains and websites (sometimes referred to as "inbound links"). An example of an inbound link might be when your local newspaper website or community calendar links to a library event page. Google uses information stored in the structure of the inbound link to help contextualize the page being linked. These kinds of inbound links help inform Google how other websites are using the information on your page, which helps to indicate how it might be useful or relevant for searches.

SOCIAL MEDIA AND SEO

While there is some debate over the extent to which inbound links from social media influence Google's PageRank algorithm, it is generally agreed that a robust and engaged social media presence is beneficial for SEO. In a 2013 survey, SEO professionals indicated that they believe Google +1s (recommendations to a Web page through Google's social media service Google+) to be a key component of Google's PageRank algorithm (Moz 2013). However, not all social media links are created equal. In the same survey, SEO professionals also indicated that they believe Google assesses certain characteristics of recommenders (such as the size of the user's Google+ "circle" of social media contacts) when incorporating social media recommendations into a Web page's rank.

While there is some dispute about the algorithmic importance of social media links, a strong social media presence can still contribute to driving traffic to your site. Some recognized social media best practices for SEO include these:

Engage your users with shareable content. While it may seem like a good strategy at first, pushing out links to content via various social media platforms is not the best way to drive traffic to your website. It is believed Google's PageRank algorithm considers more subtle "social signals" than volume of links alone: variety and quality of link sources is also essential (Demers 2013). A library's lone social media channel broadcasting content outward won't provide significant benefits. However, when your patrons *share content* with others, your SEO ranking may benefit as well as your library's word-of-mouth brand. Social media content should meet your individual user's needs, and it should be interactive. Engage with your patrons through social media: answer reference questions, recommend content to your patrons, and help your patrons solve problems. Ask questions of your patrons; for example, ask a weekly trivia question on Twitter, or ask your patrons about their favorite books or video games (Dowd 2013). Not only will you gain more traffic, you'll also build relationships with your patrons.

Give your patrons a reason to "follow." Facebook Likes, number of Twitter followers, and the number of Google+ users that have a particular brand in their "circles" are all thought to be beneficial for that brand's website ranking (Search Metrics 2013). These kinds of indicators require you to not only *get* your users' attention, but that you *sustain* it. Update social media channels regularly with interesting content. A solid, user-centered content strategy is the best way to engage your users and give them a reason to keep coming back for more.

Be consistent (but not predictable). Ensuring that you have the resources and time available to devote to sustaining an engaging social media presence is an essential part of a social media strategy. Plan out the amount of time you can realistically devote to keeping your social media presence updated and fresh. However, be careful of spamming your users. Pushing out a handful of links every morning on Twitter is not a social media strategy that will benefit your patrons or bring traffic to your website.

FURTHER INFORMATION

Google frequently updates its algorithms to adapt to changing user preferences, and so must libraries. In order for libraries to stay relevant to users, and to ensure our patrons know about the great content and services libraries provide, we must ensure our pages are visible and retrievable through Web search engines. To keep up with this changing topic, follow websites such as Moz.com and Searchenginewatch.com. Google offers learning resources on Google Analytics through Google Analytics Academy (https://analyticsacademy.withgoogle.com/course) and Webmaster tools support (https://support.google.com/webmasters/). Finally, consider joining the Search Engine Optimization Interest Group offered through the American Library Association's Library Information Technology Association (LITA) division (http://www.ala.org/lita/about/igs/seo/lit-igseo).

REFERENCES

Becker, Danielle, A. and Lauren Yannotta. 2013. "Modeling a Library Website Redesign Process: Developing a User-Centered Website through Usability Testing." *Information Technology & Libraries* 32 (1): 6–22.

Demers, Jason. 2013. "The Three Pillars of Social Media in 2013: Content, Links, and Social Media." *Forbes,* May 23. http://www.forbes.com/sites/jaysondemers/2013/05/23/the-3-pillars-of-seo-in-2013-content-links-and-social-media/.

Dowd, Nancy. 2013. "Social Media: Libraries Are Posting, but Is Anyone Listening?" *Library Journal.* http://lj.libraryjournal.com/2013/05/marketing/social-media-libraries-are-posting-but-is-anyone-listening.

Fishkin, Rand. 2012. "How People Interact with Search Engines." *Moz.com.* http://moz.com/beginners-guide-to-seo/how-people-interact-with-search-engines.

Fishkin, Rand. 2014. "The Basics of Search Engine Friendly Design and Development." *Moz.com.* http://moz.com/beginners-guide-to-seo/basics-of-search-engine-friendly-design-and-development.

Google. "Google Adwords Keyword Planner." http://adwords.google.com/o/KeywordTool.

Google. "Overview of Demographics & Interests Reports." https://support.google.com/analytics/answer/2799357?hl=en.

Google. "Search Queries." https://support.google.com/webmasters/answer/35252.

Google. "Set Up and Configure Site Search." https://support.google.com/analytics/answer/1012264?hl=en&ref_topic=1031951.

Google. "Set Your Preferred Domain (www or non-www)." https://support.google.com/webmasters/answer/44231?hl=en.

Google. "Sitemap Formats and Guidelines." https://support.google.com/webmasters/answer/183668?hl=en.

Google. "Webmaster Tools." https://www.google.com/webmasters/tools.

Georgas, Helen. 2013. "Google vs. the Library: Student Preferences and Perceptions When Doing Research Using Google and a Federated Search Tool." *Portal: Libraries and the Academy.* 13 (2): 165–85.

Killoran, John B. 2013. "How to Use Search Engine Optimization Techniques to Increase Website Visibility." *IEEE Transactions on Professional Communication*, 56 (1): 50–66.

Miller, Miranda. 2012. "Google Wants You to Use Keyword Metatags . . . No, Really." *Search Engine Watch*, September 20. http://searchenginewatch.com/article/2207067/Google-Wants-You-To-Use- Keyword-Metatags...-No-Really.

Moz. 2014. "Meta Description." *Moz.com.* Accessed May 24, 2014. http://moz.com/learn/seo/meta-description.

Moz. 2013. "2013 Search Engine Ranking Factors. *Moz.com.* Accessed May 24, 2014. http://moz.com/search-ranking-factors.

Nielsen, Jakob. 2013. "Conversion Rates." *Neilsen Norman Group,* November 24. http://www.nngroup.com/articles/conversion-rates/.

Search Metrics. 2012. "Facebook and Twitter Shares Closely Linked with High Google Search Rankings." June 7. http://www.searchmetrics.com/en/searchmetrics/press/ranking-factors/.

Chapter Nineteen

Seniors in Cyberspace

RoseAleta Laurell

Today there is a growing body of information regarding senior citizens and their use of the Internet and technology in general (see Span 2013). Most librarians and library workers have encountered their share of seniors expressing a desire for training. As librarians, we can embrace this opportunity for delivering new and innovative services or we can shun it for a variety of reasons. There are any number of perfectly sensible arguments for why we cannot do it, but there is an equally, if not more compelling argument that it is an imperative.

SeniorNet, founded in 1986, is the largest and oldest organization that provides training exclusively for senior citizens. Nevertheless, it was not until the early years of the new millennium that library literature and librarians began to take the issue seriously. Today, whether you are providing one-on-one e-mail assistance to patrons, or you are providing organized formal classes, libraries are in the forefront of training the senior population in the use of a variety of technologies. Prevailing wisdom suggests that this need is not going to diminish, but rather will increase as technology changes and evolves, therefore it seems important to begin a discussion on best practices, lessons learned, and how to learn from past experiences, successes, and failures.

Over ten years ago, I had my first encounter with seniors while training them in using computers. The library had begun a new series of computer classes, under the assumption that these classes would attract young to middle-aged people in the workforce. Much to our surprise, over 95 percent of our students turned out to be senior citizens, ranging in age from late sixties to their nineties. Lesson plans were quickly scrapped, the entire curriculum had to be reworked, and we devised as many creative ways of training as we could come up with. What were the lessons we learned from our early mistakes?

- Test-drive a program before making a large investment in equipment or long-term commitment.
- Classes are best offered during the morning or early afternoon hours.
- Repetition is imperative.
- Keep each session to one simple task.
- Use analogies and examples that seniors can relate to.
- Use examples to demonstrate how technology can improve their lives.
- Do not assume anything regarding their understanding of technology or the lingo used.
- Begin at the beginning.
- Make the classes fun, relaxed, and enjoyable.
- Handouts should be simple—one page with screen shots and large type.

Making the decision to offer a computer training program will be based on your own unique community, resources, and personnel. Since none of us can expend precious resources on non-starter programs, it is advisable to "test drive" the program before you make any investment in technology. We began our program by closing down the adult section of the public access computers for an hour to do training. We had no wireless hotspot and we had not considered buying equipment. Obviously, this is not the ideal situation, but it does provide a testing ground for the project. When we provided classes in this setting, we averaged between four to six attendees per session. Starting this way provided us with the statistics and experience to begin seeking out grant opportunities. We received very few complaints regarding the inconvenience from other patrons. It also helped us publicize the program. When people came into the library and saw a class in action they were usually curious and asked questions about what was going on. Holding classes out in the open is an excellent public relations tool. Another approach might be to offer one-on-one assistance. A possible structure would be to set aside one or two hours per week or a day if you have trained staff that would be available to work with patrons needing assistance. You could offer it on a first-come, first-served basis or students could call and book a session in advance. This type of program would allow you to gather statistics and provide an opportunity for students to give you valuable feedback about their needs, and their desire for a structured training program. It will also give you experience working with this demographic and their unique needs. This will provide excellent firsthand experience in working with seniors. Do not be afraid to start small.

Experience has shown that seniors, like many of us, are more alert and energetic early in the day. Offering classes at night presents challenges for many seniors who cannot drive at night or are simply too tired to function in the evening hours. Remember that many seniors nap in the afternoon, so consider that when selecting the time for offering training.

Be prepared to repeat the same classes multiple times. Each of us has our own personal learning styles, but all of us benefit from repetition. There are many different ways to teach the same skill and as a trainer, you should never be afraid to try different methods for teaching the same material. The method we use is to introduce a new skill; explain when you would use it and why it is important. We then demonstrate it to the entire class using a computer attached to a projector so they can see the steps; then let them try it on their own. Often this will take several times of doing the same thing over and over. We also walk around the students to monitor their progress. If they are confused or struggling with the task, we point to their screen while they complete the exercise. We spend a great deal of time pointing at their monitors and saying, "click here."

Another technique we have found effective is we invite the students to do the exercise on the computer attached to the projector while the rest of the class watches. Usually we let everyone in the class do the exercise in this manner. We have found that being in the spotlight is a mighty motivator. We also come up with games, scavenger hunts, or contests to help students retain the information taught. The Internet is packed with great ideas for teaching beginners. We will spend as much time as is needed until we are sure the student has mastered the skill, and we will often go back and cover the same materials a week or even a month later.

We also build on the skills the students already have. For instance, we will teach them how to save a picture to the hard drive from the Internet. In later classes, we will have them attach those pictures to an e-mail or use them in creating a simple greeting card.

Another lesson we have learned is to keep each session to one single topic. Do not try to cover too much territory in one session. If you have developed a training that covers creating a new file, saving a picture or document, and using it to create and send an e-mail, then you probably need to rethink your lesson plan. Consider dividing that into three separate sessions. For most beginners that is too much to cover and will be overwhelming. We all know there are many different ways of doing the same thing on the computer, but trying to teach all the different ways of copying and pasting is a waste of your time and theirs. Settle on one way of doing things and teach that. Obviously, you will want to tell them of other ways as well, but do not dwell on it.

Using analogies and examples that seniors can relate to is important. Most seniors do not understand what the "Enter" key is on the keyboard. When teaching the keyboard, I like to draw the following analogy: using the "Enter" key on the keyboard is like hitting the return handle on a typewriter. This is something seniors can relate to and remember. For cut, paste, and copy, I actually use typed text, a glue pot, and scissors. I literally show them each of the steps of cut and paste and copy the way it used to be done. In teaching files and folders, I actually bring in a small filing cabinet; file folders; and labels, documents, or pictures; I then show them how the physical act of organizing a file folder inside a file cabinet relates to doing the same function on a computer. You might think these examples are extreme or even silly, but we have found them to be very helpful. Never assume that a student grasps a concept that seems obvious to you. Be creative in the use of examples and analogies they can relate to in their daily lives.

Studies have shown that one of the greatest barriers to seniors embracing technology is that they fail to understand how it relates to their lives. Many seniors do not understand the many benefits that using technology brings to their lives, usually because no one has ever told them. So be sure in your training that you concentrate on teaching skills that they will use and find useful in their lives. There is no need to teach Excel to someone who does not intend to maintain a simple database or establish a household budget. They simply will not benefit by being taught a skill they will not use. When we teach Excel, we have students create a database of their medications, dosages, and pharmacy prescription number; or we create a simple address book of friends and family. This is when it is so important for you to really listen to the feedback. Be ever mindful of the requests and questions they are bringing to the class. These questions are often the clues to what subject to teach next.

Do not assume anything about a student's depth of understanding. Many people have no idea how to turn on a computer. We had one gentleman in his eighties, who attempted to use the mouse as if it were a TV remote. Keep in mind that some seniors have never been exposed to this technology, and they have no way of relating to the vocabulary, jargon, and technical terms you are using. We understand what it means when someone says "Press enter," however, they have no idea what that means.

By begin at the beginning, I mean begin with the basic vocabulary. Any learning that goes on has to share a common understandable vocabulary. Take every opportunity to stop the class and explain or demonstrate what is meant by a term you are using. This makes an excellent way to start a new class, by providing instruction on terminology and being sure that everyone knows and understands the terms you will be using. Making up games and contest to master the lingo is quite easy and a fun way to help them learn the vocabulary you will using. Using a mouse and keyboard is often very taxing and hard. If you have students struggling, give them Internet exercises to practice. Solitaire is a great way to learn to use the mouse and so is jig-zone.com. There are many websites with interactive mouse training exercises.

Make the classes fun, entertaining, and enjoyable for everyone. Do not be so rigid and inflexible that getting "off topic" upsets or flusters you. Go with the flow, let them talk about their lives, laugh with them over mistakes, and build on past successes. Set up every opportunity to have students succeed. This might involve the simplest of tasks like learning to click inside a search box. Celebrate that accomplishment, do not spare the "atta boys," and encourage every class member to celebrate each other's successes. After a rather lengthy training session of about four weeks using PowerPoint to create a presentation, we held what we laughingly dubbed the "First Annual Gala Slidie Awards." We had judges look at each of the slide presentations and then choose a winner in a multiple of categories, with everyone winning something. We previewed all the presentations during a regular class period, served refreshments, and awarded "Oscars" to each participant, the class voted for their favorite and the winner was given the "People's Choice" award. The two trainers dressed in evening gowns, we bought a cheap "red carpet" and presented the awards. Everyone loved it and wanted to do it again. This is a simple and inexpensive way to celebrate students' success. Seniors also like field trips. In our town all the servers and hardware that operate the city technology infrastructure are located in the IT center at the police department. We arranged with the chief of police to give our students a tour of the facility and explain the technology being used both in the police department and across the city. The students loved it and wanted more experiences like this. A trip to the local high school or grocery store to view their technologies would make a good field trip.

Handouts are very important to seniors. They like to have something to take home to help them remember the class material. You do not want students wasting class time taking notes, when they could be using the time to practice. Handouts should be simple and cover only one simple subject, like creating a new folder. Use screen shots and large text so students can easily read the instructions. We use PowerPoint slides to create handouts and then print them with two slides per page for easy reading. Try to avoid ten-page handouts, since it will usually just discourage the student.

So you have decided that you want to provide computer training for seniors, but you might be concerned about the skills and aptitudes of a good trainer. These have been identified as the most important:

- The right attitude
- Patience, patience, patience
- Praise lavishly
- Never underestimate your skill level
- Understanding and empathy for someone struggling to learn a new skill

When preparing for a class, the most important thing you can take into the classroom is your attitude. If you are bored, your students will be too. If you are worried or upset, your students will notice that. Do not be afraid to laugh at your mistakes, celebrate victories, and get excited. Be sure to have fun. Build fun into your classes. Attitude is contagious and your students will catch on to your attitude quickly. I start all my new classes with a basic set of rules:

Ask stupid questions. Chances are if you are thinking or have questions about something, someone else does too—so ask questions. Usually they will respond with "I have a stupid question." Give them a Hersey's kiss or the prize of the day. And then acknowledge that it was not stupid at all. Sometimes I will even say, "Does anyone have a stupid question?" just to break the ice.

Cheat! What do I mean by cheat? Tell them to feel free to look on their neighbor's computer screen and to ask each other for help. This encourages learning and helps both students. It also serves to build camaraderie in the class.

Make mistakes. We all learn from making mistakes. There is nothing wrong with making mistakes. Keep reminding them that you appreciate that what they are learning is hard, but they will master it. I will often relate my own despair and frustration when trying to learn something new. We recently purchased a Mac after being PC-centric for over three decades, and that experience reminded us of just how difficult new technology can be. We reassure our students repeatedly that we understand that technology is confusing, irritating, and maddening, but they *can* learn it. Repeatedly assure them that they have the capacity and the ability to learn a new skill. We try to acknowledge in every class that we are proud of their progress and proud of what they have accomplished and they should be proud of themselves.

Patience is an absolute must. Older people themselves often lack patience, whether they say so or not, and they want their time to be their time. We have found seniors can quickly become frustrated and irritable at themselves and other classmates. However, it is important that they know you are willing to do whatever it takes to help them. It is not a foot race to see who can finish first. Assure them repeatedly that you appreciate how difficult technology can be and remind them at some time everyone in the class is going to struggle with something.

I can assure you that after teaching files and folders for the forty-fifth time, it can get pretty boring and routine, but patience is required if you want to be sure they master a skill.

Praise goes a long way; good feelings and a sense of accomplishment make everyone feel good about themselves. Do not ever think you can overdo handing out praise.

Never underestimate your skill level. If you know how to create an e-mail, how to save a file to a folder, how to highlight, or select text, you are a potential trainer. Often, just teaching a senior a single simple skill will be sufficient to meet their needs. Many studies have shown that e-mail is the single most popular use of the Internet in the sixty-plus-year-old demographic (Pew Foundation 2012). Providing training and assistance with e-mail could well serve as a library's sole offering for training. Family members tend to consider e-mail as the most important thing Grandma or Grandpa can learn.

The benefits to your library will accrue as you work with this population. Our library has experienced increased usage by seniors, increased volunteer time, increased donations to the library and the program has been recognized with several national and state awards. It has proven to be one of the most satisfying and gratifying experiences I have undertaken. We have made dear and lasting friends and so have most of our students, while these are not our identified objectives, it has proven to be a source of pride. All you need to be a good trainer is a willingness to teach someone something they did not know before. It really is that simple and the rewards are abundant.

WEBSITES WITH GENERAL BACKGROUND INFORMATION ON COMPUTERS AND SENIORS

- http://www.his.com/~pshapiro/computers.and.elderly.html
- http://voices.yahoo.com/teaching-senior-citizens-computers-398697.html?cat=25
- http://www.helium.com/items/1435507-teaching-seniors-how-to-use-computers
- http://web1.squidoo.com/trainable (Provides some great links to training materials and general help for trainers.)
- http://www.pewinternet.org/Reports/2010/Older-Adults-and-Social-Media.aspx
- http://www.uni-ulm.de/LiLL/5.0/E/teaching/teachingframes.html
- http://www.seniorsguidetocomputers.com/
- www.webwiseseniors.com (An e-zine for and about seniors and technology from WebWise Seniors, Inc.)

WEBSITES DEVOTED TO ISSUES AND CONCERNS FACING SENIOR CITIZENS

A simple Google search will bring up hundreds of these. Beware: some are blatantly trying to sell products.

- http://www.go60.com/
- http://seniorjournal.com/index.html
- AARP: http://www.aarp.org/

TECHSOUP RESOURCES

Another gold mine of resources for the trainer.

- http://techsoupforlibraries.org/blog/tags/the-accidental-technology-train-er-series
- http://www.slideshare.net/TechSoupGlobal/presentation-designing-and-delivering-tech-workshops

ASSESSMENT OF SKILLS RESOURCES

- WebJunction: http://www.webjunction.org/explore-topics/computer-inter-net-basics.html
- California Library Association: Technology Core Competencies for California Library Workers: https://infopeople.org/sites/all/files/past/2006/managing/Handout-CLA_Core_Competencies.pdf.
- The Pioneer Library System competencies: http://alalearn-ing.wetpaint.com/page/pls+training+tracks

ONLINE SURVEY TOOLS

- http://zoomerang.com
- http://surveymonkey.com

SITES DEVELOPED FOR, ABOUT, AND BY SENIORS

- http://www.silverfoxnetwork.com/teaching-senior-citizens-about-comput-ers
- http://www.seniornet.org/
- http://computersavvyseniors.blogspot.com/search?updated-min=2010-01-01T00%3A00%3A00-08%3A00&updated-max=2011-01-01T00%3A00%3A00-08%3A00&max-results=50 (A blog created by seniors.)

SITES THAT PROVIDE INFORMATION THAT CAN BE USED FOR HANDOUTS AND CONTENT DEVELOPMENT

- http://www.cfscapecod.com/aboutcfs.htm
- http://abbyandme.com/
- http://help.yahoo.com/tutorials/cg/
- http://www.dynamicwebs.com.au/tutorials/email.htm
- http://www.anniston.lib.al.us/computerinternettutorial.htm
- http://www.free-computer-tutorials.net/
- http://necseniors.net.au/

MOUSE / KEYBOARD TUTORIAL

- http://www.mesalibrary.org/research/mouse/page01.htm
- http://www.seniornet.org/howto/mouseexercises/mousepractice.html
- http://www.pbclibrary.org/mousing/
- http://www.jigzone.com/

ASSISTIVE SOFTWARE/HARDWARE

- http://www.disabledonline.com
- http://www.chestercreek.com/seniorsProducts.html
- http://www.in2l.com/index.cfm
- Eldy: http://www.eldy.eu/
- Skillful Senior: http://www.skillfulsenior.com/
- Microsoft Accessibility: http://www.microsoft.com/enable/aging/tips.aspx
- GCF Learn Free: http://www.gcflearnfree.org/internet

COMPUTERS BUILT FOR SENIOR CITIZENS

- http://www.aplusseniorcomputer.com/
- http://www.telikin.com/

BOOKS

- Basic Computers: Windows 7 Basics of the PC & Windows 7 ($34.95)
- Basic Computers: APPLE Basics of an Apple Computer ($34.95)
- Internet for Beginners: IE 8 Basics of the Internet & IE8 ($34.95)
- Internet for Beginners: SAFARI Basics of the Internet ($34.95)

The following resources are from a series of books entitled "Computer Books for Seniors."

- Windows 7 for Seniors: For Senior Citizens Who Want to Start Using Computers ($12.95)
- Google for Seniors: Get Acquainted with Free Google Applications: Google Earth, Maps, Reader, Docs, Sites, Chrome ($15)
- Internet and E-mail for Seniors with Windows Vista: For Senior Citizens Who Want to Start Using the Internet ($12.95)
- Interesting Online Applications for Seniors: Get Acquainted with Thirteen Free Internet Applications ($13) (Includes a chapter on Facebook.)

FREE SOFTWARE FOR DEVELOPING HANDOUTS AND TUTORIALS

- Camtasia is a program to capture and record your computer screen. Very useful for putting tutorials on line: http://www.techsmith.com/camtasia/?gclid=CNWA-rXZiKcCFchl7AodzlSUeA
- Jing is an open source software that can be used to capture your screen or record for providing online tutorials. Both products are by Techsmith.com: http://www.techsmith.com/Jing/?gclid=CIfbvffZiKcCFY5N2godY23jgA
- Good old reliable and free Screen Capture (the keyboard "Print Screen" button) works well for use in handouts and demonstrations.

REFERENCES

Pew Research Internet Project. 2012. "Older Adults and Internet Use." Pew Research Center's Internet and American Life Project. June 6. Available from http://www.pewinternet.org/Reports/2012/Older-adults-and-internet-use.aspx. Accessed April 15, 2013.

Span, Paula. 2013. "Online Habits Coming Slowly to Older Adults." *The New Old Age*, April 8. http://newoldage.blogs.nytimes.com/.

Part Five

Networking

Chapter Twenty

Celebrating Achievements

Facilitating Networking, Learning, and Camaraderie

Sharon Miller

Gather any group of readers in a library and you will discover that many of them are writers seeking to emerge into print themselves. Since the fall of 2007, Mechanics' Institute Library (MIL) has been supporting writers from the exploration stage to publication, from peer-support writers' groups to book launches. From this support for the writing community in its midst arose a formal program of events called the *Authors' Carnival*, a re-creation of the literary activities sponsored by the Mechanics' Institute from 1879 to 1882 in San Francisco.

The first writers group started in late 2007, under the management of library director Inez Shor Cohen, when a half dozen library members began meeting twice a month to provide encouragement, support, and peer criticism for each other. Six years later there were seven groups, involving more than fifty people, meeting regularly while applications continued to arrive from others seeking to join a group. The groups' greatest strength, report those involved, is the accountability to present material for critique on a regular schedule. Members of each group agree on the protocol for reading and critiquing a set number of pages of new work from a set number of writers at each bimonthly session.

Support for the emerging writer, as a participant in one of the library-sponsored groups, was initially not much more than a dedicated space to meet on a regular basis, and access to a well-developed library collection of materials on the craft of writing. As we librarians began to meet regularly with the groups it became evident that we could develop human resources to provide additional ways to assist writers in our midst.

DEVELOPMENT OF THE AUTHORS' CARNIVAL

Participants in our library-sponsored writers' groups write for a variety of reasons and with a variety of goals. Not all seek publication. Many of these emerging writers are retired professionals who seek to fulfill a dream of writing poetry or a private memoir, or are trying their hands at creative storytelling. Others are capturing a piece of their own experience in a book for children. Still others are attempting the discipline of writing as a test of their ability to become a serious author. Many of their objectives could be met if we provided opportunities for them to engage with the readers of our library.

This discussion between writers and librarians occurred at a time when library use was diminishing, and the sense of community at low ebb. A turnover in staff, including my appointment as library director and the hiring of two new librarians with a vision for enriching the community experience, and a new focus on technology upgrades, all coincided with increasing numbers of people who indicated their interest in writing. There was no corresponding increase in budget for activities or instruction, but that was no impediment to the flow of ideas.

Mechanics' Institute has always been a promoter of networking, seeking to engage members with each other in community-building and lifelong learning endeavors. The emphasis on both literary events and support for emerging writers has a long history in Institute activities both within its membership and in the city of San Francisco. Named the *Authors' Carnival* after events that honored and celebrated world literature at the Mechanics' Pavilion in San Francisco from 1879 to 1882, Librarian Taryn Edwards created a new series of literary activities in support of writers in our midst.

Advertising for the programs was enhanced by informative flyers posted throughout the building, full information on the MIL website, and the development of a new weekly email news message that highlighted and offered registration links for all activities in the coming week. Rather than paying a graphic designer, Taryn used a contest format to solicit designs for the logo, which is used on all marketing materials for *Authors' Carnival* activities. We gained an attractive logo at no cost, and the designer received attention from our adoption of the logo.

One of the first in a series of programs I hosted was a "reading night" for each of the writers' groups, meeting once a month for several months. (Not every group chose to participate.) Even the writers who did not intend to publish welcomed the opportunity to read from work in progress in a public setting, with family and friends in attendance, a printed program with his or her biography, a microphone, wine and cheese, and appropriate marketing materials. We heard some remarkable poetry, stories, bits of memoir, and even a song.

The library's efforts to create community around individual creativity did not go unnoticed. Taryn heard from writers with a variety of works in progress, and arranged programs to highlight an online magazine, with accompanying art show; an independent film maker who focused on one period of Mechanics' Institute history; a writer who crafted a high-tech mystery around an audio tour designed to be listened to while aboard San Francisco's cable cars; and play readings of a work in progress by a member of our original writers' group. Each program was designed as an educational presentation, with the author talking about the production of the work and lessons learned, but the highlight of each program was the audience enjoyment of a portion of the finished product.

Another avenue for learning the disciplines of writing was the library's participation in organized programs such as *NaNoWriMo*, National Novel Writing Month (November), and *Flash Fiction*. From the first November (2010), when a handful of writers supported each other in writing a novel, to the second when participation more than tripled, *NaNoWriMo,* now established as an annual activity, became a way to highlight fiction writers. Annual *Flash Fiction* workshops offered yet another opportunity for writers to share with each other and listeners to learn about this different genre.

One of the more unusual events planned in 2012 was a visit to a local small press, Heyday Books in Berkeley, a successful independent publishing house since 1974. Twelve writers were given a tour of the site, and then shared lunch around the table with all of the employees, including founder Malcolm Margolin. Each member of the publishing house staff explained his or her job responsibilities to writers who were eager to learn how manuscripts were selected for publication, and what every step of the publishing process involved. Our purchase of lunch for the Heyday staff seemed a small price for such a wealth of helpful information from this reputable source.

Learning from each other has been a constant theme of the *Authors' Carnival* programming. As word of the library's increase in support for writers got out to others in the Bay Area, professionals in the publishing business offered to share their expertise. Book agents, editors, e-book publishers, and representatives from small presses provided workshops, including demonstrations of editing, cover art, blogging software, and the basics of e-book publishing. To date, twenty-nine public presentations of new works, combined with instruction on the craft or business of writing, have been well attended. The measure of each successful workshop was the buzz of information sharing that continued as people exited the building together.

THE SELF-PUBLISHING WORKING GROUP

It all started with a simple sentence. The two women seated across my desk had asked for an appointment to talk about their idea, and they had prepared their speech. "We want to learn all about self-publishing." They were both participants in one of our peer-support writers' groups, both had completed manuscripts, both had too many rejection slips to count.

By the end of December 2010 we had writers in several of our biweekly groups with finished manuscripts. The downsizing of the publishing world made the idea of self-publishing popular. Writers Carol and Allegra had composed a plan to form a group for all who commit to learn together, pool their knowledge, and tiptoe into the do-it-yourself publishing arena, with the goal of having books in hand to sell by the December holiday season.

I was impressed with the scope of their planning, Carol's ability to lead a group, and the amount of time they were prepared to dedicate to the project, tentatively called the *Mechanics' Institute Self-Publishing Working Group (SPWG)* . By the time they left my office we had set up a marketing plan, reserved the library's classroom for their use every Wednesday evening for six to eight months, and established one more avenue of interaction in our community of writers.

We immediately moved to get the word out to all who might be interested: posting on our website, making informative flyers available in the library, and sending emails to the contact people in each writer's group. The first meeting of the *SPWG* on January 5, 2011, filled every chair in the room. Twenty-five people showed up; another half dozen indicated interest but could not attend. Under Carol's direction they talked about their writing projects, their goals for publishing, and in some cases, their experience in having work published in the conventional way. They shared their understanding of what is necessary to self-publish—at this point a fairly limited perspective.

Various members of the SPWG made contacts with professionals in the field of self-publishing: company principals, technology experts, book editors, cover designers, copyright attorneys, publicists, social media specialists, and representatives from professional groups of writers such as the local Bay Area Independent Publishers Association (BAIPA). Working in cooperation with Taryn and me to plan formal programs open to others in the local writing community, the group hosted many speakers who freely shared their expertise.

I was invited to speak to groups of writers who were involved in indie-publishing endeavors. For most of the writers it was their first opportunity to hear from a librarian what libraries do in support of writers. The "buy one book and lend it to dozens of people" was the model the writers saw for libraries, and that does not look like a money-making model to the authors—

until I reminded them that the more than 29,000 public libraries in the United States spend over $360 million on books annually (Library and Book Trade Almanac 2012, 425–45). If a writer can convince one local librarian to love his book, it could easily go on display in a library, the author could be asked to come in and talk about his book, a discussion group might be formed to read and talk about it, and the library may keep every book the author publishes on their shelves. Furthermore, I told each audience, "librarians will fight to protect your copyright." Librarians have always been, and continue to be, matchmakers between readers and writers.

When not meeting as a formal instructional program, the group used their Wednesday meetings to share individual successful and not-so-successful forays into self-publishing. These successes occasionally translated into an evening program that consisted in a panel of writers reading from a completed work and talking about their learning experience to an audience of writers who were not a part of the SPWG. As the spring progressed and more books were independently published, evening programs were planned at the library to introduce them to the readers of MIL and provide an opportunity for writers to sell their books.

We librarians were impressed with the scope of the development of self-publishing knowledge by the SPWG members and with individual success stories. By August, books were arriving in the library, brought to librarians' attention by writers who wanted their books on library shelves. Taryn and I talked about ways to further support self-published authors in their efforts to market their books while, at the same time, keeping an element of professional quality control in effect. As librarians read through some of the earliest books it quickly became evident that editing was needed in many, and that not all met our library's collection development statement.

I sought volunteers with professional book review experience to become a review panel for the works of authors within the library community. Eight people responded to an article in the MIL monthly magazine and six have reviewed fifteen books to date. The ground rules were simple: the reviewer should not personally know the author; if a reviewer could not find anything positive to say about a book it would go to a second reviewer; if the second result was the same Sharon would return it to the writer with constructive criticism from one or both reviewers. All reviews were to be descriptive in nature rather than critical due to the lack of a body of work by any author.

The review panel was professional in composition, including a retired professor, a writer/editor of renown, a published poet who also worked as a reviewer, the fiction buyer of our library staff, and others who had published professional reviews. The panel followed the guidelines established by the *Library Journal* for their reviewers. Completed reviews were presented to the writers anonymously at first, and then I "introduced" reviewer and writer to each other for more conversation if they requested that contact. The amount of effort the reviewers put into the project, and the articulate analysis evidenced in each review, was impressive.

Due to positive reviews the librarians added many self-published books to the library's collection. Our catalog staff created a local subject heading that identified books by MIL member authors. When requested by the author, this subject heading is used for all materials in our library collection, including many professional authors whose fiction and nonfiction, including academic works, have been purchased over the years.

With a good review in hand, what next for the self-published author? Taryn and I could only provide so much marketing opportunity for the writers via the evening "reading and selling" events that we planned. As librarians we were not in the book-selling business, and we were conscious that we must be fair to all the writers in our midst, both emerging and established. After some brainstorming we decided that our last endeavor on behalf of the SPWG would be to make contact with local independent book stores.

By 2011 the big chain bookstores were disappearing in San Francisco, and a very popular large independent book store only two blocks from MIL had closed as well. Fortunately for all of us who live here, books are still very popular and local bookstores are still available in the area. I contacted the owners of Green Apple Books and the manager of the closest branch of Books, Inc., after reading about them as supporters of self-published books in an issue of *Publishers Weekly* (Werris 2011). Both bookstores agreed to accept our writers' works on consignment if the authors provided reviews first and agreed to their terms.

From a finished manuscript to a bookstore shelf—as librarians we felt as proud of our library's writers' achievements as any parent. The SPWG had truly grown into a network of information and sources of assistance to support of individual creativity. The word had spread about this unique group, and people were continuing to ask to join the group and learn from them. It seemed that the next logical step was to ask someone, or a team of people, to offer formal classes as a way of sharing the knowledge and expertise gained in eight months of exploration. Carol stepped up and offered to teach an eight-week class, *Introduction to Self-Publishing*, that would encapsulate the necessary information for success. Fees were established, of which she would earn 85 percent, as per our standard teaching contract. The schedule was advertised, and the class filled up very quickly. She has offered the class, with great success, two more times in 2012, refining the content to four to six sessions instead of the original eight.

The SPWG continues to meet twice a month, attempting to stay abreast of the rapid changes in digital aspects of self-publishing. The group changed its name at the one-year anniversary to Indie-Publishers Working Group, reflecting the changes in the growing industry. Their pattern of inviting speakers as an education for all interested writers continues, and individuals submit new publications for review periodically. From within the group, members have come forth with expertise to teach classes on blogging, marketing, and "*Face Time with an Editor*," all of which have been very well received by the library's writing community.

BOOK'TOBERFEST

After all of the work, there had to be a grand party. *Book'toberfest* was born as a way to celebrate the success of the SPWG. Our support of emerging authors had netted us a wide network of publishing professionals in the local area. To tie into the time of year and highlight our own independent nature, I approached two local independent breweries for beer donations, two independent bookstore managers to speak, and two local successful independently published authors to talk about their works. Everyone was eager to participate, and our first annual "celebration of local writing and reading" was scheduled for October 5, 2011, in the library's spacious second floor reading room.

The theme of the first *Book'toberfest* was "The Local Connection: Getting Your Book Reviewed, Sold, and Read in the City." Participants were invited to "put the 'pub' back into 'publishing'! Hoist a stein with local authors, indie publishers, booksellers, reviewers, agents, editors, and representatives from the publishing industry as we toast our members' recent publications." Plans for the evening included introductions of all newly published authors who had books to sell, and the unveiling of one addition to the library's *Authors' Carnival*.

The infusion of new energies and skills into the library staff in recent years included two librarians with web development skills: Jeremy Snell and Matt Montgomery. Their contribution in support of emerging writers was a website that would allow each writer to showcase his or her work. In keeping with our model of building the new upon the endeavors of the old, we named this *The Mirror*, which was the title of the daily paper published during the nineteenth-century Mechanics' Institute fairs that showcased local entrepreneurship in developing San Francisco.

Fourteen authors were introduced in person to a full house of interested readers, family, friends, and people engaged in all aspects of the world of book publishing. Each spoke briefly about his or her development as a writer, talked about the newest—or in many cases, only—book, and watched their personal Webpages open on *The Mirror*, projected on the screen overhead. *The Mirror* pages featured a brief biography, excerpts from work in progress, links to authors' blogs, reviews, schedules of speaking engagements, and other information pertinent to marketing one's work. The writers update their pages by contacting Jeremy as needed, and since that time more writers have established their Web pages on *The Mirror*.

Locally brewed beer and snacks contributed to a fun atmosphere, but the panelists who spoke to the theme of the evening also kept the mood positive with an "I was able to do this and you can too" attitude. While this no-budget evening was a lot of work for the librarians, they immediately determined that it had to become an annual event.

The second annual *Book'toberfest* in 2012 highlighted local small publishers and their authors, and set up a trade fair of booths by individuals and local companies in the book business. Some of our own indie publishers had a second book for sale. Our local breweries provided donations a second time, so we were able to keep the "'pub' in publishing" once more. John McMurtrie, editor of the *San Francisco Chronicle Book Review*, one of the few remaining book review sections in an American newspaper, moderated a panel of small publishing house editors on the topic of "brewing up a good book"—examining the issue of quality selections for publication.

As this book goes to press, we are working on the program for the fourth annual *Book'toberfest*, scheduled for September 2014. While the 2013 program included an examination of the explosion of e-books in publishing, *Book'toberfest 2014* will feature a trade show for those in the book arts, including representatives from the Squaw Valley and Napa Valley Writers Conferences. Our plans focus on our goal of supporting writers in the context of a library in which readers are the core clientele.

CONCLUSION

Mechanics' Institute Library's support of emerging writers is not done in a vacuum. Readers also want to understand the creative process. As with all libraries that support a myriad of community endeavors, our largest and most engaged clientele is the group of readers who use our library's collection day after day. This sense of engagement propels me, and our librarians, to support our creative members as they network to produce poetry, books, plays, films, and other cultural products with the audience in mind.

Challenges before us now branch out in two directions. One is in the area of quality control. Our library collection development standards require professional reviews, and that has been a deterrent to adding self-published works to our shelves. While our educational programming aimed at writers has stressed the need for editing, and our review panel has rejected some poorly written work, individual authors don't always see their work with the necessary critical eye. The second challenge before us is finding ways to make independently published e-books available via our library catalog, or on a library-owned electronic book reader. These challenges keep our library staff thinking creatively.

Learning from each other continues to be our model. We did not know where we were going when the Authors' Carnival started, but we have enjoyed the buzz of creativity and the satisfaction of seeing goals achieved. The writers, the readers, and the library staff of Mechanics' Institute Library are committed to learning all we can, and staying engaged as a community.

REFERENCES

Authors' Carnival. 2013. http://www.milibrary.org/writers.

Library and Book Trade Almanac. 2012. Medford, NJ: Information Today.

Library Journal. 2010. "Guidelines for *Library Journal* Reviews." http://reviews.libraryjournal.com/about/guidelines-for-library-journal-reviews/.

Mechanics' Institute. 2013. www.milibrary.org.

The Mirror: Reflecting Bay Area Creativity. 2013. http://mirror.milibrary.org/.

National Novel Writing Month. 2013. http://www.nanowrimo.org/.

Werris, Wendy. 2011. "Booksellers Reveal Secrets to Self-Published Success: The West Coast." *Publishers Weekly* Select 258(13): 4.

Chapter Twenty-One

Supporting Success

Thinking Outside the Box via In-State Sister Libraries

April Ritchie

WHAT ARE IN-STATE SISTER LIBRARIES AND WHY DO THEY MATTER?

In order to ensure smooth day-to-day operations, those managing public libraries with limited resources are often forced to find creative strategies. The various aspects of running a facility, from workflow to maintenance, are often the responsibilities of one or two people, perhaps the director and the assistant director or some similar combination. I know directors who, out of sheer necessity, wear many hats on any given day. Pulled in multiple directions, librarians may have to choose working the circulation desk or dealing with a broken furnace rather than focusing on strategic planning or creating exciting new programs.

Besides impeding creativity, working in a situation with limited staff can also be an isolating experience. As reported in *Library Journal*, "Librarians in small and rural communities can often feel isolated—geographically and professionally—and overwhelmed by the variety of roles they must play at their small libraries" (Kelly, Rapp, and Warburton 2011, 11). With no one to cover if you are gone, it is difficult to break away for workshops, conferences, and meetings. Even if you can find staff coverage, money may not be available for travel or professional development. In fact, a 2011 national study shows that 26 percent of rural libraries have had their budgets cut, despite increasing demands for library resources ("Technology Demand Up, Budget Cuts Limit Access,"*American Libraries* 2011).

Although I work in a larger library, I am aware of the challenges that librarians in small and rural libraries face. Several years ago I began thinking more about this issue, for I had a hunch that members of the Kentucky library community could do more through a structured program to help one another. And, by extension, libraries across the country could do more to help one another. However, I knew I had to start with my own state and work from there.

The concept behind the Kentucky Sister Library Project (KSLP) came to light in early 2010. This idea was intended to help build up all libraries in Kentucky, especially the ones with the fewest resources. As I discussed in *American Libraries* (Ritchie 2012, 40), we, as a larger library community, are only as strong as our weakest member. The status of libraries in Kentucky, and those beyond our state's borders, is up to all of us in the larger library community; it is a reflection on our ability to be creative, to work together, and to be interested in removing obstacles that stand in the way of serving all our patrons. To use a cliché, if we are not part of the solution, then we are part of the problem.

How does the KSLP serve as part of the solution? It accomplishes this by pairing two Kentucky public libraries so they can assist one another in achieving more than if neither were engaged in the partnership. The original vision was to align a larger, better-funded library with a smaller, underfunded library, usually a rural one. The pairing is completely voluntary, and libraries are not randomly joined together. Potential partnerships are analyzed with the help of the libraries themselves and ultimately approved by their boards of trustees. With this approach in place, library directors can rest assured that their libraries will be partnered with the best possible match.

Some may be familiar with the American Library Association's Sister Library Initiative, which is international in scope. A brief statement on the Initiative's webpage explains further: "To promote the concept of a global community of libraries, the American Library Association (ALA) is encouraging U.S. libraries to form partnerships with libraries in other countries." The big differences between that program and the KSLP are geography and the international cultural aspect. The KSLP is solely focused on the idea of matching libraries within the same state. One venture need not negate the other; the library world has a need for both types of programs. In fact, one of the participating sister libraries in Kentucky has a sister library in Japan.

The goal of the in-state partnerships concept is for the libraries to fortify one another by working on tasks and events together. Strengthening each library also strengthens the communities served by those institutions. Having stronger communities throughout the state is a desirable goal that directly impacts the quality of life for residents.

WHAT SORTS OF SOLUTIONS CAN A "SISTER" OFFER?

Library administrators and managers are always on the lookout for creative, frugal, and simple solutions to the myriad issues they face on a daily basis. Sometimes, standard solutions are costly or not practical in certain circumstances. Developing a sister library relationship is a win-win for both participating libraries, as it offers an alternative for overcoming obstacles. Frequently, both large and small libraries face the same dilemmas with the only difference being scale. More common ground can easily be found between a large, urban system, and a small, rural one than is obvious at first sight. One library may be strong in a certain area, while its sister library may be weak in that area and vice versa. In the relatively short history of the KSLP, collaborative efforts have included the following activities:

- Staff training
- Mentoring
- Professional development activities (co-authoring articles; joint conference presentations, etc.)
- A shared drop box for returned items
- Graphic design services for a logo
- Grant writing
- Collection development
- Weeding
- Cataloging
- Policy development and consultation
- Community-wide reads

Time constraints and travel distances sometimes come into play. However, often an inability to see the power and potential of the partnership hinders efforts. Being able to think outside the box and look at creative strategies for working together is essential for a successful partnership. Once the potential is tapped into and fully experienced, the results are empowering to both sides of the partnership. With any sister library pairing, the results depend on how much effort is put into it.

The positive outcomes of the project have been encouraging for the participating libraries as well as those considering a partnership of their own. Repeatedly, the directors of the smaller libraries have commented on how much they appreciate the fact that they can call upon their "sister" when they need help dealing with an issue. The camaraderie and support system inherently built into the sister library concept is beneficial to those who would otherwise feel more isolated in their responsibilities. Conversely, directors of larger libraries emphasize that the benefits run both ways. Staff members from bigger systems gain fresh perspectives on problem solving, opportunities to lead projects, knowledge of new communities and geographical regions, experience in building goodwill and fostering long-term working relationships.

The challenges faced by smaller libraries are not always major ones. One rural library director reported that when her library was considering the purchase of a digital scanner for microfilm, her sister library sent staff members to her building to sit in on discussions with the salesperson. According to her, the visiting staff members brought up questions that she would not have thought to ask. Sometimes, the challenges are larger and more complex. For example, two of the KSLP participating libraries, which are located in adjacent counties, share many of the same patrons, yet they are completely separate entities with different integrated library systems (ILS). In order to provide convenience for their patrons, the two systems decided to start a joint book drop. Materials from either library can be returned to the book drop, and employees from both systems share responsibilities for collecting the books and returning them to their respective buildings. This is a win-win situation that benefits the community and libraries alike.

MOVING BEYOND KENTUCKY

The framework for starting a sister library program in other states has already been laid. The Kentucky Sister Library Project website, hosted on the Kentucky Public Library Association site (KPLA), contains useful resources, including a how-to manual, a downloadable agreement form, articles, and videos. The informational manual could easily be modified to suit the needs of a newly formed program. The agreement form is a document signed by the presidents of both participating libraries' boards. It is not a legal document, and either library is free to leave the partnership at any time. Its main purpose is to formalize the pairing by putting it in writing. It outlines the terms of understanding and expectations. Just as the manual could be adapted, the agreement form could be tweaked to serve a new initiative. Any library considering such a program would benefit from looking at the resources on the KSLP website.

For any library interested in experimenting with a sister library program in their state, a pilot test is a practical way to proceed. This is the way the project unfolded in Kentucky. The first partnership was immediately successful, therefore library directors throughout the state noticed and became interested. In fact, the partnership had been in place only a few weeks when other libraries expressed interest in becoming a sister library. This was outstanding news, as it meant the original goal of the project might be obtainable. The challenge, though, was the absence of a blueprint for the infrastructure of the program. Since it had been underway such a brief period of time, all of the details had yet to be worked out.

If an initial pairing is successful, what is the next step? The model used in Kentucky could easily be used as a template in other states. Ultimately, the KSLP found its home under the umbrella of the Kentucky Public Library Association (KPLA). This was a perfect match because it gave the KSLP a boost in stature in the Kentucky library community and it gave the KPLA an innovative, one-of-a-kind enterprise to call its own. As a result, the KSLP was given its own Web page, serving as a clearinghouse for anyone seeking more information on the program. With its newly found clout as part of an official library association, the project was primed for growth.

In order to flourish, a project needs to have someone at the helm who will advocate for it. In Kentucky, I became the statewide coordinator for the project. This type of role is similar to serving on a state library committee, being the editor of a state library journal, or holding office in a state or national library association. In other words, it can be viewed as service to the profession and a professional growth opportunity.

The project coordinator will have a number of responsibilities. First and foremost, the main task is to try to recruit libraries to participate. This is one of the most challenging and rewarding parts of the coordinator's duties. The recruitment aspect is much like working in sales. Library directors need to be convinced that entering into a partnership is the right decision for their library. Another task of the coordinator is to collect and maintain all of the agreement forms for partnerships throughout the state. In addition to these duties, my experiences as coordinator have had a heavy emphasis on giving presentations at state and regional conferences about the project. This is really another extension of the sales aspect of my role, since these conferences are one of the best ways to meet and interact with library directors.

One observation I gleaned early on in my role as coordinator is that libraries' reputations, personality conflicts, regional competition, along with various other factors, can make or break the decision of one library to partner with another one. Anyone embarking upon this project would be wise to enlist the assistance of those who are informed about these hurdles and are in the best position to help create alliances. In most states, the goal would be to involve the state library or a consortium. In Kentucky, the state's regional library consultants informally assist with facilitating sister library pairings in conjunction with the potential partnering libraries' directors and myself.

A FEW PRACTICAL CONSIDERATIONS

With any new undertaking, there will inevitably be a few unexpected twists and turns. I have found these serendipitous events to be some of the most interesting aspects. Because this was a new venture, I knew all of the answers had yet to be found. This lack of completeness was not troubling because I knew that as more partnerships got underway, the entire library community would learn from the collective experiences of all the participating libraries.

As an example of an unexpected situation, the term "sister" received some pushback when the program first started, but no one thinks twice about it now. The term is clearly a take on the "sister cities" moniker, which seems to have achieved universal acceptance. Some people were worried that the term was too feminine to appeal to the potential male participants. Fortunately, this concern has not turned out to be an issue. The male library directors, board members, and administrators who are involved have not expressed any apprehensions about using this terminology.

Typically, it is recommended that partnerships involve libraries that are no farther apart geographically than about a two-hour drive. Therefore, another unexpected occurrence was the pairing of two library systems that are located approximately four hours apart. Without commitment on both sides, the distance could have posed a serious challenge. To the contrary, the director at the larger of the two libraries feels the distance has been a plus to his sister library pairing. "In fact, the distance gets us completely out of each other's regular 'comfort zone,' which has advantages in terms of swapping ideas," said JC Morgan of the Campbell County Public Library in an e-mail to the author.

By far, the most amazing, unforeseen, and welcome twist to the original concept of pairing an underfunded library with a better funded one has been an idea generated by the library directors and their staff members. What I discovered was that some directors, usually from smaller libraries, were interested in being part of the program, but for various reasons, were not comfortable being paired with a much larger system. Some directors felt more comfortable partnering with a library closer in size to their own. The idea of two equally sized libraries becoming partners works especially well because each can benefit from the strengths of one another, and likewise, they can help one another with the weak areas.

This concept was taken a step further when one tiny library gained not one, but four sister libraries. What had been happening was that all of the libraries had been informally helping one another to some degree already, since they were fairly close geographically. The four new sister libraries were slightly larger than the one they were becoming partners with, but they were still fairly small. By banding together, all of these libraries were able to assist one another by becoming a family of "sisters." By signing the sister library agreement form, they simply put their commitment to one another in writing.

These are but a few of the unpredicted occurrences in the sister library program so far. Of course, more are sure to follow, but the anticipation of that happening means that the initiative is still in its youth, with much room for growth. When it begins to take root in other states, it will no doubt emerge slightly differently in each new case.

YOU CAN'T FIND SUCCESS ALONE!

For anyone who might be considering trying to launch such an effort, it is important to keep in mind that a project of this magnitude can get off the ground fairly quickly with enough support from the library community around the state. Gaining that support will be much easier if you have experimented with a successful pilot test partnership because it helps spark interest and gives you concrete examples of collaborative efforts that have benefited the sister libraries and their patrons. Once others hear about your partnership's accomplishments, they will likely be inspired to start their own alliances with other libraries.

Networking is an essential component to spreading the message about your new undertaking. Every state will be slightly different, but there are several entities with which a connection is vital.

As mentioned earlier, if your state library has regional consultants, their assistance will be vital to the success of the new venture. Of course, their help will need to be sanctioned by their supervisor, so it is important to go through the proper channels in order to gain their support.

Most states have a statewide library association. In Kentucky, the Kentucky Public Library Association (KPLA) is a division of the Kentucky Library Association (KLA). By aligning with the KPLA, the sister library project gained stability and greater recognition. A state's library association is a natural home for a sister library endeavor, as the resources of the association will help the project in its growth, and likewise, the growth of the project will benefit the association in reputation, and possibly memberships.

Friends groups are an invaluable resource. Your library's Friends group may be receptive to footing some expenses that would not be appropriate for the actual library to cover. For example, if your sister library's staff are traveling to your location for training with your staff, they may need to stay overnight. Since small, underfunded libraries cannot afford expenses such as this, your library's Friends group may be able to assist. Minding expenses related to your partnership is critical; any library spending that is not appropriate endangers the entire project.

In addition to local Friends groups, there may be a statewide Friends organization, which helps the local chapters. In Kentucky, the Friends of Kentucky Libraries have supported the KSLP for the past two years by awarding grants to help fund activities related to the sister library program. Together, we worked out the grant criteria and put an application on their website and on the Web page of the KSLP. "With the assistance of the last year's sister library grant, our shadowing visit allowed us to streamline our data collection and analysis as well as identify several small projects that we could manage. With this added insight via our sister library relationship, I personally feel that it made a difference in the over $6,000.00 in other grant monies we have been able to acquire to promote the use and importance of a public library system in Carter County," said Nellie Jordan, director, Carter County Public Library in an e-mail to the author.

LOOKING FORWARD

As stated on the KSLP's Web page, the goal "is to strengthen public libraries in the state by creating partnerships that prove mutually beneficial through the sharing of information, experience, and ideas. Libraries with more resources partner with libraries with fewer resources. Through this collaboration, libraries with unmet needs will have access to resources that will assist them in achieving their goals." This unique slant on the idea of sister libraries has been successful in Kentucky.

If a statewide sister libraries program is to become a reality elsewhere, then some important factors will come into play. Advocates for the program will need to work with other entities such as the state library, the state's library association, and Friends groups, to name a few, in order for it to reach its potential. Additionally, fostering an atmosphere that embraces unexpected twists will help keep the program invigorated.

Administrators seeking innovative strategies now have an option with demonstrated success. The sister libraries concept is an ideal problem-solving tool because it is a win-win proposition and a blueprint for the program is already available. With nothing to lose, and everything to gain, those willing to experiment with this fresh perspective are likely to reap benefits beyond their highest expectations.

REFERENCES

"ALA / IRRT Sister Library Initiative." American Library Association (accessed September 20, 2013). http://wikis.ala.org/sisterlibraries/index.php. /ALA_/ _IRRT_Sister_Library_Initiative.

Kelley, Michael, David Rapp, and Bob Warburton. 2011. "ARSL Conference: Overcoming Isolation and Becoming Community-Centered." *Library Journal* 136, no. 16: 11. Master-FILE Premier, EBSCOhost (accessed August 23, 2013).

Ritchie, April. 2012. "O Sister Library, Where Art Thou?" *American Libraries* 43, no. 1/2: 39–41. Library, Information Science & Technology Abstracts with Full Text, EBSCOhost (accessed September 15, 2013).

"Sister Libraries Project." Kentucky Public Library Association, accessed September 20, 2013. http://kpla.org/about/sister-libraries-project/.

"Technology Demand Up, Budget Cuts Limit Access." *American Libraries* 42, no. 7/8 (July 2011): 12. Library, Information Science & Technology Abstracts with Full Text, EBSCO-host (accessed September 19, 2013).

Part Six

Fundraising

Chapter Twenty-Two

Beyond the Book Sale

Creative Fundraising for Your Small Public Library

Portia Kapraun

The Friends of the Library book sale is the traditional bread and butter of library fundraising. No matter the size of your library, the Friends are liable to rake in a good deal of money on your discarded or donated materials with little or no strain on staff time. Although the book sale is a tried and true method of consistently raising funds, some libraries, big and small, are beginning to raise funds in new, innovative, and exciting ways. These approaches often involve partnerships with the Friends of the Library as well as other community groups. Some libraries may sell flowers or hold silent auctions for items donated by area businesses, others might sell tickets to a wine tasting or dinner featuring local wineries and chefs, and still others might put on a benefit concert or even a dance. In this chapter, we will look at three ways to raise additional funds: working with the local Chamber of Commerce, hosting an art fair, and putting on a murder mystery dinner theater. While these may seem like tasks too big for small public libraries, they are easily managed through effective planning and preparation.

CHAMBER OF COMMERCE

Many people see the local Chamber of Commerce only as an organization for local business owners with no place for a not-for-profit. While the Chamber is designed to support the business community and further the interest of local businesses, it can also be a great way for your library to further its own interests.

Often the Chamber will hold a regular meetings or even luncheons for networking and sharing of information. By sending a library representative to these meetings, the library can strengthen connections to area leaders. Not only will library staff be better informed about what is going on in the business community, but the business owners will learn more about what is going on at the library. By keeping local business owners informed on all that the library offers, they will likely learn about services and materials at the library that will benefit them. See about giving a presentation to the Chamber when the library institutes a new strategic plan, and make sure to alert the Chamber to any new services or materials that will be especially important for business owners.

Additionally, members of the Chamber are often quite involved with the community and may be candidates to sponsor and donate to library programming and funds. This becomes even more likely when library staff has created a personal connection to the business owners through attending Chamber functions.

The best way to reach the largest number of donors through the Chamber is an appeal letter. Contact your local Chamber director to find out the best way to contact members. He or she may have a mailing list or email list for member businesses. Many businesses set aside a budget line for donations, and enjoy using the donations in the community. Some businesses plan a whole year of giving at the beginning of their fiscal year, so it is best to send out your appeal letter early in the year. Highlight the impact donations will have on each event and how it positively impacts the community. If you are asking for a sponsorship of a yearly event, include the average number of attendees. Offer a variety of donation levels and options. In the letter, be sure to list the ways each sponsor will be acknowledged (on flyers, announced at the event, in a newsletter, etc.), and remember to follow through with your promise.

Building relationships with area business owners can be done with an hour or two a month by attending your local Chamber of Commerce meeting, and the rewards for both the businesses and the library will be felt throughout the year.

HOST AN ART FAIR

An art fair in the library can be not only a lucrative fundraiser but also a source of culture for members of the community. Depending upon the proximity of your town from a metropolitan area, many residents may not get consistent exposure to art. This is especially true for those without reliable transportation including the working poor and the elderly. Keep both of these aspects in mind when planning an art fair.

As with most successful ventures, it is important to have a clear vision of what you want to achieve before beginning. This is where a thoughtfully assembled committee is imperative. The committee will guide the show from inception to conclusion, keeping everyone on track and ensuring that all aspects are thoughtfully considered. When gathering committee members, consider both the role each member will play as well as his or her ability to complete tasks in a timely manner. Each organization involved with the fair will need representation. More than likely the committee will include library department heads, board members, and friends of the library representatives. If possible, include a member of a local artist group or an art teacher from the local school. By recruiting committee members from these various groups, you will gain valuable insight and experience that would not exist in a committee made entirely of library staff.

Once a committee is assembled, a few things will need to be decided:

- When will the art fair take place? *Make sure to look at other art fairs or shopping events in the area. Planning an art fair for the week of or week after a nearby sale will make it much more difficult to entice buyers. If applicable, plan the fair around the local tourist season. It may even work well to partner with a nearby festival or street fair. It is easier to get shoppers in when they are already out and about.*
- Will the fair be hosted in the library or another location? *It is best to host the fair inside the library if at all possible. Patrons will appreciate the exposure to local art and art lovers who haven't been inside the library in years may be pleasantly surprised to see all that the library offers. If the library is absolutely out of the question, try to find a location that is centrally located and has adequate security.*
- What type of art will be included? *This will be determined both by the artists in the area as well as the taste of the buyers. Some committees may choose to stick to "fine art" while others will lean towards "arts and crafts." The important thing is to be consistent in application and advertising.*
- How will the library make money and who will handle the transactions? *There are two main ways to raise funds from an art fair. The first is to charge artists for booth space, essentially guaranteeing a set dollar amount from each artist. The second is to take a commission on all sales, usually 30–40 percent. Keep in mind that it may be more difficult to get artists to agree to pay a fee to enter a new show with unknown sales results. If the library is taking a commission on sales, it works best to have library staff handle all sales and write a check to the artist after the sale is over to ensure that the commission is properly factored.*

Check with an accountant or a tax attorney to see if the library is liable for sales tax or issuing 1099s to artists for items sold. Also, be sure to consult the library's insurance agent to ensure that insurance coverage is adequate and up to date for such an endeavor. He or she may suggest wording to include in an artist registration form excusing the library from liability for theft or damage.

Once these questions have been answered, it's time to start looking for artists. Begin by contacting arts organizations in the area. Many of these groups have a large mailing list and would be happy to send out information to the artists. Local businesses are also a great place to look for talent. While art galleries are great places to make connections and find artists, local coffee shops, restaurants, and boutiques may also feature local artwork. There are also websites such as Zapp (www.zapplication.org) and CaFÉ (www.callforentry.org) that allow online recruitment of artists. Additionally, artists who are recruited for the show often have a network of friends and acquaintances to refer. It will take a few years to build a solid base of artists from which to pull, but it is also important to continue to look for new talent to keep the fair fresh. Set a goal of recruiting a few new artists each year so buyers always have something new to discover. Also, don't be afraid to try out an artist whose work is less traditional. If the work doesn't sell, it will only help to gauge what types of work appeal to the community.

Some libraries choose to offer a private opening reception for patrons who pledge to spend a certain dollar amount at the fair, usually $50 or $100. By promising to purchase art, these patrons get first look at the artwork. These pledges help by guaranteeing sales at the fair, which can convince artists who may be hesitant to try out an unknown show.

After the recruitment of artists gets underway, the committee will need to begin advertising. Hang flyers around town, including local tourist destinations or hotels. Talk to area radio and television stations to see about getting an on-air interview. Often, stations are looking for human-interest pieces and the library will get free advertising. Make a budget to spend on banners, newspaper ads, and other advertising. Banners can be used for multiple years if specific dates are replaced with a time frame, such as "the first week of August."

As the show gets closer, final preparations will need to be made. Every library's show will be a little different, but a task list will keep everyone on target. Here are a few things everyone will need to do:

- Recruit volunteers to help with set up and tear down.
- Create a map of where each artist's works will be.
- Set a time for delivery and set up art to ensure that everything is in place before the doors are opened. If staff will be hanging framed pieces, ask artists to drop these off a few days in advance. Other artists should be

given a deadline of at least a few hours before the show begins to allow for unexpected emergencies.
- If the show will take place while the library is operational, ensure that there is enough staff and volunteers on hand to operate the show without adversely affecting the normal library operations.

After the show, set a time for the committee to meet to review the show. Look at what went well and what will need to be changed for the next year. Be sure to send thank-you notes to donors or patrons who pledged as well as to participating artists.

An art fair can be both a fun cultural experience for your community and a profitable and innovative way to raise funds for long-term goals. While it may seem like a lot of work, working with a committee can make it a doable endeavor for a library of any size.

MURDER MYSTERY DINNER THEATER

Every public librarian knows the popularity of the mystery genre. Hosting a murder mystery dinner theater in the library is a surefire way to raise funds for the library and have a lot of fun in the process.

The first step in planning your murder mystery is to find a script. Many murder mystery scripts can be found online. Many vendors allow a partial script to be previewed before purchase to help determine if the script is right for your library. The four sites listed below are examples of quality shows for a reasonable price:

- Penny Warner Library Mysteries: *Agatha Award–winning author Penny Warner offers up four fun-filled scripts for a library-themed murder mystery that have been successfully performed in libraries since 1987. The scripts do not require memorization, and work well for actors with little experience. Script packets also include costume suggestions, stage directions, props, crime scene layout, and instructions for hosting your dinner theater.*
- Library Mystery Night Programs by Ted Kavich: *Ted Kavich offers nine library-themed murder mysteries to choose from. Each script has a unique library setting and cast. Packets include suspect dossiers, secret clues for the detective, audience handouts, suspect biographies, and instructions for making the event a success.*
- Murder Mystery Scripts: *With 15 scripts with a wide variety of themes and settings to choose from, there is something for everyone here. The plays are not library-themed, which may appeal to a wider audience. Written and performed by the Country Gate Players out of Belvidere, New Jersey,*

these scripts are more involved than the previous two listed and will require more of a time commitment from the actors.

- Sherlock's Mystery Dinner Theatre: *Written for the Sherlocks' Mystery Dinner Theatre in Columbus, Georgia, these scripts allow flexibility in casting, allowing for a performance to be successful with as few as two actors. The scripts also encourage audience participation with 12–21 parts to be distributed the evening of the show. Writers Dr. Kate and JJ Musgrove keep the humor clean for a family friendly show.*

Once you've found a script, it's time to begin further planning. Dates, menus, and pricing must be set, and actors and a director need to be recruited. Rehearsals will need to be scheduled, and volunteers rounded up.

As soon as you know what script you will be performing, assess whether or not the play can be successfully performed in the library. Is there enough space for the actors to move freely? Will there be room for an audience to sit and eat comfortably? If the play cannot be performed in the library, consider working with your local high school, community theater, or even a restaurant with a larger room. Where the play will be performed will determine when it will be performed also. If in the library, make sure not to schedule the performance too close to other major events such as summer reading so as not to overstretch staff. If you will be performing outside of the library, the venue's schedule will dictate performance dates.

Of course, what is a dinner theater without the dinner? Menus can be as simple or fancy as you'd like to make them. A simple buffet-style meal created by library staff may suit your event, or a catered meal may be served for a more formal affair. Some libraries choose to offer two performances, one with a full catered meal and the other a coffee and dessert reception, which allows for two different ticket prices to be offered. Other considerations may include special diets and the size of the kitchen in the venue used. Performances in a restaurant have the added benefit of a built-in caterer (and clean-up crew).

The cost of your script and dinner menu will be the two biggest determining factors in the cost of a ticket price. To determine the base price of a ticket, divide the cost of the script by the number of tickets to be sold and add in the cost of the meal per person. After that, two things will need to be considered: how much audience members will be willing to pay and what type of profit will make the fundraiser worthwhile.

There is no need to have professional actors for most of these shows, instead recruit volunteers. If your town has a community theater, begin by contacting the group to look for a few veteran actors as well as someone who might wish to direct the show. If there is no community theater, that does not mean there aren't any actors in town. Most of these shows by the vendors listed above do not require any acting experience, so think outside the box when recruiting. Casting local community leaders can make the event enjoyable and profitable. Audience members enjoy seeing people they know on stage. Who wouldn't pay to see the mayor or fire chief in a play? Need someone to play a newspaper reporter? Call the local paper or radio station. Don't forget to ask library staff, too. Often a play can be cast without hosting auditions, which can be time consuming.

Traditionally a rehearsal schedule is set early on, before auditions are held. You may find that it is easier to work with your actors to set a rehearsal schedule. Set a realistic time frame to ensure that everyone involved has time to learn lines and stage directions. The amount of time needed will vary greatly depending upon how demanding the script is. Some require little or no line memorization and only require a meeting or two to run through the play, while others will require both lines and complex stage direction to be learned. No matter the time commitment involved, find some way to show appreciation for your actors: provide pizza during rehearsal one night or give a small gift to each at the conclusion of the show.

Include the actors and director in all advertising. Some people who may not normally be inclined to attend a play will attend to see a friend, family member, or well-known public figure. Also, talk to local newspapers about getting an article with pictures in a week or two before the show, as readers may recognize a face better than a name. All print advertisements should be clear and concise, listing the title of the show, dates, times, ticket prices, and how to purchase tickets. The number of seats you have available will be a big factor in determining the amount and type of advertising you do. If seating is limited, there is a good chance that there will not be a need for paid advertising. Flyers in-house and around town as well as press releases to area media may be enough to sell out. For larger venues or multi-night programs, paid advertising such as print ads or radio spots may be necessary. Public radio stations offer competitively priced programming sponsorships and reach an audience more likely to attend live theater. Ultimately, word of mouth is usually the best form of advertising, so encourage everyone involved to talk up the show with patrons, coworkers, family, and friends.

Most murder mysteries ask the audience to try to solve the mystery before the truth is revealed. Determine whether or not prizes will be awarded for correct answers. Prizes need not be expensive; a small token such as a box of chocolates or even a certificate naming the winner can be enough. Another option is to contact area businesses for donations of small items or gift cards. Look for something that follows the theme of the evening, if possible. Prizes may also be given for most original answer, if you choose, allowing audience members to show their own creative side. Make sure someone is chosen ahead of time to read the submissions and choose the winners.

After all of the details are set, it is time to begin planning for the night of the show. Create a list of tasks to be performed the day of the show, such as setting up furniture, serving food, and so on, and make sure each task is assigned to a staff member or volunteer. Live theater rarely goes off without a hitch, but your evening will run much more smoothly if everything has been carefully considered beforehand.

CONCLUSION

While most small libraries wouldn't initially consider teaming up with the Chamber of Commerce or trying to pull off an art fair or murder mystery dinner theater, these can be enjoyable and profitable endeavors. Effective planning and preparation ensure that these three fundraising techniques can be accomplished without affecting normal library operations. Working with community members and business leaders as well as the Friends of the Library can help your library go beyond the book sale.

Chapter Twenty-Three

Fundraising

Filling the Gap without Grants

Judith Wines

In this chapter, we'll look at how fundraising fits into the big picture, steps to take to prepare to fundraise, and how three types of library fundraisers can work together in order to create a fundraising program that maximizes the potential of your community. These three types of fundraising are as follows:

- community events
- gala events
- direct appeals

Your needs likely fall into at least one of two categories: projects with a onetime cost, such as a new building, a remodeling project, or a new audio-video system; and improvements to library services with ongoing costs, such as an increase in hours or staffing. Fundraising is a great solution to the first need and a treacherous solution to the second. Ideally, your local support will cover your ongoing operating costs. Before you look to fundraising to keep your doors open, be sure you have examined all means of increasing your local support: requesting an increase from your funding municipality, seeking an increase from your existing taxpayers or forming a special district or other entity where the public can vote on levying a tax to fund your operations.

While more money is always nice to have, if you are going to ask your community to give it to you voluntarily, you need to have a purpose, and to be sure that your community is supportive of the plan. Be able to articulate your plan both in short and in full. Once you can do this, you need to be able to demonstrate the community's support for what you want to do. Your evidence can be from focus groups, surveys, or simply anecdotal, but you must have evidence.

Once you have a project and can demonstrate its support, you need to create buy in. The good news here is that creating opportunities for your community to support a project both benefits the project and builds support for it. These we'll call community events. They provide the opportunity for supporters to get involved with a cause at a low cost to themselves and learn more about and possibly become more involved with the project. These events include many traditional fundraising events, such as chicken BBQs, book sales, bake sales, and 5k races. While these events all are effective fundraisers, they are also great opportunities to educate the community about your project. Have poster boards up at your bake sale that illustrate how great/necessary/transformational your project is. When community members pick up their chicken BBQ, thank them for supporting your cause. If circumstances permit, make your fundraiser a community event: find local musicians who will work for a free dinner and ask them to play in the park where your BBQ is held. Families will linger and have a great time and the BBQ can go from a way for the library to make some money and parents to grab a quick dinner, to a community event that families look forward to.

The particulars of these events are too varied to go into any of them in great detail, but there are some caveats that apply to them all.

Retail style fundraisers are labor intensive. You may need to remind your library board that procuring adequate funding for the library is a key part of their role and they need to pitch in for fundraisers—it cannot be a staff-only job.

This is a great time to revitalize your friends group/library volunteers list. Have a sign-up sheet at the circulation desk and collect e-mail addresses of people willing to bake/sort books/wear a chicken suit to publicize a BBQ. Give patrons the opportunity to demonstrate that they do love their library.

Plan ahead. Lots of local businesses will donate bags/paper goods/beverages or other items you need, but they often need lead time to get approval from management.

Remember that these events are not just about the money. You may not make a huge amount—our library raises an amount equal to 1 percent of our operating budget at each event of this nature. They raise the visibility of your project and provide a low friction way for the community to support you. They can also become events your community will look forward to annually, almost an extension of library service.

Once members of your community see themselves as library supporters, you have a starting point for more lucrative events. While smaller fundraisers can provide the community the opportunity to support the library by paying the going cost of a good or service, and having it benefit the library, the next level of fundraising, which I will call gala events, asks library supporters to pay for an event or service, knowing that the amount they're paying may be well above the retail value. There are many iterations of events of this sort—cabaret nights, dinners, wine tasting, art events, and so on, but most have something in common. Participants purchase a ticket, a portion of the cost of which may be tax deductible. (Any library putting substantial resources into fundraising needs to procure for itself or its foundation or friends group 501(c)3 status. This is the IRS designation for groups that can receive donations, which can be deducted from the taxes of the givers.) Frequently, the event is paired with an auction—live or silent—which both adds to the appeal of the event for attendees and can provide a substantial portion of the event's proceeds.

You should expect to raise a larger amount of money at a gala event than at a community event and spend more time preparing for it. A gala event generally has a dedicated committee that should be comprised of board members, staff members, and community members with experience in event planning and deep social connections in your community. You will want months of lead time to secure your location, prepare your theme, get your date on people's calendars, secure donated auction items, and arrange for food and/or entertainment.

Here are a few things to consider:

Encourage attendees to dress up. The event will feel more special if attendees are in festive attire than if they show up in jeans and t-shirts.

Connect the event to the library. Have a slide show running in the background showing your library at its best. If you have speakers, ensure that they talk about the library.

Consider an honorary committee. You'll want to price your tickets at a point that is profitable, but doesn't price out too many potential attendees. The two-tier pricing system that an honorary committee affords allows those who are able to pay more to do so, and be recognized for their support.

Keep your costs low. This is the financial side that is under your control. If you can use a municipal space at low cost, and decorate it to the nines, you will start off in a much better position than if you had to hire a country club at great expense. This is a challenging area because is it important for your event not to feel cheap. But creativity and talent can go a long way in creating the type of space you want.

A gala event should be something that gets your library buzz in your community, generates substantial income (we have raised close to 20 percent of our budget in one evening), and strengthens the bond between you and your donors.

The third type of fundraising is the direct appeal. Here you are working with your strongest supporters and asking them to make an unreciprocated gift to the library. This category includes bequests, pledges, and gifts. The most important aspect of seeking gifts is to ask. Your "asks" should be both passive and active. Be sure to ask about the possibility of employers who match gifts.

Your website should have a downloadable gift form, and the functionality to accept gifts online (there are many services that can accept online donations at a low cost, including Amazon Payments and Google Checkout.) Your library should have brochures and giving forms easily available to the public. You'll want to provide recognition to your donors—both to thank them publicly and to remind others of the option of donating to the library. A donor wall, with levels of giving, serves this function well.

In addition to making your donation opportunities easy to learn about, your library may choose to directly ask for money. Draw upon the knowledge and connection of your staff and board to identify community members who have the means and motivation to support the library. Draft a letter asking for money. Consider sending it toward the end of the year when many people make the majority of their donations. Ask the person who identified the prospect to write a short personal note that goes along with your letter. You have the option of sending the letter out to a very targeted audience, or to a broader one, such as all registered borrowers.

For more specific ideas about fundraising, the internet is a wonderful resource. A few websites with library specific fundraising ideas are listed below:

- The Libri Foundation: http://www.librifoundation.org
- Friends of Libraries USA: http://www.folusa.org
- For information on holding a gala or other event, the website the Chronicle of Philanthropy has resources on event fundraising: http://philanthropy.com/section/Fundraising/268/?eio=32739
- For a start in setting up the infrastructure for your patrons to remember the library in their wills, use search terms such as "public library bequests" to see examples of how other public libraries facilitate this process.

Depending on the scope of your project and situation of your library, fundraising can be anything from a small, one-off endeavor to an enterprise that requires significant resources from your organization. Wherever your needs fall on that spectrum, having a well-thought-out and articulated strategy is key to success.

Chapter Twenty-Four

Grantsmanship Methods and Strategies for Rural and Small-Town Librarians

Dwight McInvaill

When I recently told a buddy at the Winyah Fitness Center in Georgetown, South Carolina, that I'd be writing a grantsmanship chapter in a book for rural librarians, he said, "What's grantsmanship?" When I explained, he retorted, "Just tell those folks to fill out the forms; to turn them in on time; and to do the applications creatively." So that's that! But seriously, there's somewhat more than that to an effective grantsmanship process.

I. BACKGROUND

I've got a lot of experience in writing grants. I've enjoyed writing grants for over thirty years. I started in college by winning a Rotary Foundation scholarship to study for a year in France on the Riviera and in the wine country of Bordeaux. When I won that grant, I was definitely sold on writing more. During the last two decades, I've made millions of dollars in grants for the Georgetown County Library of South Carolina while directing that institution.

I've gotten grants for construction (the latest being a $500,000 Community Development Block Grant thru the South Carolina Department of Commerce); grants for equipment (recently $120,000 through the United States Department of Agriculture for computers and a bookmobile); grants for digitization ($350,000 from the Gaylord and Dorothy Donnelley Foundation for a digital library); grants for using technology creatively with young people ($600,000 from the Frances P. Bunnelle Foundation); grants for investment education ($180,000 from the FINRA Foundation); grants for e-book readers and then for a small business center ($42,000 from the South Carolina State Library), and many others ranging from emergency-disaster preparation ($60,000 from the International City/County Management Association) to thousands of dollars repeatedly for humanities programming. I'm continually looking for funding, because like most rural and small-town librarians, I'm always faced with funding challenges, especially for innovative programs.

II. RESOURCES

There is a lot of money out there, and there exists a variety of ways to find it. For online sources, I often explore sites like the Foundation Center (http://foundationcenter.org), eCivis (www.ecivis.com), and Grants.gov (www.grants.gov). At my headquarters library, we've recently established a Cooperating Collection of the Foundation Center. Generally, there are a number of such centers in each state. By visiting the Foundation Center website you can find them. These centers have great grants-getting materials, online access to grant resources, and trained, helpful staff. I'd advise that you go to a nearby Cooperating Collection soon to learn of these Foundation Center resources. Here are some other ideas:

- Government Agencies: I locate information on grants regularly from the websites of the State Library and from the federal Institute of Museum and Library Services (IMLS; www.imls.gov).
- Professional Organizations: I keep up with grant news from the American Library Association (ALA; www.ala.org), the Public Library Association (PLA; www.ala.org/pla/), and the Association for Rural and Small Libraries (ARSL; http://arsl.info) via websites and blogs.
- Personal Contacts: I cultivate a lot of acquaintances in foundations and through my professional life. I actively seek such contacts out whenever and wherever I can.

III. ART OF GRANTSMANSHIP

To obtain grants, I see it as an art with three main elements:

- Grammar: That's the nuts and bolts of submitting a sound, well-written proposal: composing, drawing, and filling in the color and details of your project through nearly a basic paint-by-numbers approach.
- Landscape: That's the awareness of your surroundings, which may enable you vividly to distinguish your proposals from others. This mindfulness

comes from a mixture of research in the closed-in confines of the library office and also from work in the open air.

• Vision: That's the imaginative leap—based on solid, prior study mixed with some lucky serendipity—which may permit you to use grants for creative purposes to position your organization strategically in distinctly advantageous ways. Although I think that Vision should come first, we will save that for the end of the discussion, since some of you may be interested mainly in fundamental techniques to obtain enough money just to keep going as long as possible, which is also a valid concern.

IV. GRAMMAR

Follow this basic approach in writing a grant proposal to cover the main bases:

Instructions from grant providers. Review grant guidelines carefully to know if you are eligible and to understand precisely what's required. If no grant application form is provided, use the provided grant guidelines to create your own detailed form with headings and subheadings to be sure to cover every single desired point. Watch for elements in the critical-path timeline in completing your proposal. For example, is there a letter required from another entity which may take you some time to get? If so, then prioritize what you'll need to do and then commence work soon. Set aside plenty of time if possible. My rule of thumb is to take the number of hours that I think I'll need and then to multiply them by three.

Budget (and budget narrative). Rather than immediately jumping in to write prose, start with the budget to delineate clearly the overall composition of your project. Defining things precisely in a numerical way is a disciplined approach to envision everything clearly. This initial approach will give you a sharp view on how to proceed efficiently.

Timeline. Continue your application by working next on the timeline. This section flows logically from the budget. You will essentially be transforming the two-dimensional numerical approach into a three-dimensional universe incorporating actions being undertaken by specific people in definite places in sequential processes. You are fleshing things out further in a logical, clear way based on time.

Evaluation. Once you have listed your action steps in the timeline, consider how you will gauge your success in accomplishing them. The traditional approach is to measure inputs and outputs numerically. Outcome Based Evaluation (OBE) is a newer approach that focuses on changes of attitude, knowledge, and behavior. See the Institute of Museum and Library Service's (IMLS) website for a good summary of OBE.

Goals and objectives. Now look for general patterns in the budget, time-line, and evaluation. These contours should suggest your overall key goals and major objectives. You should be able to use these main points and the outline and details that flow logically from them to create narrative para-graphs characterized by definition. You learned how to write paragraphs of definition probably in the eighth grade of grammar school, but for a quick review of this basic approach, just consult any English composition book. It's somewhat like writing an entry for a dictionary. Just explain succinctly and clearly what you'll be doing.

Action plan. Next, refer back to your timeline to write the narrative action-plan section that will essentially be one characterized by processes undertaken through time. This is also a good place to list and comment upon the project's personnel and to describe why they are excellent people to undertake this work. Do so by writing quick sketches of individuals here. But don't meander. Relate such characterizations back to the project and keep them short. In this narrative action plan, you'll be explaining how your project will proceed step-by-step. Just think how you'd explain to someone how to bake a cake using ingredients, tools, and processes. Doing the action plan works basically from the same approach.

Impact on needs. Needs and impacts may be covered in a couple sec-tions, but they relate closely to each other. If you've thought of applying for a grant, then you will likely already have an idea of what deficiencies will be addressed by getting the grant or what strengths will be enhanced with grant funds; if someone has assigned to you the task of writing a grant, then you should discuss needs and impacts with that person to get their ideas. To buttress your argument in this narrative section, you'll need statistics and anecdotes. The United States Census is always a good standard source. But others exist depending on your needs, and since you are librarians, you will already know how to find them and you will be one step ahead of many other grant seekers, won't you? In part, this section will also be characterized by definition, but it also lends itself to comparison and contrast between where you are now and where you would like to be at the conclusion of the grant period.

Your organization and partners. Treated together or separately, these two topics both are founded on definition. Typically, when you define your organization, you may refer to your mission statement which provides a brief, formal announcement of what you do. Your next aim should be to communicate to a potential funder the stability, fiscal prudence, and account-ability of your operation. You want the funder to know that you will be a very good steward of the grant. But this section also gives you the chance to sing your own professional praises and to distinguish yourself as highly as possible from other potential applicants.

But here's a caution: don't undercut your expressed need by emphasizing your strengths in the wrong way. You may be strong, but you must remember to emphasize, too, that you need help. As for partners, check with them before listing them in the final proposal. Make sure they are on board. Also, when you ask your partners or others for letters of support, provide them with some suggested points to express in their letters. Or if you are really comfortable with a partner, provide this supporter with a nearly prepared letter to sign. That way, you can control the message more precisely. Here's one that I helped an elderly lady to compose. It was later quoted in January 2008 by First Lady Laura Bush at the White House when my library won a National Medal for Library Service:

Dear Members of the National Museum and Library Services Board:

Recently, I celebrated my 90th birthday; so, I have been many places and I have seen many things. I wanted to let you know that our Georgetown County Library is very fine. I had the pleasure several years ago to serve as the President of the Friends of the Georgetown Library, and I know firsthand about many details of the library's innovative projects and activities. Most recently, the library hosted the South Carolina Humanities Festival, but it has successfully coordinated many similar events, also.

In 2001, the library helped with the visit of the Amistad during a wonderful time when we celebrated together our rich cultural heritage and discussed deeply the issue of racial reconciliation. But the library didn't stop there. During the following year, it did an oral history video project entitled "The Women of Georgetown County." And in 2003, it did another on the men, too. For the past several years, it has also been working on an original documentary series entitled "African American History in the South Carolina Lowcountry." The first 60-minute part was entitled "When Kings Became Slaves," and the second is on the verge of coming out. It will be "Slave Revolts and Insurrections." The library is helping to give voice to a significant part of our history. It is my understanding that the library will soon start on an important digital library of historical photographs, too.

Personally, I really appreciated being interviewed for "The Women of Georgetown County" series. Through it, I was able to leave a record of my experiences for future generations. Will they believe that the Wall Street financier Bernard Baruch really tried to make me dance as a child for his guests at Hobcaw Barony, where he entertained the likes of FDR and Winston Churchill? Will they understand how I later helped to build liberty vessels during WWII in the shipyards up north? Will they learn how I took preschoolers to camp on the lawn of Eleanor Roosevelt's home? Will they appreciate why I was jailed trying to register folks to vote? Yes, the library has given me a voice for many future generations to come. It's definitely a very important part of our community.

These letters of support can have more impact than you might reason. I learned this fact the hard way as a young man in college when I wrote my first grants abroad. I devoted hours then to grant writing and research, and I even got my roommate interested. So, both he and I applied in tandem, although not always to same exact sources.

But his applications seemed to move further along, while mine went nowhere. But the quality was comparable. He won a Fulbright Scholarship, and I was in the dumps! Then I discovered that a professor I'd asked for a reference—because he was the head of a department—had actually been writing almost negative ones on me! When I dropped him from the roster, I immediately won a Rotary Foundation scholarship from Rotary International. I have always remembered that lesson and have henceforth always controlled that part of the process closely—taking no references for granted.

V. LANDSCAPE

To develop better grant proposals, improve your in-depth awareness of your locality:

Basic elements worth knowing. These include geography, people, socioeconomic conditions, and history and culture.

Geography. What makes your setting distinct? How would you describe its contours, its systems, and its flora and fauna—both actually and figuratively? How has this geography evolved due to the passage of time and because of the influence of humanity? How does this understanding relate to problems and strengths; to deficiencies and opportunities? How would you like to see this environment changed or strengthened?

People. What kinds of people inhabit the terrain? Where did they come from? How are they a part of a general pattern and how are they individually distinct? How has the physical environment impacted them? How have they changed; how have they remained the same?

Socioeconomic conditions. What are the groups within the landscape and where are they located? Who are their leaders and how can you interact effectively with them? What do people do and how do they benefit from it? How has this changed during time? What is the outlook for the future? What do you think should be done to produce or to continue prosperity for the greatest good or conversely for certain special-needs persons?

History and culture. What are the key shared experiences of the people of your landscape? How have these occurred during the passage of time? What values have arisen and subsided? How have these values been expressed creatively? How is this inheritance unique to the inhabitants of this terrain? Why is it worth encouraging? What needs to be changed?

Learning about the landscape. Learn about the landscape through secondary and primary means:

1. Secondary approaches involve narrative definitions and overviews; statistical sources; specialized atlases; journalistic essays; and popular stories, art, and music.

2. Primary methods include immersing oneself in the landscape through participation with others ranging from the nearly passive to the strenuously active. By rubbing shoulders and making connections with others, you'll really learn how things work in your rural and small-town locality.

Proven "shorthand methods." Surveys and focus groups are formalized ways of seeking views and opinions. There's a great deal of information on such methods in books and on the Internet. But basically, this process consists of seeking people's opinions and writing them down for future comparison. Look for trends and also for some great new ideas.

Effective active ways to understand your locality. These include collaborations, competitions, and creative associations. In our case, here are some examples: the visit of the Slave Ship Amistad, the All-America County Contest, and the hosting of the SC Humanities Festival. Each of these involved individuals representative of the county's socioeconomic and cultural spectrum brainstorming and creating together under pressure. That's when you really get to know one another!

Importance of this awareness. Knowing your landscape will enable you to develop a good framework for a composition that's appealing to the intellect while providing a stimulating and colorful experience to draw readers into your narrative through movement through place and time while providing pauses at the necessary focal points for emphasis of main points.

Here's a sample of how I used landscape in a recent National Endowment of the Humanities Challenge Grant submission:

> The Georgetown County Library system seeks, with this grant's help, to create a Heritage Complex at its new Waccamaw Neck Branch Library. This project would involve two key aspects: constructing a heritage room along with an auditorium in this impending replacement for an older public-library facility while also creating there an expanded collection of books, materials, and technology assets focused on humanistic values related to the historical and cultural significance of Georgetown County, particularly its coastal 28-mile-long peninsula: the Waccamaw Neck.
>
> The special heritage of Georgetown County and the Waccamaw Neck derives in large measure from the passage of this land and its people through time. This district lies on South Carolina's seaboard midway from Myrtle Beach to Charleston. Ringed with development, it remains essentially rural, particularly in its interior. Its low-lying areas flood easily and are often covered by water: consequently, it has been called "the Lowcountry" for generations. The county's 517,120 acres comprise the heart of the Winyah-Bay and Santee-Delta ecosystem. This vast juncture of six rivers and the Atlantic Ocean

encompasses myriad wildlife habitats. Its rivers' names echo tribal heritage—Waccamaw, Sampit, Pee Dee, and Santee. According to Paul Quattlebaum's book, The Land Called Chicora *(1956), and other sources, the Spanish may have settled here temporarily as early as 1526. In the frontier days of the 1750s, people throughout the British Empire and elsewhere called Georgetown County and its Waccamaw Neck home. South Carolina was then known as one of America's most liberal colonies; so, there occurred an influx of religious groups escaping persecution including Jews and French Huguenots. Tolerance, as a value here—especially in regards to worship—consequently has deep, local historical roots.*

As George Rogers noted in The History of Georgetown County, South Carolina *(1970), this locality is also linked firmly to the establishment of the principle of freedom in America. A Georgetown planter, Thomas Lynch, for instance, who John Adams referred to as "a solid, firm, judicious man," attended for South Carolina the Stamp Act Congress in New York in 1765. Lynch later participated in the Second Continental Congress in 1775 and then played a conspicuous part in organizing the Continental Army to invest British forces in Boston. A contemporary, local resident General Francis Marion, meantime used fluid guerrilla warfare tactics in Georgetown County and elsewhere to spar with British Colonel Banastre Tarleton in the swamps around the district in episodes celebrated two centuries later in* The Patriot, *a movie partly filmed here in 1999. Additionally, on June 13, 1777, the Marquis de Lafayette set foot for the first time on American soil when coming ashore on Georgetown County's North Island with the Baron De Kalb. After two days of local hospitality, he wrote his wife, "The customs of this world are simple, honest, and altogether worthy of the country where everything reechoes the beautiful name of Liberty." It was here that he swore to conquer or die in freedom's cause.*

The value of freedom did not extend to everyone locally. Georgetown County's early national influence was due to wealth from an enormous human tragedy related directly to the American Civil War: slavery. Antebellum chains scar our very landscape, even today. A view from the sky clearly shows these links etched deeply into the terrain: canals and dikes extend for countless miles like vast fetters on the Waccamaw Neck even after generations of disuse. In the 1840s and 1850s, Georgetown County produced, through these devices, one-half of the total rice crops of the United States. As the nation's principal rice-growing area, the district also existed—from 1810 to 1860—as the place in South Carolina with the highest percentage of slaves. Almost 90% of the population, during the 50 years prior to the Civil War, was bound in Georgetown County in the shackles of perpetual servitude. Michele Obama's ancestral family, for instance, was amongst this enslaved number here, a fact underscored recently by journalist Anderson Cooper's usage of the Georgetown County Library's existing digital resources in a special report on First Lady Obama's antebellum lineage. For at least three centuries, this interchange between Blacks and Whites has resulted here in the singular Gullah/Geechee language and culture along with rich values and traditions, as noted in The South Carolina Encyclopedia *(A project of the Humanities Council SC 2006), "especially in the areas of folklore, storytelling, literature, and the visual arts."*

VI. VISION

To really create well and to make positive key changes in your organization and your community, be sure to keep up with the best of the old and with the brightest of the new to relate your locality to the broader flowing context of things innovatively and effectively. Then, take some time each day to be keenly aware, to focus quietly, to think about things deeply, and to dream. Turn off the TV, the cell phone, and the computer. Block out everything, and just sit! You really don't have to be always connected or always accessible, do you? Actively deny others access at times to you. Go find your favorite country spot, and sit there alone. To connect deeply, you must disconnect.

As the French Scientist Louis Pasteur once noted, "Fortune favors the prepared mind." To innovate, one benefits from a familiarity with the broader world. Such knowledge combined with openness sometimes leads to wonderful occasions of serendipity when the mental connections come together somehow with wondrous results. To achieve that aim professionally, there are many ways—from attending conferences to perusing the professional journals to visiting others and to seeing things firsthand. But to keep things simple, I'll share with you one of my favorite sources: *The Christian Science Monitor*. Nothing beats that newspaper for a balanced world view and for an ongoing commitment to life-long education. It has wonderful sections on contemporary culture and books, of course. But even better, it always emphasizes technology in an easily understood manner. In our busy age, it's an accurate way of quickly keeping up. It's where I've gotten a lot of the impetus to create innovative programs at the Georgetown County Library.

As a librarian, I've also been influenced deeply by the Da Vinci Institute study titled *The Future of Libraries: Beginning the Great Transformation* by Executive Director Thomas Frey, which came out online in 2005. It points out that although currently valued, the library, like many institutions and businesses, is faced with societal changes related to technology. It identifies key trends to watch closely such as the following ones:

- Rapidly evolving communications systems
- Life-style time compression
- Increased reliance on verbal interactions over print communications
- Exponentially growing demands for global information
- Coming new age of global systems
- Transition to an experience-based economy.

It concludes that libraries will change generally from information centers into cultural commons. It recommends most importantly that libraries adopt these approaches:

- Become locally attuned by learning what things matter most in one's own community
- Remain flexible and current by embracing new technologies continually
- Connect deeply with one's own area by actively preserving community memories
- Experiment creatively with interior and exterior library spaces as the library's role evolves

There are a lot of similar studies throughout our loquacious profession. The need is to read and to consider some of them carefully—the ones that somehow speak to you—and then to act purposefully. This point must be underscored: active persistence is the key to everything good. Nothing happens easily. You've got to work smart and work hard again and again and again. And then be prepared to dust off and spring back up quickly if you get knocked down. That leads to one final point: when you do succeed, please remember to broadcast your success to the entire world. Don't be shy! Others should know what you've done, and you should be rewarded for it publicly. Most importantly, your funders will love it if others recognize and emulate you. So, go forth briskly, strive well, and shine brightly!

Chapter Twenty-Five

Programming Turned Fundraisers from a Library Board Trustee Member/ Librarian Perspective

Linda Burkey Wade

This article will cover some new and exciting programming that has been done at the Brown County Public Library District (BCPLD) while working fundraising in those events from the perspective of a library trustee board member. I will tell you how our library got started on our road to get employees and the community excited about the library.

BROWN COUNTY PUBLIC LIBRARY DISTRICT

The district library has a main building and one branch library in another small rural community in Brown County, Illinois. The library serves around 6,926 residents with a property tax supported budget. The libraries' staff positions include a homebound assistant who delivers to the elderly and disabled; two staff members at our branch library; the marketing/events librarian; an outreach coordinator who delivers books to surrounding smaller towns within the county; a summer reading coordinator and the library director. Lastly, we have a seven-member elected board of trustees of which I am a member. None of our staff works full time and the marketing position is only allotted sixteen hours per week. Our library just recently created a marketing/events librarian position to promote the library to our community and raise funds for a new building. The board has not provided a budget for this position so, obviously, this employee has many challenges making our small library more noticeable and valuable to the community while promoting library services, our new building, and programming events. Following is an account of how our library has worked to meet the informational needs in our small rural town while fundraising.

MOTIVATING STAFF, CREATING EXCITEMENT, AND POSITIVE ATTITUDES

Motivating your library's staff is one of the first steps to better customer service and marketing, which is the beginning to any programming and fundraising your library will do. Because frontline staff provides the first and lasting impression your patrons will have of your library, a motivated staff is essential to good customer service. Empowering your employees with training and autonomy while promoting team effort and fun at work will give your staff the confidence and feelings of trust essential to customer service–oriented employees. It is important to encourage continued education in which your library staff learns new skills. Don't forget to keep your staff informed of changes and solicit their solutions for problem solving, and changes to workflow or services. They may have ideas you wouldn't think of since they do the tasks regularly. These simple techniques help employees feel they have ownership of their job and that they are valued by the library board.

You would like your staff to be eager to learn new skills. But how do you know what to have them learn? A good way to make sure they will engage in training is to ask them what new skills they are interested in learning. This past year during evaluations our library director had staff complete self-evaluations and asked them what new skills they would be interested in learning. The employees said they wanted to be trained to search the online catalog, to assist patrons with reference questions, and to help them access e-books. This was a nice surprise to the director and the board. The present staff is an older generation who had not seem concerned about learning new technology skills in previous years. Sometimes training has to be mandated for equipment or software changes, but how nice it is when your staff is willing to learn something new. Because the staff asked for training in these specific areas of customer service the BCPLD director provided training and opportunities for them to attend staff development sessions.

"Effective employee recognition programs provide many benefits" for bosses and employees including improvements to staff morale, productivity, and loyalty to the library (Lake-Bacon et al. 2013, 1). The most inexpensive motivation tool is simply saying, "Thank you." It is the most underutilized and frequently overlooked reward. Be sure to be sincere in anything you try and follow up with ideas and issues as they arrive. What motivates one employee may not motivate another. Get to know your employees' interests and it will go a long way toward providing a reward each one finds motivating and satisfying (Lake-Bacon et al. 2013, 19). With just a few simple techniques and little cash, you can motivate and promote positive employee attitudes that lead to good customer service, events, and marketing:

- Learn employee interests, give them autonomy
- Ask the employee what they would like to learn, provide training
- Communicate information so staff doesn't feel left out
- Be sincere in any employee recognition that you do
- Say, "Thank you," or any phrase that tells employees they are doing very good job

MARKETING IS EVERYONE'S JOB

Marketing is the responsibility of your entire staff and the impression your staff makes with customer service (Hakula-Ausperk 2013). First, hire an eager, outgoing person for your marketing position. Then watch as your staff and patrons get excited about the library. Sometimes events need to be simple, and the easiest ideas get customers into the library. Our first event occurred during National Library Week, when we gave prizes away. All the prizes were donated by local businesses that our marketing/events person had contacted in the community. Prizes included gift cards for food and gas, and other donated merchandise. An invite was placed in the library's weekly column of our county newspaper and on our Facebook page. The BCPLD saw its first turnout of over sixty customers just coming into the library registering for door prizes.

As the enthusiasm and positive attitude from the new marketing/events coordinator became contagious, other staff became interested in learning new skills working various events, and promoting the library. The director found herself with a renewed passion for her work and wanted to do more. Even the library's board was thrilled about the library and agreed to fund various projects. It took boldness for the library director and the new staff member to set a proposal before the board requiring a holding fee for a band concert as part of our Big Read programming. However, it does help when your board of trustees are as excited as you are to create new and innovative events. Look for innovative ways to fund your events such as selling t-shirts or concert tickets. It will make the proposal go a little easier with the board if the staff already knows where the money is coming from for special programs. And before we knew it, our events were becoming fundraisers.

LOOKING FOR MONEY IN THE RIGHT PLACES

Our marketing librarian didn't waste any time in applying for grants to enable him to purchase various items the library needed. He applied for the United Way grant, which the library had not received for quite a number of years, the Dot Charitable Committee grant, and Build-A-Bear grant. Look around your area for potential grants to help you meet your library's goals and needs. The marketing/events librarian applied for five grants and received four of them totaling just under $9,654. The library received half of the monies needed to purchase a Smart Board from the United Way aiding us in our outreach to our local schools. The Dot Charitable Committee grant of $3,000 allowed us to purchase a new children's computer for ages two to eight. The Build-A-Bear grant will be used to purchase a second children's computer for ages nine to twelve. These grants allowed us to update our technology and continue our outreach to the public and home schooled learners in the area.

More importantly, grant writing isn't a one- or two-person job; it belongs to the board as well. The BCPLD board members applied for the Illinois Library Construction grant, the Tracy Family Foundation grant and the Gladys Brooks Foundation grant. The first grant contained our plans and specifications to build our new library. The Brooks grant, if received, will be used to purchase our new library site, clear the debris, and fill it with dirt to make it foundation ready.

By now, you are wondering how we have been so successful at obtaining these grants. Here are our suggestions based on what we did:

- Match grants to your program needs. Find grants that will fund specific projects or has certain goals so your request will most likely be funded. There is no guarantee (e.g., don't request computers if the grant says it will not pay for technology).
- Fill out the application and create a budget.
- Follow directions when filing grant applications; don't provide more information than the grant requests.
- Have other people look at your work and double check it.
- Don't just sit and wait to hear back; apply for more grants.
- Don't expect just the marketing person and the director to write grants.

You won't receive all the grants your library applies for, but don't get discouraged. We did not receive the construction grant and, at the time of this article, our library is still waiting hear about the Brooks grant. At this point, I'll say it again: "Don't put all your eggs in one basket." Keep applying for grants and moving forward. For example, our marketing person has applied for two separate grants to fund our children's laptops. While we are waiting to hear about these grants we continue to work identifying funding sources and other grant opportunities to help us build our new 10,000-square-foot library.

TIGHT SPACES: FUNDING, PARTNERING, AND PROGRAMMING

Build your library up. Sell it to the community by meeting customer needs. In addition to finding local community grants, the library needs to continue popular programming and provide new innovative opportunities for the community to come to the library. Finding new donors involves more programming and outreach activities too. Just as you match grants to your programming needs, do the same with potential donors by matching their passion with library projects. Participate in local parades and ask local businesses if they are interested in helping with library sponsored events.

Don't forget to thank your donors and business contributors. Much like motivating staff, recognition for donors is a must and can be done in the form of a simple "Thank you." Gratitude for various donations goes a long way to making the person or business feel like they have made a difference. Choose appropriate forms of appreciation; for example, younger people would love a mention on your website while older donors would prefer something printed. Our library uses thank-you cards and plaques for larger items.

Just because your library is limited by space doesn't mean your programs should be constricted with the same events or certain types of happenings. You've got to get customers to come in to find out what your library is doing. Partner with local organizations and co-host movie night, vendor booths, or a concert. Here are some example fundraising activities:

- Parade entries
- eReader training
- Table fairs
- Movie night with the Y
- Silent auction
- Music concert
- Book signings
- Private tours
- Exhibits
- Hosting meals
- Miniature golf at the library
- Bake sale
- Book club
- Trivia night
- Book sale

- "Sponsor a Book"
- "Buy a Brick"
- Business promotions (e.g., Christmas on Main Street)

Our library works hard to support our local schools since there is not a school library. Our staff attends the YMCA's health fair and the annual school fair. Our booth at these events provides information about our services to teachers, parents, and children. Also, we sign up new card members and hand out bookmarks and library bags so participants can fill them with the various vender goodies. Furthermore, our marketing librarian goes to the school or classroom promoting summer reading and other opportunities for school-age children. He talks about the library, reads a story, and hands out promotional items. Last summer the library sponsored a bookmark contest to kick off the summer reading program, and prizes were awarded to four children.

This last winter our library participated in "Christmas on Main Street" by remaining open past our usual hours the Friday night of the event. We took this opportunity to provide snacks and read Christmas stories, which brought in seventy-five new visitors. Likewise, our library holds a fall and spring book sale. From the proceeds we have purchased new computer chairs and a nice wooden cart for our donated Keurig coffee maker. Additionally, these funds allowed us to secure a band for the Big Read events that I will be discussing in the next section.

One other programming event that is becoming a staple of our outreach is e-reader training sessions. Our patrons receive various e-readers for birthdays or other holidays, and then would like to know how to access and download e-books. Our marketing/events librarian covers the various types of readers in about an hour. Later sessions are geared toward certain readers because we learned from the first session everyone had purchased a different e-reader.

New to the lineup this summer is the Teen Movie Club and the Adult Movie Club. The movies are shown at the Mt. Sterling YMCA once a month. This event includes a different genre every other month and a trip to a blockbuster movie. Discussion and rating sessions are held after the movie event.

In the spring we had a trivia night at the library. Forty-five participants came. Everyone had fun eating donated hotdogs, making jokes, and winning rounds despite the packed room. The library made $450 that night. It just goes to show you that even though your library has limited space you can still hold events and pack them in. Sometimes these events are at your library and other times you will find places around the community to hold the programs. We have utilized the YMCA and the American Legion. These are just a few of the programs we have done to get our name out in the community and prove our value to our county.

TURNING YOUR EVENTS INTO FUNDRAISERS

Silent Auction

Our largest fundraiser to date was the silent auction we had after spring cleaning. Items up for bid included an old record player, records, prints, and books. The event netted $850 just for items we wanted to get rid of—not bad for cleaning out the closet. Also, our local newspapers, the *Democrat Message* (*DM*) and the *Quincy Herald Wig*, provided free publicity about the silent auction. In addition, the events librarian posted the Wig's interview link and information about the auction on our Facebook page.

The Big Read

Our biggest project was the Big Read with the Quincy Public Library. We had agreed to be a part of this reading experience if Quincy Public received the grant from the National Endowment for the Arts. The Big Read is a program intended to encourage reading and revitalize the role of reading in American culture. Quincy was one of seventy-seven nonprofit organizations to receive the grant to provide programming for the Big Read in the fall. BCPLD received some free advertising in exchange for hosting events and purchasing books to hand out. The book we used for the Big Read was *True Grit*, which gave us our country-western theme. Events will kick off in September, and we will hand out copies of the book at the first home football game along with a flyer of our programs for the Big Read through October.

Line Dancing

One event is line dancing with local dance teachers who volunteer their time to teach the dance to be held at the American Legion with Quincy patrons attending the event. The cost to our library is around $5,000 including paying the band and our staff, purchasing 210 books, and printing flyers and T-shirts. Almost all the advertising is handled by Quincy Public with our events mentioned. To help fund this programming of various events our library applied for the Dot Charitable Committee grant to cover the staffing and other costs of the Big Read events. (Dot Foods is a local food distributing business.) At the Fall Festival we will have a booth and promote the big finale, a concert the following week. The Banksters, a blue grass band, will be promoted throughout the area and we only need two hundred people to show up to cover the band and T-shirts cost. Any sales after that goes toward our new building fund. Many local businesses helped to fund the upfront costs for the programs and fundraisers. Our library did have to pay $2,000 for some purchases, which included reserving the band. With the grant, and T-shirt and concert sales, we hope to make a minimum of $1000.

CONCLUSION

Working on staff motivation will help any library improve customer service, which promotes your library and lends to successful fundraising and programs. Give your staff autonomy, communicate with them, and ask them for solutions to old or new problems. Provide educational and training opportunities for your staff and board members. Everyone is responsible for how the community views the library and not just the marketing person.

Hiring an enthusiastic marketing/events librarian will go a long way to help energize the entire staff. Set priorities for your library and communicate with staff any changes in services or policies. Locate local grants and other funding opportunities that help you extend or support your programming. Look for ways to partner with other institutions and businesses in your community. Here are a few tips to make your library successful and turn programs into fundraisers:

- Motivate and energize your staff.
- No one can do it alone; marketing is everyone's job.
- Partner with other institutions to increase your outreach.
- Get involved in community projects.
- Turn events into fundraisers.

Sometimes you have to start internally by building up positive staff attitudes and improving morale so that customer service is at its best. When that is done, branch out and participate with your school, YMCA, and community groups. Look for funding locally and in other sources that have similar goals, such as improving literacy or hosting community events. Above all, don't forget to be appreciative of your staff, as they are your most precious asset. Also, don't forget to be grateful to donors by saying, "Thank you."

SUGGESTED READING

Shanker, Adrian. 2012. "Beyond the Booksales: Fundraising for Public Libraries." *Insight & Outlook*. September 5. Accessed May, 2013. http://www.wolper.com/2012/09/beyond-the-book-sale/.

REFERENCES

Lake-Bacon, Deborah, et al. 2010. *IUPI Library Employee Recognition Program: A Project in Partial Fulfillment of SPEA V522 Human Resource Management in Nonprofit Organizations*, 1–100. Accessed May 30, 2013. http://www.ulib.iupui.edu/files/MasterCompiledHR_Project.pdf.
Hakula-Ausperk, Cathernine. 2013. *Marketing for Everyone.* Webinar moderated by Janet Nelson. (Demco GoWebinar. May 15, 2013).

"99 Ways to Say, 'Very Good.'" Career Lab.Com. Accessed June 7, 2013. http://www.careerlab.com/99ways.htm.

Part Seven

User Services

Chapter Twenty-Six

The After School Café

Amy White

Every library has them. Every librarian knows who they are. The ten-year-old boy who comes into the library every day after school and every Saturday morning to play one particular game on the computer. The nine-year-old girl who stands at the circulation desk but doesn't have a book to check out or a question to ask. Someone's little sister who doesn't want to stop coloring at the table. The twelve-year-old twins who wreak havoc on the puppet collection in the children's section.

They come in after school in the fall, winter, and spring—rain or shine—and stay until the library closes, whether it's 5 p.m. or 8:30 p.m. In the summer, they're waiting by the door for the library to open. They don't read. They don't do their homework. They just need a place to be. They don't want to go home. And they're hungry. Have they always been here? Have there always been this many of them? Is this particular segment of the population growing in number? When did I start noticing them more?

Since I became director of the public library in Lisbon, Iowa, in 1989, the population of the town has grown by a little over 30 percent. Lisbon went from a town where everyone knew or was related to everyone else to a place where new families either moved annually through rental housing and the school system or purchased new homes on the edge of town and commuted to larger towns close by. The transient population was more likely to find the library first, usually living within walking distance of the main street building where the library is located. The addition of movies to check out and computers for public use was of particular interest to this group of patrons.

During times of economic stress, the library serves as a place to pass the time for adults who have lost their jobs and are looking for work. Although this growth has generally been good for the town in terms of a tax base—Lisbon has its own school—not much of it has translated into a thriving downtown. Currently, the main street is dominated by the library (located in an 1875 storefront building), the History Center (across the street in another old storefront), the post office, the bank, and a couple of struggling cafés. For those on foot with little or no spending money, there's not a lot to do except to hang out in the library.

Besides the computers and the DVDs, the addition of wireless Internet access at the library has been another draw for library users of all ages. For several years, Lisbon Community School has participated in the One on One incentive program, in which each student in grades 6–12 is given a laptop computer for the school year. Since many local families don't have Internet access at home, students are able to connect to the library's Wi-Fi. The student computers have somewhat alleviated the waiting in line to use the two designated student computers (almost exclusively used for gaming and Facebook), but simply finding a place to sit—either at the table, on the floor, or in one of two "comfy" chairs is a challenge for the laptop users. More adults are investing in laptops and tablets as well, making space even more valuable. For a library with only 1,200 square feet of space, twelve teenagers with laptops take up a lot of room.

For these young patrons, the library has begun to serve more as a social hub than a place to read or a study area. We're open after 5 p.m. on just one night a week, and that is a popular time to visit the library. We noticed that many kids were staying through the dinner hour, parked in the library from the time school was out until the library closed at 8:30 p.m. They either don't want to or can't go home after school. In most cases, there isn't an adult at home, and in other cases, the adult at home is sleeping because he works at night or is otherwise not receptive to having kids around. Kids are noisy. They want and need to talk to other kids. The YouTube videos that they are watching on their laptops (with headphones) are extremely hilarious and need to be shared with someone their age.

But a small library has to be shared by everyone in the community, and sometimes the loud presence of the preteen crowd is intimidating to parents with young children or to older library patrons. We wanted to encourage this underserved population of children ages 9–13 to use the library (although sometimes we wondered why) but had to keep the library available to others and more like—well, a library.

Luckily for us, a resource for more space was under our noses. The rear door of our building is attached to the Southeast Linn Community Center, which houses the county's food pantry and offers congregate meals and deliveries to senior citizens. They also accept donations of clothing to sort and give away to anyone who needs them. Their activities are done by 3 p.m., and the building sits empty until groups come in to play cards or hold meetings in the evenings.

What if we extended the library into the congregate dining room for an after school program that featured snacks and games? Besides having plenty of tables and chairs, the community center also has wireless Internet access and, being a modern building, many more electrical outlets to plug in laptops. Because a long hallway divides the dining room from the library back door, noise is not an issue. There are monthly and weekly donations of perishable and nonperishable food, enough to share with hungry preteens. And, perhaps most importantly, there was a qualified person who was willing and available to supervise the program.

The director of the community center was receptive to the idea of serving youth, but was initially concerned about liability issues and whether or not he would have to conform to daycare regulations. He and I met with a community center in nearby Cedar Rapids that was providing a similar program for after school students and we had many of our questions answered. We were under no obligation to provide daycare or conform to daycare regulations. The space was going to be used no differently than the space in the library— it was merely an extension of that space. Since we already had the space, and the community center could get food through their regular donors, the only expense would be paying someone to develop and supervise the program. The easiest solution to the question of who would hire and pay the program supervisor was to make it a partnership between the community center and the library. The community center could do the hiring and take advantage of grants from social services organizations, and the library could request and provide some funding from the city.

So far, so good. The kids love it. We started up the After School Café on Wednesdays and expanded after a few months to include Mondays. The plan is to continue during the summer months and to serve lunch and play social games like Bingo. One of our library's board members also serves on the local arts council and convinced them to provide artists and supplies for monthly workshops. Because the students in the program are not typically involved in the programs offered by the town's parks and recreation board due to lack of support or transportation, we are hoping that that board will provide some activities on site as well.

Perhaps the most important element of our success has been the enthusiasm and kindness of the program supervisor. I highly recommend paying a caring, accepting, kid-friendly individual in this role and not just relying on volunteers. Volunteers can definitely be utilized, but our emphasis is that this is an educational program offered as an extension of the library, and this job should be seen as that of a social services professional.

Already there have been success stories of children finding out about services offered by the community center—pool passes, free clothes at the Clothing Closet (stocked by donations), school supplies—and have confided in the program supervisor about conditions at home. The community center is pleased to include more active programming for children because they bring in more families to the center and spread awareness of services. Children who are struggling socially in school find friends at the library and at the After School Cafe.

Although ours was a smooth startup with several months of success under our belts, I can imagine that not all libraries have the resources or support that we found. We were lucky to have a community center, but other libraries have partnered with churches, schools, or other public or private institutions. You must have the approval of your staff, library board, and city council, and they all need to be in on the plans from the beginning, along with the partnering space. I initially called a meeting about the possibility of an after school program and invited our city administrator, parks and recreation director, the director and staff of the community center, and our mayor.

You may be able to think of more representatives that need to be included—it's important not to leave any group out that may want to be involved. We met with overwhelming approval and support, but have also fielded a few complaints. Why does the library have to provide this service? Isn't this the responsibility of the parents? Is it our mission (or the city's, or the school's, or the taxpayers' mission) to fill the needs of someone else's children? It depends on how you look at it. It may be a parent's job to teach their children responsibility, but it's not my job as a public servant to teach responsibility to parents. My job is to serve the needs of the community. We know that children who are supported and fed do better in school and in life. Their failure will not serve as a lesson for their parents. It is the mission of everyone in any town to make sure that the basic needs of its children are met.

Chapter Twenty-Seven

Instructional Design and the Public Librarian

Melissa Cornwell

With technology constantly changing and becoming accessible, public librarians have to teach their library users not only how to find and use information but also how to use the technology to find the information. When you begin a workshop or other instructional session, ask yourself these questions:

- First ask "What is the challenge that my library users face? How can I help them to meet it?" (Booth 2011).
- "What questions are most common from customers? What is an obvious need in my community?" (Groene-Nieto 2013). Anticipating the needs of your community always involves a certain amount of risk but your library users will appreciate your attempts.
- Then consider yourself, the educator, and your skills. "What are you interested in teaching?" (Groene-Nieto 2013).
- "Are there knowledge, skills, or attitudes that you as the librarian need to acquire?" (Booth 2011).
- Do you have the skills to teach this workshop or do any of your coworkers? If not, how can you get the training for this kind of instruction?
- "What resources can I review and reuse to assist me with this project?" (Booth 2011).
- Assuming you do have the skills to explain about e-readers, you can then consider some questions about your audience; for instance, What knowledge do you assume your users already have?
- "What knowledge do I require of my library users in order for the material to be useful?" (Booth 2011).

- Does your workshop require that your library patrons have basic computer skills or know how to connect to the Internet?
- Always clearly list any prerequisites your audience will need to have before they can attend your workshop. The next step is to look at the context in which you will present your material. Where will you teach this? Do you have the technology available to give this kind of workshop in your library?
- Above all, ask, "What do I know about the instructional environment, and how can it be shaped to create a positive learning experience?" (Booth 2011).

LESSON PLANS

The final component to consider is the content, and you can focus on this when you create a lesson plan. Although lesson plans have primarily been used in education, they can also help serve public librarians to collect their thoughts and organize what should go into a workshop or instruction session. The basic lesson plan includes the following components:

- a description or overview
- learning outcomes
- an outline
- an assessment

The description gives information on the workshop or session such as how long it will take, who your audience will be, the equipment your class will require, the location for the session, and what you will be teaching; you will also include any prerequisites your library users will need to have before they can participate in your session or workshop.

LEARNING OUTCOMES

Learning outcomes are perhaps the most important part of building a lesson plan and are defined as what learners will know or be able to do as a result of your instructional session or workshop (Wong 2013).

You start by "examining the type of knowledge learners will build during the interaction" in order to define your goals (Booth 2011); your goals are what skills or concepts you hope your library users will know by the time they leave your workshop. You already started forming your goals in your mind when you started reflecting on your workshop but the overall best question to ask is "What do I hope to achieve in this interaction?" (Booth 2011).

Learning outcomes must be learner-focused and ability-focused; they must also be specific and measurable (Wong 2013). What do I mean by measurable? When learning outcomes are measurable, it means that you are able to evaluate to see if your library users did in fact learn the concepts you were teaching them.

A good structure for learning outcomes is to put a verb phrase in the outcome. For example, by the end of the workshop, library users will be able to navigate the e-book provider's catalog in order to download e-books for offline reading. Always start with learners (or students or library users). The following formula is a good template to use when building learning outcomes: "'Library users will be able to' + verb phrase + 'in order to' + why" (Wong 2013).

I've also seen other librarians create learning outcomes (or objectives) by just saying, "At the end of the class the student will," and then only have the verb phrase. Here's an example: "At the end of the class, the student will know how to work an e-reader."

Find whatever method works best for you to create these learning outcomes depending on the needs of your staff and library users. After you've created your learning outcomes, you need to look at how you will outline your workshop or instructional session.

- What kind of instructional session are you doing?
- How will you present your content?
- What activities will you have?
- Will it have more lecture or more hands-on work?

ACTIVE LEARNING

When giving workshops at the Camargo Township District Library in Villa Grove, Illinois, I tried to incorporate both lectures and active learning as it worked the best for my library users when they were trying to learn new technology.

But what is active learning? "Active learning describes techniques that engage audiences and invite them to interact meaningfully rather than passively" (Booth 2011). I've always found it easier to teach technology by interacting with it than just lecturing on it.

For instance, when giving the workshop on e-readers, I encouraged my library users to bring their devices with them, and I built time into the lesson plan for them to engage with their devices and to ask me any questions they had. You can have this be what the whole workshop will be about or you can build in some time for a lecture.

From personal experience teaching technology, I have found that a simulation is the best kind of lecture. I set up my computer, turned on the projector, and then proceeded to show my library users step-by-step how to download e-books from the library. In between different stages, I had my library users do the actual step with their own devices, and after they'd completed that step, I proceeded to the next. If a library user doesn't have a device, I still ask them if they understand the steps I've taught, and I might ask one of the other participants to share their device.

TIMING

Once you know how you are going to teach your content and in what stages, put those stages in your outline. You'll want to break out each stage in terms of the time you think it will take to complete it.

Always start with stating the time it will take you to prepare for the class and then spend that amount of time. For instance, you might need thirty minutes before the workshop starts to set up the computer and the projector, set up chairs and tables, or print out any handouts you want to give to your participants.

Next, you move on to the introduction; you might take five to ten minutes to introduce yourself and what you'll be teaching in the workshop. After the introduction, break your topic down into subjects.

- Your first subject might be an introduction and simulation of how to access and navigate the library's e-book provider, which is followed by your participants actively learning the concept by doing it on their own devices. You may allot twenty minutes for the first subject.
- Looking at your next subject, you do the introduction and simulation, again followed by an activity, and you give yourself twenty minutes again.
- Repeat this process for as many times as you need until you've covered all of your subjects.
- The amount of time you give each subject obviously depends on how much time you have for the instructional session. I don't recommend covering more than three subjects in any given instructional session as it may overwhelm your participants.
- After listing your subjects and activities, you should have time allotted for a conclusion to the workshop where your participants can ask you questions before the workshop ends.

ASSESSING YOUR WORKSHOP

After you've built your outline, you then need to think of a way to assess (or evaluate) your workshop to see if your learners (or library users) did indeed learn the concepts you were trying to teach.

You will want to make sure that the learning outcomes were met and that your library users are at least somewhat confident in their abilities with the new knowledge before they leave your workshop. Assessment is also a good way to gather feedback on your workshop so that you will know what worked and what didn't for the next time you give the workshop.

Much of the assessment you will do will probably be through observing your participants as they go through the workshop. As you go through the workshop, do your library users seem to understand what you're teaching? A good way to do this is to teach a concept and then ask your library users if they have any questions; let them know that there are no stupid questions and they will appreciate your willingness to help them.

Another form of assessment might be to give a survey at the end of the class to see how your library users felt about the workshop; you could also give a few questions to ask about the concepts you taught. If you taught a skill and you noticed that your library users are still having trouble with that skill, you could build in an activity that lets them work with the challenging concept more thoroughly in future instructional sessions.

Finally, make it clear to your library users that you are there to help them and that they can follow up with your any time after the workshop if they still have questions.

HANDOUTS

In addition to the lesson plan, you will also need to create a handout to give your library users. Always, always have a handout to give out in your instructional session as it will help to reinforce the concepts you are teaching.

Make the handout simple to follow and include information on the concepts you will teach; even giving a brief outline of what you will be teaching will help your library users to follow along. As you prepare your lesson plan for your instructional session, you should also be preparing your handout.

You can also incorporate handouts into your instructional session in the form of worksheets or guides. When I gave workshops on e-readers and e-books to my library users at the Camargo Township District Library, I had also made guides for the step-by-step process of getting e-books through our e-book provider. I made the guides using a combination of both text and screenshots, and my library users loved the screenshots as it helped them to follow along with my simulation and they could take notes. Always include both text and images when possible as this will make your content more accessible for your library users (especially if you want to put your guides on your library website).

In this section, I have tried to give a very brief overview of the instructional design process and the phases that go into designing a workshop or any other instructional session. There are several authors who have written excellent books and training materials should you want to pursue the topic of instructional design further.

ITERATIVE LESSON DESIGN

While working at the Camargo Township District Library in Villa Grove, Illinois, I could not find any methods for creating workshops that seemed to work for a public library. Then, I found the Iterative Lesson Design plan.

The Iterative Lesson Design was first created by two public librarians who work in the Community Technology Center at the Denver Public Library: Simone Groene-Nieto and Nate Stone. It is an instructional design model that can be adapted by any library, regardless of size, for teaching technology to both library users and staff.

ITERATIVE LESSON DESIGN CYCLE

"Design is iterative—it informs itself in an ongoing cycle. A cycle of reflection and adaptability is built into the instructional design approach, while evaluation and feedback revise the facilitation of learning" (Booth 2011). The iterative lesson design focuses on five steps:

1. play
2. write
3. edit
4. teach
5. evaluate

The Iterative Lesson Design method is excellent whether you need to train your staff on new technology or explore it for a patron's sake, and there are a couple of options on how to use it to teach technology to your staff.

• The first option is to have one librarian on the team learn the technology and then teach it to the rest of the staff using the Iterative Lesson Design cycle.

- The other option would be to have the staff go through the Iterative Lesson Design cycle together, instead of just one librarian learning the process and then teaching it to their coworkers.
- After the staff has learned the technology, you can then use the Iterative Lesson Design plan to build instructional sessions for your library users.

STEP 1: PLAY

For any new technology that is not previously learned, a librarian would come to the material as a learner (Groene-Nieto 2013). There is no way that you would be a master of a technology straight away; you will have to play around with it first. However, by starting out with a new technology, you can put yourself in the learner's role and explore the technology as a beginner would (this will help you when you start to build the lesson plans for your workshops).

First, you should familiarize yourself with the topic or tool and explore other training materials already out there from other libraries (Groene-Nieto 2013). If you know of a library that has materials online, ask for permission to adapt the materials to your own library's situation. Use these materials to train yourself on the device and use Google to search for online tutorials.

Remember to fully engage with the technology in order to learn its ins and outs. An important part of this step is to record the steps you took in learning how to use the device or tool; record any problems you encountered and make note of them as you begin designing your workshop's lesson plan as your participants will likely have had similar problems (Groene-Nieto 2013).

STEP 2: WRITE

This step is about actually writing out a lesson plan for your workshop or instructional session. You first need to write learning objectives for your library users (Groene-Nieto 2013). What do you want them to learn from your workshop? What should they be able to do when they leave your workshop?

Then, create and order topics to match your learning outcomes and fill in the topic content in a session outline (Groene-Nieto 2013). The goal of the writing step is to "aim for project-based lessons with multiple activities" (Groene-Nieto 2013). Examples of these activities include demos, solo activities, or group tasks (Groene-Nieto 2013). Mainly, look at how you want your users to interact with the device and with each other.

Another key component is the comprehension check for each topic, which includes a question and answer and another activity for your users to try out their new knowledge (Groene-Nieto 2013). The comprehension checks are a great way to assess if your participants are learning the concepts you are teaching throughout the workshop.

STEP 3: EDIT

Once you have written the lesson plan, it's time to get some feedback from your co-workers. Since they also interact with the library users on a daily basis, they will be able to help you decide if your lesson plan is best meeting the needs of your library users. By making the evaluation of the lesson plans a group effort, your colleagues will also feel like a part of the process (Groene-Nieto 2013).

Edit your lesson plan based on the decisions you've made with your colleagues. You should also consult your own feelings (Groene-Nieto 2013). Do you feel that the lesson plan will work?

STEP 4: TEACH

Once you have agreed on the lesson plan, it's time to teach it. Let the lesson plan be your guide but don't be afraid to be flexible and change things in the classroom to suit the needs of your participants.

STEP 5: EVALUATE

The main purpose of this step is to get feedback. After you've taught the instructional session, you should evaluate your participants to make sure they've understood the concepts. See if they have any lingering questions, and see how effective your instructional session was. You can get input from the students themselves and also from surveys, in-class comments, or even from just simple observation (Groene-Nieto 2013).

After you've got feedback, it's time to edit your instructional session for the next time you teach it. Run your lesson plan by your family or friends and ask them for their input (Groene-Nieto 2013). Take your time on editing the lesson plan, and figure out what subjects and activities were the most beneficial and which ones were not.

STEP 6: TEACH

Have another librarian teach the next instructional session as "different people bring different methods of teaching" (Groene-Nieto 2013). Always remember to focus on the end goal, which is the achievement of the learning outcomes.

CONCLUSION

While I was writing this chapter, the Illinois State Library has made it a requirement for public libraries in Illinois to participate in the Illinois Edge Initiative in order to qualify for a state grant.

What is the Edge Initiative? The Edge Initiative is "a management and leadership tool for public libraries. It provides a snapshot of the library's current public technology services along with steps to make improvements and better serve communities" (About the Edge Initiative 2014).

The Edge Initiative allows public libraries to assess their community needs for technology and then helps them to create strategies for meeting those needs. Participation in the Edge Initiative is free and could be of some use in helping those small and rural public libraries that do not have staff members or the budget to assess the technology needs of their community.

In this chapter, I have looked at the general components of an instructional session and a lesson plan. I've also looked at the Iterative Lesson Design as an approach coming out of a public library on how to teach about technology. If you are simply developing a workshop to train your staff and not just teach your library users, the information in this chapter will still help you to develop those training materials.

REFERENCES

"About the Edge Initiative." 2014. *Illinois EDGE Initiative Resource Page.* March 19. http:// www.finditillinois.org/edge/Resource-Page.html (accessed February 23, 2014).

Booth, Char. 2011. *Reflective Teaching, Effective Learning: Instructional Literacy for Library Educators.* Chicago: American Library Association.

Groene-Nieto, Simone. 2013."Play, Write, Edit Teach." Champaign, IL: Graduate School of Library and Information Science, April 24.

Wong, Melissa. "Learning Outcomes." 2013. Champaign, Illinois: Graduate School of Library and Information Science, February 6.

Chapter Twenty-Eight

Library Services for Users in Their Twenties and Thirties

Samantha C. Helmick

Echo boomers, also referred to as millennials or generation Y, represent a significant demographic of potential library users. Their unique characteristics have been described as more open and culturally tolerant, proficient in information retrieval, and perpetually connected to the digital world. The echo boom group constitutes the largest population growth since the baby boom following World War II and is the first authentically emerged tribe of digital natives.

For the purposes of this discussion, echo boomers are defined as the nearly 86 million Americans born between 1982 and 1995, who share attributes which may not be conducive to initial library engagement:

- About 15 percent of echo boomers between the ages of nineteen and twenty-five are married in comparison to 65 percent of baby boomers at that age.
- Studies indicate that echo boomers purchase more books than all previous generations and account for approximately one-third of the bookselling market.
- Echo boomers are opting out of having children or waiting significantly longer than their parents to begin a family.
- Thirty percent of echo boomers have obtained a four-year degree, which makes them the most educated generation in American history.
- Nearly 70 percent of echo boomers are relocating from their birthplaces often to more urban areas.

The generational shift in values and practices has excluded many library services from the life of a typical echo boomer. As an example, if an echo boomer waits to start a family until their mid to late thirties, the library may not see them for nearly two decades once they leave the Young Adult department. The time between obtaining their driver's license and returning for their child's first storytime is expanding. Tech-savvy echo boomers, proficient in obtaining information and entertainment through digital means, may not see the inherent value of resources and materials available with a library card. The nomadic lifestyle of echo boomers, who frequently choose where to live before deciding their profession, decreases the numbers of lifelong and intergenerational library membership (Wasserman 2011).

Similar to the push for young adult library services in the late 1980s and early 1990s, libraries are perceiving the need for focused services geared to echo boomers. Public and academic librarians are championing for services dedicated to engage to those in their twenties and thirties. Librarians are embarking on programming for the user group that professional consensus may eventually refer to as New Adults (O'Connor 2012, 26). However, this uncharted territory has yet to meet mainstream practices of librarianship or enter the dialogue of major information technology organizations.

For the sake of sustainability and equitable access, emerging trailblazers are rising from the field to create library space for echo boomers. The Burlington Public Library in Burlington, Iowa, began a monthly Adults After Hours series of programs that introduced popular culture events to the rural community. Well attended events include a *Doctor Who* gathering and co-splay, *Big Bang Theory* Trivia Night, Bollywood Film Fest with a Chaat recipe exchange, and an Apocalypse Party on December 21, 2012, the end of the Mayan calendar. The eschatological event organically became an end-of-the-world date night at the library and received statewide attention from new outlets.

Rather than advertise Adults After Hours specifically to the twenties and thirties in their population, the library staff use outreach to market their services to echo boomers. Information tech librarians furnish their services to local employment agencies for online application and resume skills and share flyers about echo boom services. The outreach librarian speaks at community groups such as Rotary, Kiwanis International, Young Professionals, and Optimist Club to poach potential library echo boom users. Adapting the tactics used for attracting tweens and teens through school visits is also successful when applied to echo boomers during lunch and learn presentations, employee meetings outreach, and by volunteer associations. Posters are distributed to area bars and gyms to catch the age range the library is seeking to engage. Social media is another primary resource for informing echo boomers about library happenings.

The Birmingham Public Library System in Alabama has a "twenties" and "thirties" advisory board. Their members have collaborated on library concerts, I Heart the '90s events, mixology classes, mini golf in the library stacks, literacy-themed pub crawls, and an adult spelling bee. A great advantage to Birmingham's approach as an echo boomer advisory board is their voice among the electorate. Echo boomers comprise nearly one-third of the United States' voting population. Engaging this group of constituents is crucial for continued support of tax-funded library services throughout the nation (Pew 2013, 36).

Ohio State University Library along with many other academic information centers are building open source services and interactive hackathons. These variations on content manipulation and data creation range from new students forming teams to complete new projects in a twenty-four-hour timeframe to universities participating in Open Data Day as they encourage students around the world to write applications, liberate data, create visualizations, and publish analyses using open public information. Echo boomers are more pragmatic than previous generations, but they are deeply invested in open access to the Internet and transparency in government. Hackathons and open data classes show support for echo boomers' interests and their adoption of open information policies by the world's local, regional, and national governments.

Open data classes like CoderDojo at the Iowa City Public Library in Iowa City, Iowa, help young people learn how to code, develop websites, apps, programs, and games. Their content is hosted through the public library as an evolved digital preservation project for the community and identifies library users as content producers as well as consumers. One of the benefits of open source information is that it can be utilized by patrons in a rural library in Iowa or in an urban information center in New York. Open Book Hack Weekend at the New York Public Library, in New York, New York, joins forces with NYPL Labs, Readium Foundation, O'Reilly Media, Perseus Books, Hypothes.is, Google, and Datalogics for digital book open source and content development based on HTML5, EPUB, and the Open Web Platform.

New York library users are asked to organize teams of developers and register ideas for software and content projects to pursue a weekend of creative app, service, and content hacks to improve the future of digital books and advance open source building blocks for authors, designers, publishers, booksellers, and readers. As the walls between content consumer, producer, and distributor begin to crumble, libraries can play a significant role in the access amplification through their collaboration with echo boomer ethics, ideals, and skill sets.

In the past, echo boomers have been marketed for their consumer power. Libraries embraced the collection pitches of "try it before you buy it" and implemented library value calculators that allow users to see how much money they saved from checking out materials rather than buying them. With the availability of economic software and data, echo boomers are able to develop content, mash, and adapt information and dispense their work with considerable ease. Potential users in their twenties and thirties consider libraries as repositories of the community zeitgeist, which includes the development of a collection solely created by the service area. Academic libraries have been gaining relevancy with their twenty- and thirtysomething users as they provide space for web portfolios, resumes and projects for students. Public libraries are picking up this momentum (Dwyer 2012).

Makerspaces are part of the library movement to capture a generation of designers, tinkerers, and inventors. Science, Technology, Engineering, and Mathematics (STEM) programs are becoming normative additions to book clubs and crafternoons, which support a workforce relying heavily on these fields for the future. By 2018, 20 percent of jobs in the United States' economy will require a degree within the STEM fields. Workshops on coding, copyright, and design-oriented innovations are cropping up for teens and echo boomers. Resources such as 3-D printers and software applications for 2-D and 3-D computer-aided design are becoming obtainable within library budgets and echo boomers are visiting for edutainment (Robertson and Jones 2012, 15).

London's Barbican Music Library is expanding on the idea of library users as content creators to connect with echo boomers. The Barbican Music Library won the 2014 International Association of Music Libraries (IAML) Excellence Award for Music Libraries and the Award for Outstanding Personal Contribution in part for their innovative access to user-created content. Their Unsigned London initiative permits musicians who are not signed to a record label to place their work in the library's circulating collection. This service gives the artists exposure and allows the community to discovery local influences and genres. The underground element of the collection has attracted many echo boomers who are keen to uncover emerging media and ally with other artists. While the Barbican Music Library has not created an official makerspace, they do provide two practice pianos for users on which they can learn and compose while at the library (Foertsch 2013, 17).

Embracing lifelong education rather than lifelong learning may sound like a play on semantics, but the libraries that are applying passive programming and active services to assist self-paced experiences for their users are popular. Education is an easy buy-in for most current and potential library users. Libraries are learning from the echo boomer generation that connectivity, integration, and fun makes the memory sticky and enhances education. Perhaps this is why library programs that ask the participants to share ideas that are crowd-pleasing to echo boomer patrons. Events like Movieokie at the Oak Park Public Library in Oak Park, Illinois, asks attendees to recreate their favorite movie scenes—karaoke style—on a monitor. Library's Adult Lego clubs and video game tournaments are simply a reflection of a generation that uses Pecha Kucha at the bar and the board room or board games as part of professional development (Ellin 2014, 63).

The University of Manchester in the United Kingdom has tapped into the eagerness of echo boomers to crowd source ideas with their Eureka: Library Innovation Challenge. By taking the academic focus group or usability study into the twenty-first century, the University of Manchester invites their students to submit ideas to make their library experience richer or more convenient to them. Some of the winning ideas have included a traffic light system to indicate when a study space was free and a "Refresh Zone" where students can rest and recharge their batteries. Other quick-win suggestions have been a mobile app allowing users to see where books are shelved using a satnav-style display and even a robot that retrieves items for faculty and students. The cooperation between echo boomers and library professionals has enhanced library services, established a long-term relationship between students and their academic institution, and given the University of Manchester international promotion.

Echo boomers are too large of a group for libraries to ignore. They are a major influencer of scholarly precepts and global politics. Echo boomers are the founders of the startup revolution and crave meaning through contribution. Libraries and echo boomers have much to offer each other. Cultural and economic factors make information access and library services crucial to the echo boomer lifestyle:

- The retirement rate in the United States is at a twenty-three-year low, which blocks echo boomer movement into the job market.
- Echo boomers have the highest turnover employment rate of any generation with an average tenure of 1.5 years.
- A shift in perception shows that echo boomers value time and job satisfaction over money.
- The American job market is rife with tech inefficiency and lacking in tools readily available to echo boomers during their college experience.

Echo boomers cannot afford to let libraries drop services such as resume help and interview prep from their regular programming. Libraries extend prime real estate for the communal start-up business market and a space for remote interviews. On-going job searching and renewal of marketable skills are library service staples that support the rapid career changes of the echo boomer generation. A library's partnership with (or substitute for) state employment agencies, gives it the advantage of helping employers and job seekers from both ends of a professional spectrum to connect, converse, and collaborate.

Recruitment fairs and job-seeking library guides are growing in popularity in British public libraries, but have been trending in American libraries for several years. The City of Manchester Council has created physical and online spaces for young people, single parents, and differently abled groups to utilize the library for mutual professional support. A pattern in successful career information services for libraries has been the synergistic approach through group programs. Career-advice coffee klatches and work clubs are just some of the ways that echo boomers can combine efforts, and they are well received in both the United Kingdom and United States.

Echo boomers' focus on the quality of life has opened the door for experience programming in libraries. Twenty years ago, those in their twenties and thirties would visit the library and check out a book of recipes. Five to ten years ago, "twenties" and "thirties" would copy the recipe out of the book or print an online recipe during a library visit. Today, twenties and thirties like to experience cooking the recipe at the library with a group of their peers. For the same reason Betty Crocker asks the consumer to add the eggs to a cake mix, libraries are morphing into learning annexes. The quality of knowledge gained is defined by methodology. The power of communal education and hands-on learning leaves a lasting impression with echo boomers.

Life skills programming has shown itself to be fruitful in public libraries across the country. Health certification in cardiopulmonary resuscitation and emergency first aid are offered at the Way Public Library in Perrysburg, Ohio. Working with their county fire division and the American Heart Association has allowed their library to open life-saving training to library users. The series has expanded to Community Emergency Response Training (CERT) through their local division of Homeland Security, safety procedures for babysitters, and basic life support for family members of a home health care patient.

The Pierce County Library System in Tocoma, Washington, conducts classes on planning for college, buying a first car, acquiring credit, mortgaging a home, studying for the SAT, and exploring alternatives to college, such as apprenticeships. Each event is hosted at the library and features community members that present personalized tips and tricks for life decisions. This library programming style reaches all audiences and can be easily modified for senior, teen, and youth interests.

Libraries in the United Kingdom have established experience-based programming that appeals to twenty- and thirtysomethings. The Guildhall Library in Aldermanbury, London, has a series of hands-on lectures during the lunch hour. Their lunch-and-learn lectures permit the employees in London's banking district to take in the culture and history of the city and interact with amazing displays that include Shakespeare's first folio and one of the few known copies of the Magna Carta in existence. This opportunity is recreated by libraries in conjunction with museums and the local historical society to make meaningful experiences for library users who have an interest in the past, present, and future of their community.

Primary services that teach basic digital skills will always be necessary at the library, advocating for users ranging in socioeconomic backgrounds. While echo boomers have never lived in a world without the Internet, they are susceptible to the pitfalls of the information age and the complications of the digital divide. It could be argued that the stakes are higher for echo boomers, as they navigate their employment data, health information, and news through digital means; handle the rapid release schedules of operating systems and browsers; and acclimate to growing lists of media types and mobile capabilities of their day-to-day data. Echo boomers are described as incredible multitaskers. This translates into more information and platforms for distraction.

The onus of librarians and information specialists is to vigilantly update their knowledge in order to help users understand and analyze the enormity of data. Echo boomers need the library's help when Firefox updates automatically, they register on the Affordable Care Act site, or locate their district representative to express how much the library does for their community. A case for services for adults by any name, echo boomers, millennials, New Adults, or generation Y, should be made because generally it is not made. Library services for adults are assumed, which can leave them vulnerable to devaluation and cuts. Without the assessments of adult programming from qualitative and quantitate data it can be difficult to justify services to the echo boomer user demographic to outside groups. Without the financial, social, and political support of echo boomers, libraries will have less resources to serve users that are incapable of voting for library growth.

Methods to meet this obligation to echo boomers and to engage twenties and thirties in meaningful library relationships include the following:

- Invest library staff time into echo boomer community groups and objectives before introducing library services and selling points to create genuine relationships between the library and its potential user base.
- Take risks to include nontraditional or unorthodox events in the library's roster to entice echo boomers to visit and learn more about services.
- Treat each interaction as a vote lost or gained for library services. Be prepared and willing to articulate the need for echo boom library services.
- Approach reference as an experience that involves give and take between the librarian and the library user. Obtain solutions together like a temporary team.
- Embrace outreach through programming and online services to accommodate the changeable working hours on the echo boomer job force and schedule.

Adult library services do make a community greater, according to Gregory Currie, a professor of philosophy at the University of Nottingham; compelling evidence shows that adults are morally and socially better for reading. Reading gives echo boomers a stronger ability to understand others as well as empathize and comprehend various world perspectives. Values the library community ascribe to reading programs and after-school groups relate to the social causes for echo boomers. Library users can benefit from cognitive interaction and civic engagement at any age. A 2009 study at the University of Toronto reported higher levels of cognitive philosophy in adults that read books for life-long education or even pleasure. Literate activities and programs for those in their twenties and thirties can be safe, productive ways to create bonds with the wider community and gain better understanding of library services (Emanuel 2013, 25).

At this time, the significance of young adult and adult literacy is less axiomatic than early literacy, but some of the most obvious benefits of echo boomers literacy are the development of natural abilities, improved knowledge, increase in adaptability to change, self-fulfillment, and keeping consistently engaged to prevent intellectual atrophy. An echo boomer library program or service may superficially seem like an additional or unnecessary perk in an atmosphere that already promotes free access, free assistance, and free information. However, each event displays the lifelong education commitment of the community, showcases the public library in an attractive light for voters and its appropriateness to a significant fraction of our culture. Echo boomer library service is an investment toward a more sustainable future for libraries and an access privileged citizenry.

REFERENCES

Dwyer, Liz. 2012. "Generation Read: Millennials Buy More Books Than Everybody Else." *Good.is.* August 17. http://www.good.is/posts/generation-read-millennials-buy-more-books-than-everybody-else.

Ellin, Abby. 2014. "How Their World Makes Sense to Them." *Psychology Today* 47, no. 2 (March/April 2014): 63.

Emanuel, Jenny. 2013. "Digital Native Librarians, Technology Skills, and Their Relationship with Technology." *Information Technology & Libraries.* 32, no. 3 (September 2013): 20–33.

Foertsch, Andrea. 2013. "Innovation in Manufacturing: Makerspaces." *Mass Development.* April 2013. http://ampitupma.com/pdf/makerspacesreport_april2013.pdf.

O'Connor, Lisa, and Julie VanHoose. 2012. "What They Didn't Tell Me in Library School Is That Students Don't Care about Learning to Use the Library." *Reference & User Services Quarterly* 52, no. 1 (Fall 2012): 26–27.

Pew Research Center for the People and the Press. 2013. "Millennials' Lukewarm Support for Health Care Bills." Pewresearch.org. February 4. http://www.pewresearch.org/2010/02/04/millennials-lukewarm-support-for-health-care-bills/.

Robertson, Michael J., and James G. Jones. 2012. "Exploring Academic Library Users' Preferences of Delivery Methods for Library Instruction." *Reference & User Services Quarterly* 48, no. 3 (Spring): 259–69.

Wasserman, Todd. 2011. "LinkedIn Edges Out Want Ads as Job Search Tool for Millennials." *Mashable.com*. April 5. http://mashable.com/2013/04/05/linkedin-want-ads/.

Chapter Twenty-Nine

Market Research

A Vital Tool for the Survival of Public Libraries

Brian A. Reynolds

Public libraries across the nation are suffering severe budget cutbacks. Market research can and will reduce the vulnerability of public libraries and promote their long-term survival. This article provides an overview of marketing, what it is and isn't, in a public library context, and a case study involving the public library I used to direct, is included.

MARKETING IS NOT PUBLICITY

Marketing is often defined as publicity or advertising but is much more than that. In a public library setting, market research builds loyal customers, recruits new customers, and engages everyone else both directly and indirectly.

Public libraries need revenues that are higher, more diverse, and more dependable. This often means winning library funding elections/referenda. So, getting library customers and supporters to support increased library funding (whether as a budget priority or in a funding election) requires getting the entire community involved and committed, not just library users.

Marketing is research about creating viable products and services. In a public library setting, marketing requires querying three distinct groups:

- existing customers
- potential customers
- potential supporters who won't necessarily become customers

For current and potential customers, market research allows staff to create and sustain a better fit between community needs/priorities and the public library's service array. Market research examines customers in niches, also called segments or clusters. Most private businesses and some public agencies perform similar market research and community outreach. Public libraries must also engage in these activities with vigor and with an eye toward survival in the long term.

MARKET RESEARCH CHALLENGES

In troubled times, many people retreat to the old, trusted ways, not new ways. So, even though market research in public libraries is a growing trend, barriers remain as staff and supporters can be resistant to change.

A practical definition for marketing is this: the complex series of activities involved in creating products and services, promoting their existence and attributes, and making them physically available to identified target buyers. In public library terms, this involves identifying and acting upon the information needs and priorities of current and potential customers. Most importantly, what are the needs and priorities of non-customers (residents who vote and pay taxes) that the library might address both directly and indirectly to elicit these folks' support?

Selling a discretionary service that depends upon community support and finite tax revenues is not easy. Selling support for a public agency that is not used by about half of a community is even more a challenge. Proper "marketing" creates products and services that minimize the effort needed to "sell."

Staff experience and intuition are important but inadequate by themselves. Market research is useful in many ways:

- It is collected scientifically, by experts trained to do it.
- It queries both current and potential customers.
- It involves community leaders who may never become a library customer but whose advocacy and moral support matter.
- It yields new information and often counterintuitive ideas.
- It suggests ways to enhance existing services, create new services, and diminish current services that are a poor investment.
- It assures staff that new, different tasks can be accomplished without increasing workload.

This last bullet is vital: proper market research takes into account staff opinions, morale, and workload. Done with forethought, the changes proposed to staff will sell themselves, at least to early adapters within the staff. No program of change as contemplated in this article will be successful without getting support from a critical mass of staff.

Market research offers many benefits, some of which are listed below:

- Learn how to better serve existing customers.
- Attract new customers without overburdening limited resources.
- Engage and enthuse non-customers who might provide advocacy, fund raising, volunteerism, and enhanced connections between the library and community individuals, groups, businesses, and agencies.
- Better deploy staff and other resources at individual branch library locations.
- Create new services/enhance existing services while diminishing/eliminating wasteful or obsolete services, using scientific inputs and measureable outputs/outcomes.
- Empower library support groups such as Friends of the Library and a Library Foundation.
- Identify and recruit library Super Supporters.

The following list describes some built-in advantages that will improve the chances of conducting a successful market research effort:

- Many people do not realize that the public library is in a vulnerable condition. Publicity about the pending market research efforts lends a sense of authenticity, even urgency to the discussion.
- A public library is an agency, unlike some, that brings its "good name" to the table. While a significant portion of the public does not use a public library, the feelings most people have towards the library are almost uniformly positive.
- History shows public libraries to be one of the most adaptable, adaptive, and resilient of all public agencies. For example, these libraries used customer-friendly techniques (mostly around e-technologies) to improve public services years (decades?) before other public agencies.

Traditional and newer technologies hold huge potential for improvements. In particular, a public library's use of e-technologies will enable market research and community outreach to discover more about their communities, more often and more profoundly. These discoveries can then be converted into new, more customized services and public relations that will use other e-technologies for delivery, plus on- and off-site evaluation.

CREATING A MARKET RESEARCH EFFORT

Market research in a public library setting will vary based upon circumstances but the general sequence is as follows:

1. First, the planning team should think of their public library as a conglomeration of diverse products and services, not a monolithic whole. A second step would be to examine the community as a diverse collection of people and groups, in clusters or segments. A third step would be to let the needs of the customer drive the process, not library staff and supporters' preconceived notions.
2. Typically, market research begins by convening a focus group(s). The focus group is used to: (a) recruit people who are members of the target demographic and are often called informants; and (b) define and refine topics and questions that should be included or excluded in a subsequent survey. When the audience is small and/or issues at hand simple, the research can start and stop with the focus group and not include a survey (step 3). Focus groups can also be used to monitor progress and produce other needed resources such as further community contacts and advocacy, volunteers, and even fundraising.
3. The focus group leads to a scientifically designed survey. In times past, surveys have been distributed by mail or using random-dial telephone techniques. These days, especially with the advent of cell telephones and social media, an e-mail survey is more common. For a survey to be useful, it is vital that it be designed, administered, and evaluated scientifically. A bad survey leads to bad data and decisions, which one can easily be unaware of until it's too late.

Given that the focus of this article is on small public libraries, it's likely that the library itself will not have adequate resources itself to conduct the activities or to pay for the services of a professional firm. At that point, it is wise to seek outside funding such as a budget allocation from the parent jurisdiction, donations, or a grant. Market research can be a modest, home-grown effort, but caution is advised since it is a complicated endeavor.

OUTREACH

What happens on library grounds and in library buildings should be determined by market research and community outreach. Market research will affect a host of service elements on library grounds and within library buildings such as accessibility to the building (e.g., parking and open/closed signage), internal amenities such as clean restrooms and clear direction tools, and even organization of physical spaces and display cases. An efficient/effective open hour schedule is a biggie. This process starts, stops, and begins, again, with community outreach. Poorly conceived and/or executed, any and all of these elements can be customer service "deal breakers."

As noted earlier, market research and community outreach may be viewed by some staff and stakeholders as trivial or even too risky. While it is possible that market research and outreach will yield data that confirm existing expectations and practices, it is even more likely that new, counterintuitive data will set the public library on a new course altogether. Conducting market research will turn "invisible" librarians and library supporters into visible players in community affairs, no longer hidden away in the library building itself.

Community outreach to various demographic niches will require different approaches and techniques. For example, demographic variables such as education, income, ethnicity, language spoken, age, and many more, will determine the details of how the market research and community outreach should be performed. Beware of these pitfalls: choosing the wrong medium, paying too much money for a message that will not be heard, trusting a self-proclaimed community spokesman who lacks respect within the target community, and assuming library programs are popular because they are well attended (by the same people, week after week). A common mistake (especially of governmental agencies) is to promise (or over promise) and then not deliver.

The mechanics of community outreach vary. For example, staff and library supporters can do it, or a professional consultant can be used. The target audience can be visited where they gather (for work or for pleasure), in their residences, or invited to events at the library itself. E-technologies have greatly enhanced the portability of the library, such as providing library access to customers from their home or office, or library staff taking the "e-library" to community events.

STRATEGIC PLANNING

A market research and community outreach effort is a complex undertaking even if library staff have done it before and have the experience and resources necessary to succeed. If this effort is a first attempt, then the complexity quotient rises dramatically. Creating a strategic plan, or incorporating a market research/community outreach effort into an existing plan, is a good idea. As a public library director for many years, and having taught a graduate level course in leadership and management, I know that creating and using a strategic plan can be difficult and fraught with risks. Here are some common characteristics of a strategic plan:

Purpose. A strategic plan should serve as a roadmap or diary of a complex undertaking. It has little to no political value but might help in a grant application process.

Authors and participants. A plan should be written by the people expected to carry it to fruition.

Basic elements. The format of strategic plans varies, but all include goals and objectives. The sequential elements I like to include are Vision, Mission, Goals, Objectives, Evaluation, Constraints/Challenges, and Budget. Sometimes a Background section is included and Objectives can include detailed action steps. The Evaluation section measures progress on the Objectives themselves, not the Goals.

A strategic plan is not necessary for simple, short-term tasks or for emergencies. However, if the proposed undertaking is complex, or long-term, a strategic plan is essential.

The key to the plan, the litmus test, is reasonable objectives. Here is a simple example related to a goal of improving a library's youth services: The Youth Services Librarian (who) will convene a focus group comprised of youth, parents, teachers, and youth advocates to consider some youth-oriented events at the library (what) by June 1 (when). Any costs associated with this objective are included in the Plan Budget. It is surprising how difficult writing a decent objective is. The most common mistake is to omit the "who." Omitting the "who" reduces clarity, accountability, and ability to budget, among other things. Other common mistakes include not mentioning a certain date (when) and providing too much detail or background information. A properly written plan can be a huge gift, assuring the success of goals via the design, implementation, and evaluation of reasonable and actionable objectives.

A CASE STUDY

As director of the San Luis Obispo County Library in California for over twenty years, it was my job to help the library succeed. A few years ago, I became convinced that a market research and community outreach effort would be very beneficial. At a *Library Journal* directors' forum in San Francisco a few years ago, a major topic of discussion was library branding. At that forum, I met a representative of the consulting firm OrangeBoy. We began discussing a possible project. Several years later, we achieved funding for the project, funding shared by the library, our Library Foundation, and a California State Library/LSTA grant.

This market research aimed to address several challenges: The library budget, like most public libraries in California, was quite limited. For example, the books/materials budget was about half of what national standards indicate. Full-time employees levels were down about 15 percent over the past few years, luckily through attrition and not layoffs. Still, open hours have been reduced, with all large branches (seven out of fifteen) open only five days per week. These larger branches were open only one evening per week. Alarmingly, the market penetration for residents who own library cards is less than 30 percent when the national average is 50–60 percent.

Making things more interesting, several branch libraries are or have been dramatically expanded or remodeled. No additional staff or operating expense was anticipated for these larger buildings.

As discussed in the narrative, the goal of the market research was to create an ongoing data stream that will allow the library to successfully face three challenges: (1) to better serve existing customers, (2) to attract new customers (double the existing numbers), and (3) to engage residents who won't necessarily become customers but whose moral and political support are important.

It is vital to think about customers and supporters in niches or clusters. OrangeBoy calls this concept "clusters, or clustering." Clustering is the process of collecting and mining data collected directly from library customers in order to identify segments that share similar library usage behaviors and distinct needs.

OrangeBoy's process to assess library customers starts with the creation of a knowledge base, using primary research methods to gather customer and market insights. This research includes mining the cardholder database to uncover consumption patterns, demographic trends, and comparing results to market data in order to identify potential service gaps. Here are some examples of fascinating data from Phase I of our market research study:

- Many library customers use multiple branch outlets and even libraries in other jurisdictions. Scatter diagrams of this use, based upon zip code and Areas of Dominant Influence (ADI), reveal interesting patterns of use.
- Library cardholder penetration varies dramatically from one branch library to another.
- Some of the highest population growth in the county is occurring in small, rural communities near larger cities.
- Library use of our largest branch, the San Luis Obispo City Library, is hugely affected and skewed due to proximity to California Polytechnic University (Cal Poly) and its dominance in the eighteen to twenty-five age bracket.

The market research also includes surveying existing customers and stakeholders and conducting ethnographic studies to observe how customers interact with library products and services, staff, and the physical environment. These studies occurred onsite in the library's fifteen locations. All survey instruments are designed to address the issues, needs, or priorities customers might have in their daily lives to which the library might add value. From this research came behavioral clusters of branch library users. Each branch library chose the clusters with the highest priority in that particular community. One strategy that we might expect to come from this research is to encourage light or occasional users to use the library more. Characteristics of non-users will be extrapolated by looking at segments of the population that are not currently served by the library. OrangeBoy worked with the library to identify priorities and strategies and then created a dashboard to monitor ongoing progress toward more satisfied customers, new customers, and engagement between the library and the community at large.

In discussions I and others had with satisfied OrangeBoy client libraries, these outcomes stood out prominently: All of the previous clients were glad they conducted the studies. None of the client libraries felt they could have conducted the research on their own. All of them would conduct the research in an ongoing manner if they could, especially aiming at the non-users, asking the vital question, "How can non-users be engaged and enthused, become convinced that an agency they don't personally use (the public library) is worthy of their concern, their support?"

Here are some examples of how library staff hope to use the market research data yielded by OrangeBoy and subsequent community outreach:

- Better understand what library customers really want and what is trivial.
- Better understand what will attract new customers and keep them coming back.
- Enhance existing services, create new services, and diminish existing services without adding to staff workload or angering people/groups vested in the status quo.
- Reinvent and reinvigorate the library system to be more efficient and effective, especially how to offer services that maximize customer self-service and navigation (in physical buildings and online) that minimizes staff workload and maximizes staff involvement in positive service outcomes.
- Engage movers and shakers. Identify how library staff and supporters can recruit and engage Library Super Supporters. Creating attractive events is an option but events and programs are notoriously labor-intensive. Library staff hope to promote the right programs to the right audience in the right location and on the right days and times.
- Empower library support groups such as Friends of the Library and the Library Foundation in recruiting new members, forging partnerships with community groups, and increasing fund raising.
- Set the stage, just possibly, for a successful library funding measure in one or more communities. In California, this requires a local election and

approval by a super majority of voters (67 percent). Now you can see why a less than 30 percent market penetration for library cardholders is so daunting.

- Strengthening the public library's two basic roles: promoting self-improvement and self-efficacy.

SUMMARY

Public libraries matter. Public libraries, in cooperation with other agencies such as public education, and groups such as the League of Women Voters, promote a community's quality of life and a democratic and egalitarian society. The two basic roles of a public library are to promote self-improvement and self-efficacy in the context of a community or place. Many modern ills of society could be healed or even cured if more people worked together for the common good and better planned for the future. This is why the continued survival of public libraries cannot and must not be taken for granted. Two important tools in the fight are market research and community outreach, documented via a strategic plan.

Chapter Thirty

Simple Strategies for Improving the User Experience with the Library Website

Teri Oaks Gallaway and James B. Hobbs

Improving the user experience with the library website does not require a huge investment in either time or money. It can be achieved through simple, low cost, or free tools and techniques. In this chapter, methods will be described for working with staff and patrons to find ways to make your website a more enjoyable site to use. By engaging your staff and patrons in the process, you will ensure that their website needs are met. The described methods can be used as stand-alone practices or in a step-by-step holistic process.

Understanding how your patrons and staff currently use your website, what things they enjoy, and where they have trouble is best achieved by working directly with users and user-generated data. Methods to do this include website analytics, surveys, focus groups, usability studies, card sorting exercises, and observation or ethnography. Additionally, using these techniques, you will be better prepared for the political aspects of website design. Being able to offer data and patron testimony to back up your arguments will help facilitate an improvement plan or project.

Finally, accessibility standards aim to ensure that your website will be usable by a person with or without disabilities. Referred to as Section 508 compliance in the United States or Standard on Web Accessibility in Canada, these standards have mandatory aspects that publicly funded organizations must observe. Tools for reviewing your site's compliance as well as tips on how to remain compliant are offered.

GOOGLE ANALYTICS

Understanding the needs of your website visitors should take a multi-pronged approach. Google Analytics, a free service, is one tool in this process. After setting up an account and copying and pasting a short bit of code to the footer of your webpages, you are ready to begin tracking visitors to your site. Data collected includes time and length of site visits as well as what type of operating system and screen resolution your visitors have. Reports are available on the number of users visiting your site on a mobile device, how long your pages take to load, and what are the most clicked links on your pages. PageSpeed Insights, a report within Google Analytics, analyzes the load speed of your pages and then offers recommendations on how to increase the speed. Using Google Analytics should help you identify a list of priorities for further development as well as assist in identifying website content that could be better promoted.

SURVEYS

Library staff likely use and know the library website better than any of your patrons and it behooves you to gather their feedback about the site if you want their support in making changes. Your patrons may also be willing to provide valuable insight into how they would like to see the library website improved. Keep your questions open-ended and be prepared: many patrons will not differentiate between your library website and library systems. A quick email survey or anonymous web survey using your favorite free survey tool like SurveyMonkey or Google Forms allows you to quickly gather input.

Here are some potential questions to ask:

- If you could change anything about our website, what would it be?
- What feedback have you received from our patrons about the website?
- Are there features on other websites that you think we should incorporate? Please describe.
- What features of our existing website do you think work well?
- What things do you or our users have the most difficulty doing on the website?

Begin identifying themes in your responses that you can then translate into a list of priorities. It may help to keep a tally of recurring ideas or problems. Qualitative data analysis software can assist with this task if you have a large number of responses. CompendiumNG an open source tool, for example, can help identify problems that are revealed while also keeping track of potential solutions. CAT (Coding Analysis Toolkit), also open source, offers the ability to code the text in your survey responses to identify similar suggestions and responses.

ENVIRONMENTAL SCAN

Your survey results will direct you to other websites that your patrons and staff like. In addition to comparing your site to those sites, an environmental scan should assist you in identifying site improvements. Create a list of comparable sites in your state or region to review as well as some non-library sites. What ideas or conventions can you glean from those sites? How does your site compare?

Another important aspect of the environmental scan is to review trends in your market segment. What critical documents related to changes or trends in public libraries and their patrons are available? Does your chamber of commerce or local government have forecasts on job trends or population migration that would impact your services? Are you expecting to serve a larger Spanish-speaking population or the unemployed? How might you use the website to prioritize the needs of your growing population segments?

USABILITY

At first glance usability studies may seem cost and time prohibitive to the small library staff. Research has shown however that even small-scale usability studies will reveal a worthy set of user issues to resolve (Nielsen 2012). In the next sections some basic concepts on how to design and implement a manageable usability experiment are described. Although you may like to have access to screen capture and eye-tracking software in a usability lab, the following information will help you get going on your usability tests with a computer, paper, and pencil.

Identify common website tasks or questions. What do your patrons and staff need or want to do with your website? If you have already used a staff or patron survey, identify any possible questions. Begin to create a set of questions or tasks that reflect the most important functions of your site or the most problematic issues. Create descriptions of the types of patrons that visit your website, how they use it, and what types of tasks reflect their needs. If you are keeping reference logs, look to that data to find common questions related to the website. Another source of user questions are your website search logs from a Google Custom Site Search account.

Design your tasks. You probably don't want to take more than thirty minutes of your volunteers' time, so limit the number of tasks per study. You can always schedule further tests with alternate questions. Your tasks should reflect your priorities and include a mix of simple and challenging tasks.

While you may be inclined to only include questions about the website itself, keep in mind that your patrons may not distinguish between what is the website, the library catalog, and your databases or other tools. Consider whether or not you want to include questions related to your other web-based services and products that are accessible through your website. During your initial round of testing, it may be helpful to limit your tasks to whether or not your users can locate your web-based services and systems on your website. The following are sample tasks:

> Does the library own a copy of *The Old Man and the Sea*?
> What events are taking place in the library this week?
> What hours is the library open this week?
> What services does the library offer to help you with your research?
> What databases are available for business research?
> You can't get into your library account; what should you do?
> How do you request that the library buy a book?
> What services are available for children?

Learn about working with human subjects. Before scheduling and recruiting participants, learn about the risks of working with human subjects. When done properly, usability tests should have a low risk for harming human subjects. However, it is important that you are aware of the general guidelines of working with human subjects. A free online course to familiarize yourself with proper procedures is available at the NIH (National Institute of Health) Office of Extramural Research. This course will introduce you to restrictions on working with children and other vulnerable populations, and once completed you will be able to print a certificate. Depending on your institution and the goals of your study you may wish to pursue study approval by the institutional review board for your organization or confirm that you are using a methodology that is exempt from review.

Recruit participants. A small group of participants is all that is needed to identify most of the issues with your website. Between five and ten participants should suffice if you include a variety of volunteers to reflect your patron base. If you are able to offer an incentive of a small gift card, a paperback book, or library merchandise, it may be easier to locate willing participants. In the absence of library funds for the project, the author has had success with home-baked snacks as an incentive. Depending on your availability, you may want to set up appointments ahead of time or recruit participants in the building. Be sure to inform your participants about the nature of the study, how long it will take to complete, that they may end the session at any time, and whether or not you will be recording the session.

Test the site. Watching your volunteers navigate your website can be an eye-opening experience and you may be overwhelmed with the urge to help or to correct. Don't do it! Your job is to watch and listen. Prepare a script of directions and your questions and stick to it. Herer are some sample instructions:

> (Read to participant) Today we are testing how well the library website is organized to help patrons find the information they need. Some questions may be challenging, but please be aware the test is of the system and not you. All the questions can be answered using the library website and catalog. Please start at the library homepage to find the answer to each question after I read it aloud. Describe your process out loud as you go.
>
> For example: "First I'm going to click on the link that says "Research" because I think that is where I would find help with research. I'm looking around on the page and I see another link that says "Getting Started" this looks like it could be good. I'm looking over the page and I don't see what I need so I'll click the back button."
>
> If you would like to stop the test or a specific question at any point, you are free to do so. With your consent, we will record this test using screen capture software to document your mouse movements, clicks, voice, as well as video of your facial expressions and/or eye movements.

As mentioned earlier, these tests can be completed with just a computer and pencil and paper. If you are not going to record the sessions, make sure to have two testers at every session. One person will guide the volunteer and the other will take copious notes of what the person said and did. Even with screen capture software, it is useful to record your observations in this manner. At the time of publication, two standard products for screen capture were available at a relatively low cost. Single licenses of either Camtasia or Screenflow were available for $99. These products can be used not only for usability tests, but can serve double-duty for recording instructional videos.

Be prepared that some participants will ask for your assistance during the study. Politely explain that you cannot offer assistance. Below are some typical questions or statements you may hear during a usability session and some possible ways to respond:

> Question: Is this the right answer/book/item/webpage?
> Response: Do you think it is? Tell me why or why not?
>
> Statement: I don't know. I've never done that before.
> Response: That's okay. Show me how you might go about finding the answer.
>
> Question: What is a _____?
> Response: What do you think it means?
>
> Question: Why does the website do it like that?
> Response: How do you think it should do it?

As you can see from the suggested responses, your job is to get your volunteers talking and to avoid guiding them or their opinions. At the end of your session, include an opportunity for your volunteers to provide feedback about the site or study in general. Scheduling multiple consecutive sessions with short breaks in between to catch up on note taking will offer an opportunity for you to begin to find similarities in user experiences. As time permits, jot down your ideas for solutions to the problems you are seeing.

LABELING AND INFORMATION ARCHITECTURE

The results of your survey, logs, or usability studies might indicate that the words you use to describe your services or systems may have different meanings for your patrons. These efforts might also reveal that the way you have organized your site content is not intuitive to your users. A follow-up or stand-alone technique to improve these labeling or information architecture issues is card sorting. This can be accomplished with a few volunteers and some scrap paper or index cards. Determine if you want to use an open card sort, where your volunteers come up with the content labels; or if you want to use a closed card sort, where you give the volunteers the labels.

To start an open card sort, provide your volunteers with a stack of cards that are pre-written to include one service description or idea per card that represents the existing pages of your website. Have your participant sort the cards into like groupings and then name the group. For a closed card sort, follow the same procedure but create the names of the groupings ahead of time and have your participant sort into the predefined groups. Compare the results and update the organization of your website content areas to reflect how your users expect information to be grouped and labeled.

DESIGN IMPROVEMENTS

Perhaps your site is meeting your users' needs in terms of the content and organization, but it's just plain ugly. Design matters, and it has an impact on how your patrons perceive the quality of your services. If your website looks outdated and unprofessional, your patrons may perceive that your library is as well. Think about the websites where you shop. Aren't you less inclined to make a purchase on a site that is poorly designed?

If you've already completed a scan of other library websites, you probably have some ideas on how you would like your website to look. If not, have a look at the templates available in a variety of content management systems like Joomla, Drupal, or Wordpress. You might consider migrating to one of those content management systems if you do not have the expertise or budget to implement large-scale design changes. Start with your homepage layout and print out some website templates. Use scissors and tape to build a mock-up of a new homepage layout or begin sketching it out on graph paper.

These activities will help you with sizing later on when you start your design work. You can also work with free web-based mock-up tools such as Gliffy of Website Wireframe. Use these activities as group techniques to find agreement on how to put pieces of a new homepage together.

For smaller changes consider updating or standardizing your fonts and color schemes. Look at color designing websites like Paletton to select a complementary set of colors to use throughout the site. Google Fonts features an interactive tool where you can copy and paste text to see how it will appear in a variety of web friendly fonts. Consistency in use of fonts and colors will go a long way to improving a site. Preview changes in your fonts and color schemes with the built-in style editing developer tools in Google Chrome or the free Firebug extension for Mozilla Firefox.

WRITING ACCESSIBLE WEB PAGES

Writing Web pages that are accessible to the most people is not just smart, it's the law. Any group that receives federal funds in the United States must have a Section 508–compatible web site. Section 508 is a 1998 amendment to the U.S. Rehabilitation Act of 1973, which mandates that websites provide comparable access for users with disabilities. Section 508 covers visual, hearing, movement, and cognitive disabilities. Each type needs its own considerations in writing pages. The listing of requirements is available as a Section 508 checklist on the WebAIM website.

Accessible Web page design begins as pages are written and designed. It continues as pages are created, used, and tested. Accessibility is not an afterthought. Here are some code suggestions:

- Keep HTML content flow the same as visual flow. Try reading unstyled text out loud to find discontinuities.
- Use headers to set off sections, not formatting. HTML was created to provide the organization of the document, not its appearance. Cascading style sheets (CSS) give much more control over appearance, but CSS should not be used as a substitute for HTML's organizational elements, such as paragraphs and headings.
- Images should generally use alt tags, if they convey information. Images that are used for branding or layout do not need alt tags. Logos need only one set of alt text per page. An image used as a header requires additional preparation, with HTML headers preferred or used alongside images.
- All page navigation and menus are read aloud for the visually impaired when using a screen reader. Consider schemes for the reader to skip directly to page content instead of reading menus at the top of each page.

One way to accomplish this is with a link that only a read-aloud browser will find:

```
<span class="hidden">
    <a href="#content" base="#content">Skip to content</a></indent>
    </span>
```

with

```
<a name="content"></a>
```

where the content begins.

- The <class="hidden"> CSS selector should be referenced in a linked or inline CSS stylesheet with a line like: a { visibility:hidden; }.

Additional suggestions:

- Avoid frames whenever possible.
- Don't automatically start audio.
- Make a careful choice of link text, not "click here."
- Sans-serif text is preferred.
- Don't hide links to text-only versions of Web pages at the bottom of the page. Place then at the top so the screen reader can catch it early. Do the same for links to mobile versions too. If there is a link to skip to main content, place the link at top of the page.
- Provide HTML versions of all PDF documents.
- Sentences should be 10–15 words or less.
- Hover menus are invisible to screen readers.
- Provide captions for videos. Consider CaptionTube for automated caption addition: http://captiontube.appspot.com/.

Accessibility Testing

WAVE (Web Accessibility Evaluation Tool) is an extremely useful online test for individual pages. It is a free public service of WebAIM (Web accessibility in mind), a nonprofit organization based at the Center for Persons with Disabilities at Utah State University. Enter the URL of a page for a report in text and visual format showing accessibility weaknesses. It is also available as a Firefox toolbar. Besides WAVE, WebAIM also provides a color contract checker, and an article on web accessibility for designers. An API is also available with a fee based on usage. The Web Accessibility for Designers article's fourteen points call on ideas from print (use adequate font size) and ideas unique to the web (make sure links are recognizable). It is highly recommended.

The information-rich WAVE display takes some time to learn effectively. It shows the Web page at right and three tabs (Styles, No Styles, Contrast), with subparts at left. The Styles tab indicates problems with a page as it appears in most browsers. No Styles renders the page in plain text, as a screen reading browser will see it. The Contrast tab looks for problems for low-vision users. The Styles tab shows Errors, Alerts, Features, Structural Elements, HTML5 and ARIA (Accessible Rich Internet Applications), and Contrast Errors. Each category is color-coded and a corresponding icon appears on the page depiction. Items marked in red are critical, yellow, desirable but not essential. Green is the good news; your page has accessibility features built in. Alerts call attention to poor practice, but do not mean that a page is unusable. Errors, however, should be fixed as soon as possible.

Common Page Issues from WAVE

- Form label problem: there is no text label present near the form box. (Read the full info in WAVE for these errors; it tells you how to fix it.) Adding a title attribute after the input type for the form box will fix the problem. If this is the code for a search box (or any form box):

```
<input type="text" value="Enter search terms" name="searchstring"
class="textinput" size="22" onFocus="clearValue( this );">
```

  Add a title attribute so it looks like this:

```
<input type="text" title="Enter search term box" value="Enter search
terms" name="searchstring" class="textinput" size="22"
onFocus="clearValue( this );">
```

The screen reader will read about the title: "Enter search term box." The title should accurately convey to the user what they need to put in the form box.

- Be sure that labels and form field text are the same. For example:

```
<label for="last">Last name: </label>
<input type="text" name="lastname" id="last">
```

- Labels are not needed for buttons, though the text in a graphic button should be the same as the text in the value attribute.
- If a form uses validation, use specific language for the user to explain the problem, do not make a generic "there is a problem" statement and a field or message in a different color. A helpful explanatory message:

```
<p class="error">That's not an email address. Email addresses should have the
form of: user@host.edu.</p>
```

FURTHER THOUGHTS

Improving a website requires team or collaborative efforts. Make sure that you organize your team for success. Try to include individuals with creative skills, someone who is good at project management, someone who has a great eye for detail, as well as someone who is skilled at setting up an environment for collaborative decision making. Your project lead might not even be an experienced web designer. Maybe they are just good at project management and leading a team.

As you identify areas of your site to change you may run into issues in not having the expertise to make the improvements. Spend some time expanding your skills with free online training. W3 Schools includes tutorials on everything from basic HTML and CSS to more advanced training in Javascript and JQuery. The Canadian government's WET (Web Experience Toolkit) also offers a cut and paste repository of web accessible code for creating everything from tabbed menus to forms and image carousels.

Lastly, remember that you might not get it all right in one shot. Make improvements in increments and then go back and test again. Don't be afraid to make mistakes so long as you are willing to correct them. Your process should be iterative and ongoing as technology and expectations about technology are evolving.

ADDITIONAL RESOURCES

- Cunningham, Katie. 2012. *Accessibility Handbook: Making 508 Compliant Websites*. Sebastopol, CA: O'Reilly Media.
- ChromeVox: a Google Chrome screen reader extension.
- Cynthia Says: an accessibility site test.
- Firefox Fangs Screen Reader Emulator: an add-on that simulates how a screen reader would read the page.
- NNg (Nielsen Norman Group) website: a collection of reports and articles on user experience research.
- Usability.gov: Methods, templates, and guidelines on usability including project management tips.
- VizCheck: a colorblind test for your site.

REFERENCE

Nielsen, Jakob. 2012. "Usability 101: Introduction to Usability." *Nielsen Norman Group: Evidence-Based User Experience Research, Training, and Consulting.* http://www.nngroup.com/articles/usability-101-introduction-to-usability/.

Chapter Thirty-One

A Tree without Roots Cannot Grow

Creative Outreach to African American
Genealogical Patrons

Nancy Richey

Creative management of small libraries requires outreach to diverse populations that bring the neighborhood into the library. One of these diverse groups who are looking to libraries, especially the small, neighborhood library are African Americans. A recent Pew study ("Library Services in the Digital Age" 2013) notes that "African-Americans and Hispanics are especially tied to their libraries and eager to see new services" and that "African-Americans are more likely than whites to say they visit to get help from a librarian" ("Libraries in the Digital Age" 2013).

One of the outreach services African American patrons are seeking is assistance with family history/genealogical research. Most of these users may be pursuing this information as a hobby or passion, brought about by the popularity of television programs such as *Finding Your Roots* and *Who Do You Think You Are.* But many are seeking heritage, adoption, or medically essential data. Public libraries must be ready to meet the needs of these patrons by knowing the basics of African American genealogical research.

Assisting any patron with heritage research requires finding answers to standard queries: Who (names), What (events), When (dates), and Where (places.) The patron must do their part by gathering the above basic facts as they pertain to his or her progenitors. Many libraries have purchased subscriptions to commercial genealogical databases, but staff may not be knowledgeable in using these databases or in wading through the myriad of free genealogy websites and online resources available. Reaching any ethic genealogy patron who are very confused not only by the information but by the

271

reliability of the sources, gives relevance to the librarian's role in helping provide access to authoritative sources and information on how-to use those sources. By gaining familiarity with the best of these resources, librarians are able to assist in formulating successful research strategies and the best methods for access.

African American genealogy presents particular challenges for the patron and librarian. Though this is an exciting avenue of outreach for small, public librarians, it is challenging because records are limited and sometimes difficult to find. The interested researcher must first identify whether the records sought represent free or enslaved ancestors; because slaves were treated as property, the records documenting their lives will not usually be found among traditional vital records. Slaves as property were not taught to read and write, could not legally marry, own land, vote, or participate in the customary activities that usually generate the records needed for genealogical research. Furthermore, the surnames assigned to slaves could be changed with ownership and were often changed deliberately by ex-slaves after the Civil War as freed blacks sought to distance themselves from a slave owner. In both cases, the link to family names is lost. Also, racial identities might not have been reported correctly for these individuals in the records that do exist.

To begin researching African American heritage, staff should encourage the researcher to follow the basic genealogical research techniques first, and also to become acquainted with African American history, especially as it relates to the slave era. The librarian should also explain how genealogical research differs from family history but how they are inexorably tied. Genealogical research will discover documents and records for verification and location of births, deaths, and marriages. Family history will use these resources to tell the story of the lives of their ancestors. Managers must communicate the importance of these researchers and the importance of the staff's role in assisting them. We cannot, in this case, be "accidental librarians"; we must be purposeful.

THE BASIC TECHNIQUES FOR ALL FAMILY HISTORY RESEARCHERS

Write Down Your Own Information and Then Add What You Know about Others

Start with yourself and work backwards. Oral history plays a vital role in African American researching so the researcher must record every oral tradition and look for the oral memory keepers in the family. Alex Haley, the famed author of *Roots: The Saga of an American Family* wrote about his childhood in Henning, Tennessee, remembering how the oral traditions of his family were passed down to him. "Every evening, after the supper dishes were washed, they [Cousin Georgia, Aunt Plus, and Aunt Liz] would go out on the front porch and sit in cane-bottomed rocking chairs, and I would always sit behind grandma's chair. And every single evening of those summers, unless there was some particularly hot gossip that would overrule it, they would talk about otherwise the self-same thing. It was bits and pieces and patches of what I later would learn was a long narrative history of the family which had been passed down literally across generations." (Perks and Thomason 2012). The accuracy of some of this "handed-down, passed-around" information may be questioned but it can provide valuable clues.

Ask Questions and Record the Answers

Interviewing relatives, family and friends can fill in the gaps and give the researcher many paths to follow. For African Americans, oral history is an especially important part of the research process, because those interviews might provide clues that just do not exist on paper. The best questions are open-ended and cannot be answered with a simple YES or NO. Many lists of possible interview questions are available online by using the keywords "genealogy interview questions." And don't forget that family memorabilia and photographs make excellent "prompts" to get stories going during interviews. Many forms and charts are also available online to begin the process of recording family information—researchers can just Google "genealogy charts" to find them. The most common chart types are the ancestral chart (records the ancestors from whom one directly descends) and the family group sheet (records the family unit, i.e., parents, spouse, children). See textbox 31.1 for sample interview questions.

Textbox 31.1

Sample interview questions:

- Tell me about the family's surname. Do you know if the spelling was changed at any time? Was there a naming tradition in the family? Nicknames?
- Who is the oldest relative you remember?
- Ask about specific events?
- Where were your grandparents born and why did they move?
- Did anyone in the family talk about slavery or free persons of color?
- Are there stories that have come down to you about your parents, grandparents, or even more distant ancestors?

Start Finding Records and Documents

The first records all researchers should consult are those closest to them, within the family sphere. Letters, photographs, awards and trophies, family Bibles, scrapbooks, diaries, insurance papers, funeral programs, and other such "records" are the best place to start to gather names, dates, and places. Once the family-specific sources have been collected and studied, the family historian can verify and supplement that information with available vital records (birth, death, and marriage). For the African American researcher, these will include the above noted recent records, transition records (from slavery to freedom), and slave records.

Other essential sources for all family historians include census and naturalization records, city directories, church, school, and organization records, marriage and death certificates, military records, probate records and wills, real estate records, and newspaper articles (especially obituaries). Be prepared to look for separate indexes, for the records, just like the persons, were written many times, segregated, kept in separate files, or listed in the back of record books. Remember, both librarian and researcher must detach themselves emotionally from some of the material. Many of the records, particularly those dealing with slavery, will be racist, cruel, crude, and offensive.

Here is where the researcher tracing African American lineage starts to need the help of an information professional. In addition to the basic sources all genealogists need, these more specialized record sets play a role in African American research:

African American newspapers (pre-1900)
Ancestral church publications
Apprentice and indenture records
Bounty lists
Canadian and Caribbean transits
Cemetery headstones
Cemetery records
Club records
Cohabitation records
County courthouse registers
Divorce records
Employment records pre-1900
Estate inventories
Freedmen's Bureau Records of Field Offices
Freedmen's Schools
Funeral home records
Funeral programs
Guardianship records
Homestead records

Institutional records: hospitals, etc.

Insurance papers

Labor contracts

Local school records

Manumission records

Military and conscription records

Obituaries

Plantation Records

Plaques or awards

Poll tax records (AKA "head tax" or "capitation")

Poorhouse, workhouse, almshouse, and asylum records

Records of black-owned businesses

Records of historically black colleges

Records of slave burial grounds in owner's papers

Records of protectors and patrons of slaves

Register of Violence against Freedmen

Registers of Signatures of Depositors in Branches of the Freedmen's
    Saving and Trust Company

Runaway slave advertisements and legal notices

School and college yearbooks

School certificates

Sharecropper agreements

Slave Registries and Manifests

Social Security records

Tax lists

U.S. Colored Troops Records

Voter records and registrations

WW I and II discharge papers

The researcher should also systematically search the myriad records associated with the American Missionary Association (a Protestant abolitionist organization), the Freedman's Savings and Trust and the Freedmen's Bureau (both government-sponsored organizations designed to aid freed slaves). Finally, the researcher can check the records of the Southern Claims Commission, an executive-branch effort to reimburse Union sympathizers living in the South whose property was confiscated or damaged during the Civil War.

THE 1870 CENSUS

The United States government has enumerated the population every ten years since 1790. All are still available except for the 1890 census, which was virtually destroyed in a fire in 1921. The institution of slavery decimated many families and left few exact records, but the researcher tracing African

American families can usually go back successfully to the 1870 census. This was the first to list African Americans by name (previous census takers noted their existence only with tally marks on the page). Other information included address; name; age; sex; color citizenship for males over twenty-one; profession, occupation, or trade; place of birth; attended school within the year; and whether persons ten years old and over were able to read and write. Be careful to note the date and place of birth listed for former slaves and their families.

All researchers using the census should remember to search the census pages for an area one page at a time (either microfilm rolls or online images) and not rely on the index alone. Looking through the census page by page for a certain area can reveal nearby relatives and friends the researcher did not know about. Additionally, the spelling interpretation and transcription of the census taker and transcribers may cause many errors. For example, Daniel can be spelled/transcribed as David; Nathan as Matthew; and surnames, Clarck/Clark, Canady/Kennedy, Garrod/Garrett, Robards for Roberts, and Bunde for Bunch.

For researchers wanting to go deeper than the widely known "population schedules," the librarian can help them find mortality schedules and other such specialized lists, such as the 1890 schedule of surviving soldiers of the Civil War and the 1850/1860 mortality schedules, which listed slaves. Also, the Agricultural Schedules 1840–1910 can be used to document African American sharecroppers and assist in identifying free African Americans and their property holdings. A good starting place to locate these specialized schedules is through the Ancestry.com database called "Selected U.S. Federal Census Non-Population Schedules, 1850–1880." Even though this is a subscription database, many public libraries offer ALE (Ancestry Library Edition) as a service to their patrons.

In the population schedules, researchers should note white families with the same surname, and watch for black children indentured to white families. Once a slave-owning family is identified, they can be found in previous years' census, and then their land, tax, and probate records can be searched for information on their slaves. Free blacks appear by name on census lists prior to 1870; in fact, free African American heads of household were listed in the federal census beginning in 1790.

SLAVE OR FREE

It must be emphasized that not all African Americans were slaves prior to the Civil War. It is estimated that by the time of the Civil War, one in every ten African Americans were free or 476, 748 persons.

Begin by checking "Free" population schedules of the 1860 census. Free persons of color were born free, emancipated, or could earn their freedom by military service. For enslaved ancestors, the researcher should check these slave owner records: property divisions that list inventories and named slaves, overseer records, account and day books, birth and death registers, accounting lists of slaves, daily work, and financial records. Additionally, look for slave owner diaries, advertisements, bills of sale, and burial records. See textbox 31.2 for what to look for to determine an ancestor's slave or free status.

Textbox 31.2

Free person of color? Look for the following:

- Is there oral history?
- Did they live in a historically black town or area?
- Do they have mulatto ancestry?
- Were they literate
- Was there a northward migration pattern?
- Any southern residency in places known to have large classes of free blacks?

REGIONAL LIBRARIES, SPECIAL COLLECTION, AND THE NATIONAL ARCHIVES

Once local records are exhausted, African American researchers will benefit the most from other state public libraries, regional special collections, and NARA (National Archives and Records Administration). They will have unique, rare, and one of a kind records that may hold the clue needed for completing a family's story. For example, if the researcher lives in Kentucky but has traced their ancestors to South Carolina, the archives and libraries of that state must be accessed. Many libraries are creating online access to primary source materials such as the Avery Research Center for African-American History and Culture. Such libraries note that their "mission is to collect, preserve and document the history and culture of African-Americans in South Carolina and the Lowcountry region. This is a very important mission because approximately half of all African Americans in the United States can trace their arrival to this continent to this region" (Charlestoncvb.com 2013).

The records included in such local holdings include bills of slave sales that may have been separated from land deeds and donated to these types of local historical societies, libraries, and archives. The National Archives holds records, documents, and materials that were created by the United States Federal government. This will be a rich resource for the African American researcher.

African American family history is not lost, but certainly requires extra effort. For African American researchers, the most numerous and richest sources are usually found at the local level and by the public librarian who knows their collections best. Despite the challenges, many family historians have successfully traced their African American lineage, and public library genealogy book collections usually contain at least one volume about this special area of research (see below for recommended reading and acquisitions). The African American researcher must understand that they will "plowing new ground" as they will not have the benefit of already completed historical research. Public librarians who take the time to learn to assist African American family historians provide valuable outreach to a population under-represented in library collections, as well as generate community goodwill. Outreach to these diverse users through one-on-one contact or through classes is an absolute necessity for public libraries. As one public librarian noted their outreach "respond[ed] to a community need. We notice participants of all ages, cultures, and backgrounds, and have been gratified to see many of them also become frequent users of the rest of the library. We enjoy the challenge of integrating something as traditional as genealogy with modern technology, and, in the process, attracting new people to this popular pastime" (Fisher and Pankl 2012).

A successful search can provide historical evidence for many undocumented communities, neighborhoods, and individuals, and bring to light their role in American history. Finally, African American genealogy and history has not been widely researched. There is a much history to catch up with and this area is a gold mine for librarians and historians. Thus, librarians must be prepared to handle the variety of in-person and electronic requests from these growing populations. Familiarity with the above resources and this type of outreach will help meet the needs of this unique population, and these future key users, and facilitate the viability of local, public librarians as partners in this type of research. Library managers particularly of small libraries must use this type of outreach and create a valued neighborhood space that focuses on learning and service to individuals with diverse interests.

RECOMMENDED PRINT RESOURCES

This list contains some older material as these are the standards and sometimes the only works.

Beasley, Donna. *1997. Family Pride: The Complete Guide to Tracing African-American Genealogy.* New York: Macmillan.

Bunkley, Lonnie R. 2013. *Journey to Freedom: A Genealogical Study of an African American Family and the Political and Social issues that Impacted Their Lives, 1778–2013.* Los Angeles, California: The Bunkley Foundation, Inc.

Burroughs, Tony. 2001. *A Beginner's Guide to Tracing the African-American Family Tree.* New York: Simon & Schuster.

Byers, Paula K., ed. 1995. *African-American Genealogical Sourcebook.* New York: Gale Research.

Conte, Stephen, Shamele Jordon, et al. 2013. *African-American Genealogy.* (DVD). New Jersey, HomeTowne TV Production.

Gutman, Herbert G. 1976. *The Black Family in Slavery and Freedom, 1750–1925.* New York: Pantheon Books.

Hait, Michael. 2011. *Genealogy at a Glance: African American Genealogy Research.* Baltimore: Genealogical Publishing Co.

Harris, Bailey, Bernice Alexander Bennett, et al. 2014. *Our Ancestors, Our Stories.* Suwanee, GA: The Write Image.

Hill, Walter. 2000. "Documentation of Slavery and the Slave Trade in Federal Records." *Prologue 32*, no. 4. (Winter).

Lawson, Jacqueline A. 1995. *An Index of African-Americans Identified in Selected Records of the Bureau of Refugees, Freedmen, and Abandoned Lands.* Bowie, MD: Heritage Books.

Lawson, Sandra M. 1993. *Generations Past: A Selected List for Afro-American Genealogical Research* Washington (DC): Government Printing Office.

Matthews, Harry Bradshaw. 2014. *Stories Our Mothers Told Us: A Search for Roots.* Oneonta, NY: U.S. Pluralism Center.

Peters, Joan W. 1995. *Local Sources for African-American Family Historians: Using County Court Records and Census Returns.* Broad Run, VA.: J.W. Peters.

Philibert-Ortega, Gena. 2013. "Tracing Your Female Ancestors: We'll Show You How!" Toronto, ON: *Moorshead Magazines Ltd.*

Puckett, Newbell Niles, compiler. 1975. *Black Names in America: Origins and Usage.* Boston: G. K. Hall.

Rose, Christine, and Kay Germain Ingalls. 2012. *The Complete Idiot's Guide to Genealogy.* New York: Alpha.

Rose, James M., and Alice Eichholz. 2003. *Black Genesis: A Resource Book for African-American Genealogy.* Baltimore, MD: Genealogical Publishing.

Schultz, Janice Lindgren. *Finding Your Roots: Easy-To-Do Genealogy and Family History.* Chicago: Huron Street Press.

Smith, Franklin Carter, and Emily Anne Croom. 2003. *A Genealogist's Guide to Discovering Your African-American Ancestors.* Cincinnati: Betterway Books.

Thackery, David T. 2000. *Finding Your African-American Ancestors: A Beginner's Guide.* Orem, UT: Ancestry.

Weant, Kenneth. 2013. *Civil War Records: United States Colored Troops.* Arlington, TX: K. E. Weant.

Witcher, Curt Bryan. 2000. *African-American Genealogy: a Bibliography and Guide to Sources.* Fort Wayne, IN: Round Tower Books.

Woodtor, Dee. 1999. *Finding a Place Called Home: A Guide to African-American Genealogy and Historical Identity.* New York: Random House.

RECOMMENDED WEB RESOURCES

Africana Heritage Project: www.africanaheritage.com

AfriGeneas: www.afrigeneas.com

Afro-American Historical and Genealogical Society, Inc.: www.aahgs.org

Born in Slavery—Slave Narratives from the Federal Writers' Project, 1936–1938: http://memory.loc.gov/ammem/snhtml/

Cyndi's List: African-American Genealogy: www.cyndislist.com/african-american

Directory of African-American Genealogical Societies: http://haitfamily-research.com/pdf_files/A%20Directory%20of%20African-American%20Genealogical%20Societies.pdf

Kentucky African-American Griots: www.rootsweb.ancestry.com/~kya-famer/

My Slave Ancestors: www.myslaveancestors.com

Our Black Ancestry: www.ourblackancestry.com

REFERENCES

Charlestoncvb.com. 2013. "Charleston's African-American Heritage." http://www.africanamericancharleston.com/avery.html (accessed July 1, 2013).

Fisher, Jean, and Robert R. Pankl. 2012. "A Focus on the Family." *Library Journal* 137, no. 1 (September 15): 94.

"Library Services in the Digital Age." 2013. Pewrearch.org. January 22. http://libraries.pewinternet.org/files/legacy-pdf/PIP_Library%20services_Report.pdf (p. 23; accessed June 1, 2013).

Perks, Robert, and Alistair Thomason. 2012. *The Oral History Reader*, 9. Routledge: New York.

Chapter Thirty-Two

We Started a Festival

The Halloween Costume Collection

Amy White

Does your town have an identity of its own? What holidays does it celebrate? Any festivals? What makes it special?

Our little town struggles a bit with identity because it is located near another slightly bigger little town that has a college. The slightly bigger little town has more businesses, more people, and a deeply ingrained superiority complex that probably dates back to the founding of the college. It has a steadier influx of new residents who bring ideas from all over the country: ideas for festivals, contests, celebrations—ways to make that town a fun place to live. The slightly bigger little town has a Magical Night the week after Thanksgiving that includes a visit from Santa, musical entertainment and refreshments in all the shops, and a wagon ride down the main street. There is no competing with them for the small-town Christmas market, so our little town doesn't even try.

Enter a couple of librarians with a great idea.

Back in 1999, my colleague and I were wondering what to do with the Halloween costumes we had hand-sewn for our sons. They had all been worn and enjoyed multiple times, passed back and forth and lovingly cared for. The idea of cataloging them for circulation in the library came to us when we talked to other parents who had either made or purchased high-quality costumes that had more wear left in them. The library could provide a dual service to the community by accepting used costumes and making them available for checkout. So we gave it a try.

Although we were certainly not the first library to house a collection other than books, we may have been the first to offer Halloween costumes for circulation. As soon as we advertised that we were accepting donated costumes, we started receiving them, and every year we have added more. We made tags with barcodes that could be pinned to the costumes. We brought in a rack to display our collection. The rules were simple and still work for us today:

- Children had to have a library card and a parent or guardian to check out a costume, and they could only have one.
- They could try on the costumes in our bathroom.
- We put the costumes out in the library on the first day of October, and we kept them on display through Halloween.
- The costumes are due back a week after Halloween.
- After they're returned to us, I take them home and wash them. Sometimes the patrons return them laundered, which I appreciate but don't require.
- We ask the patrons to take off the pinned barcodes for wearing the costumes but to keep them and return them to us with the costumes; some are lost but most are returned.
- We keep a sewing kit at the library and my colleague makes necessary repairs and replacements of tags.
- We store the costumes in bins in a closet for eleven months out of the year.
- We accept donations of costumes year-round. We donate worn or undesirable costumes to Goodwill.

It didn't hurt that at the time we started our collection, our city administrator moonlit at the Disney Store at the closest mall. He donated at least two dozen beautiful, brand-new costumes that he bought on sale after Halloween with his employee discount. Those Disney costumes are still in the library's collection and get checked out every year. At this point, we own over two hundred costumes, so we have started to be discriminating in accepting them. We accept all donations of costumes and take what we don't keep for our collection to Goodwill. It is key to the success of a project like this that the library can provide materials to a critical mass of patrons. A larger library may not be able to serve as large a percentage of their population as a smaller library, but may have a bigger storage area for costumes, more space in the library for costume display, and a larger pool from which to draw donations of costumes. Our proximity to the town's community center has been helpful in terms of using their closets for storage of costumes, but this is something that needs to be considered when starting a special collection—especially a seasonally active one.

Another important aspect of the Halloween Costume Collection's success is that it is used and appreciated by everyone. There are no requirements or parameters attached to it in terms of income-based need, just like any other part of the library's collection, so there is no stigma in wearing a "library" costume. Millionaires could check them out. Teachers, who witness every year the full range of children—from those who come with their parents to the costume parade with lovely new handmade or purchased costumes to those who have nothing in their backpacks to change into for the party— promote the collection to parents during the Halloween season. The library costume collection is publicly advertised and enjoyed by all giving even adults with grown or no children the opportunity to share the fun of seeing children select whatever costume they want without regard to its price tag.

But getting back to our small town's identity crisis: how did the library's Halloween costume collection help?

Maybe we couldn't do Christmas, since the slightly bigger little town already had their Magical Night in place. But what about Halloween? Our little town could do Halloween! The two main streets that intersect in a four- way stop could be blocked off and set up for games and decorations. The community center could offer a soup supper in their senior dining area and the library could be open for trick or treaters. All it will take is a committee of volunteers on a very limited budget and a whole lot of candy.

Halloween Town has been operating since 2007. Some of the same volun- teers are still organizing it. They have used donations of money, materials, and candy from individual businesses, with recent help from the Community Development Group that serves both our little town and the slightly larger little town down the road. Like with just about any other idea that turns into an actual event, the success of the project depends on the passion and energy of at least one person as well as important factors beyond anyone's control— namely, the receptiveness of the public and the weather. In the last six years, we have had just about every variety of weather—nice, rainy, cold, and miserable—which is not bad, and turnout is only beginning to decline. When Halloween Town was a new event, neighborhoods in the larger little town close to our little town reported significantly fewer trick-or-treaters, leading us to believe that everyone had gone to Halloween Town for the night.

No one would give any credit to the town librarians for starting a festival like Halloween Town, nor would we accept it all if it was offered. It was one of those ideas that rises subliminally out of the community consciousness out of a need that more than one of us sees. Librarians are creative people and use what they have to help the community. They do what they're good at and that inevitably helps others reach out as well. The costume collection was a natural lead-in to Halloween Town, which has grown to include a haunted alley decorated and managed by high school art students and a Murder Mys- tery Dinner fundraiser that is held the weekend before Halloween and bene- fits the library, the community center, and the town's museum, the History Center. Halloween is now the town's big thing.

Index

About the Editor

Carol Smallwood received an MLS from Western Michigan University and MA in history from Eastern Michigan University. *Librarians as Community Partners: An Outreach Handbook* and *Bringing the Arts into the Library* are recent ALA anthologies. Others are *Women on Poetry: Writing, Revising, Publishing and Teaching* (2012), *Marketing Your Library* (2012), and *Library Services for Multicultural Patrons: Strategies to Encourage Library Use* (2013). Her experience includes school, public, academic, and special libraries, as well as administration and library systems consulting. Carol is a member of the American Library Association.

About the Contributors

Kim Becnel is assistant professor of library science at Appalachian State University in Boone, North Carolina. Becnel teaches and researches in the areas of public library management, youth services, distance education, and children's literature. She coedited the volume *Library Services for Multicultural Patrons: Strategies to Encourage Library Use* (2013), and her work has appeared in *Middle Management in Academic and Public Libraries* (2011), *Diversity in Youth Literature: Opening Doors through Reading* (2012), and the magazine *Public Libraries*.

Amanda D. McKay Biarkis is director of the Helen Matthes Library, Effingham, Illinois, which she joined in 2011. Her education includes an MLIS from the University of Illinois at Urbana–Champaign in library and information sciences as well as an MA from Eastern Illinois University in English. Amanda is a member of the American Library Association and the Illinois Library Association, serving on the latter's board for three years. She finds a lot of joy in working at a public library and helping people find the resources they need to live more meaningful and full lives.

Jan Burns has worked twenty years in public libraries and twelve years in medical libraries. She served as a public library consultant for the state of Alabama and a mentor in the SWIM Regional Collaborative Library Education Project. Her greatest accomplishment was being asked to participate in a panel discussion at the Library of Congress on how electronic subscriptions affect interlibrary loan. Jan has worked in libraries since the age of five and has gained library experience in Alabama, Texas, Oregon, Nevada, and South Dakota. She is currently a librarian in Twin Falls, Idaho.

Brady A. Clemens is the director of the Juniata County Library in Mifflintown, Pennsylvania. He began his career as the Historical Resources Reference Librarian at the Uniontown Public Library in Uniontown, Pennsylvania, responsible for managing the library's collection of local history and genealogy resources, after having completed his MLS at Clarion University of Pennsylvania. He has previously published several book reviews in the *GLBTRT Newsletter* of ALA's GLBT Round Table. The author wishes to thank Ellen Stolarski and Lisa Rives Collens for their constructive comments on an early draft of this chapter.

Melissa Cornwell was assistant library director at the small and rural Camargo Township District Library in Villa Grove, Illinois, for almost two years. She earned her MLIS at the University of Illinois Urbana–Champaign and then got her current job as the distance learning librarian at Norwich University in Northfield, Vermont. Her memberships include the Association of College and Research Libraries and the Library Information Technology Association. She loves reading manga, writing, and watching crime dramas. You can also find her blogging at the Nerdy Mindful Librarian.

Karen Harrison Dyck earned her MLS from the University of Toronto. She has managed small and medium public libraries, including Delhi, Ontario (1974–1986); Parkland Regional Library, Lacombe, Alberta (1988–1991); Thunder Bay, Ontario (1992–1997); and Coquitlam, British Columbia (2002–2006) during her more than thirty years in the profession. Currently, retired on the west coast of Canada, she has a consulting business specializing in hiring and staff training projects for smaller public libraries. She is a past president of the Canadian Library Association.

Sari Feldman (author of the foreword) has been the executive director of Cuyahoga County Public Library (CCPL) in Ohio since June 2003 and heads one of the nation's busiest and best library systems. Cuyahoga County Public Library has twenty-seven branches and serves forty-seven communities. CCPL is ranked by *Library Journal* as a 5-Star Library for the past four years. Prior to joining Cuyahoga County Public Library, she was deputy director of the Cleveland Public Library. Active in the both local and national organizations, Sari will serve as the president of the American Library Association from 2015 to 2016.

Wayne Finley, business librarian/assistant professor at Northern Illinois University Libraries (DeKalb, Illinois), earned his MLIS from the University of Illinois and his MBA from Western Illinois University. His research and public service interests include the application of marketing and management theory in public and academic libraries. Wayne's work has appeared in journals such as *Journal of Business and Finance Librarianship* and *Behavioral and Social Science Librarian*. He also authored the chapter "The Art of Personal Selling: Techniques for Library Marketing," which appeared in *Marketing Your Library: Tips and Tools that Work* (McFarland 2012).

Teri Oaks Gallaway is the library systems and web coordinator at Loyola University New Orleans. In addition to her work on user experience studies, she participates in the library's reference and instruction programs as the liaison to the sociology, criminal justice, and honors departments. She has published and presented on topics including selection of a web-scale discovery system, promoting electronic resources, and using web services APIs. Her first library job was at the public library in Ann Arbor, Michigan, where she worked as a technohost, an information desk clerk, and later as a cataloger.

Cynthia Harbeson is currently the processing archivist and an assistant professor in Special Collections of the Carol Grotnes Belk Library and Information Commons at Appalachian State University in Boone, North Carolina. Previously, she worked as the reference librarian at Richmond Memorial Library in Marlborough, Connecticut, a town with an approximate population of 6,400. While there, Cynthia was in charge of adult programming, reference, original cataloging, the local history collection, and some collection development, which she found to be memorable and rewarding work.

Samantha Helmick, customer experience and outreach librarian at Burlington Public Library, Burlington, Iowa, obtained her MLIS from the University of Illinois. Samantha's memberships include Librarians Without Borders, International Library Network, American Library Association, Public Library Association, Library Information Technology Association, and the Iowa Library Association. She has appeared in *Modern Libraries Journal* and *Public Libraries* magazine.

James B. Hobbs is the online services coordinator at Loyola University New Orleans. He participates in the library's reference and instruction programs as the liaison to the biological sciences, chemistry, mathematics, physics, and psychological sciences departments. He also oversees contracts for electronic abstracting and indexing services and provides research assistance online and at the library's Learning Commons Desk. He created the university's first website for the library in 1995 and helps to maintain the current library website. He also oversees the library's interlibrary loan services.

Joshua K. Johnson, manager of the Davis County Library's North Branch located in Clearfield, Utah, holds an MLS from Emporia State and an MA in

English from Montana State. His memberships include the American Library Association, Public Librarian Association, and the Utah Library Association. His work appears in the *Rocky Mountain Review* (Rocky Mountain Modern Language Association) and *Journal of Buddhist Ethics*. He has also presented at the Utah Library Association on statistical analysis and library mythology. Joshua has an abiding interest in examining the profession academically and pragmatically. He blogs at www.joshinglibrarian.info.

Portia Kapraun is the adult services manager at Monticello-Union Township Public Library in Monticello, Indiana. The library serves 11,000 residents and hosts over 500 programs annually, including the Broadway Art Show and Murder Mystery Dinner Theater, all with less than ten FTE staff. She has appeared in *Time and Project Management Strategies for Librarians* (2013) and *Summary of Proceedings Sixty-Fifth Annual Conference of the American Theological Library Association* (2011). Portia received her MLIS from Dominican University, and is a member of the Indiana Library Federation.

Sarah Kaufman, MLS, MPA, has worked in public libraries for over fifteen years. As an outreach librarian at Tempe Public Library in Tempe, Arizona, she teaches educational programs for all ages at the main library and outreach locations. Ms. Kaufman also writes grants and coordinates family events for the library. She enjoys attending community events and partnering with local businesses and non-profit organizations. She has received an Arizona Library Association Youth Librarian of the Year Award and teaches classes as adjunct faculty in the Library Technician Program at Mesa Community College.

Joanna Kluever, director of Julia Hull District Library in Stillman Valley, Illinois, earned her MLIS from University of Illinois and her MA from Western Illinois University. In her current position she has expanded library programming for specific user groups, increased patron attendance, and helped redefine the library's role in the community by rewriting its strategic plan. Her most recent publication includes a chapter from *The Frugal Librarian: Thriving in Tough Economic Times* (2011), "Creating and Sustaining Community-Focused Programs."

RoseAleta Laurell, library director, Bell Whittington Library, Portland, Texas, has been a library director for over twenty-five years. She holds an MLS from Texas Woman's University and a certificate of advance studies with a focus on rural and small libraries from the University of North Texas. She was a founding member of Texas Library Association's Small Community Libraries Roundtable. She has received numerous state and national awards. Her library was named a 2013 Finalist in *Library Journal*'s Best Small Library in America and was a 2013 finalist for the Institute of Museum and Library Services National Medal.

Melanie A. Lyttle is the head of public services at Madison Public Library in Madison, Ohio. She received her MLS in 2003 from the University of Illinois at Urbana–Champaign. Melanie was an ALSC-sponsored 2010 ALA Emerging Leader. She also participated in Library Leadership Ohio in 2008. In 2013, she was the Ohio Library Council's Northeast Chapter Action Council Coordinator, and she is a member of the Children and Technology Committee for ALSC. Most importantly, Melanie is known in her community as the "Crabby Librarian."

Lauren Magnuson is the systems and emerging technologies librarian at California State University Northridge. She obtained her master's in library and information science from the University of Missouri–Columbia. She also holds a master's in educational technology with an emphasis on learning systems design and development. Lauren has also worked as a systems coordinator for the Private Academic Library Network of Indiana (PALNI). Her primary interests include open-source software adoption in libraries, Python scripting, and XML/XSLT.

Dwight McInvaill, Georgetown County Library director in Georgetown, South Carolina, since 1996, has received such honors as the National Advocacy Award from the American Library Association (2005); National Medal for Library Service from the Institute of Museum and Library Services (2007); I Love My Librarian Award (2009) from the Carnegie Foundation and the *New York Times*. He served recently on the board of the Association for Rural and Small Libraries and on the steering committee of the Digital Public Library of America. He believes in the power of libraries to transform lives, especially in rural communities.

Sharon M. Miller, library director at Mechanics' Institute Library, San Francisco, California, obtained her MLIS from San Jose California State University. She is a member of the American Library Association, serves on the Library Technology Industry Advisory Committee for the Library Technology program at San Francisco City College, and has served on the board of the Bay Area Library and Information Network. Sharon's prior library employment includes Calgary Alberta Public Library and City College of San Francisco.

LouAnn Morehouse returned to school to obtain an MLS in public librarianship after twenty years as an administrator, program developer, and grants officer for agencies serving adults engaged in lifelong learning. Since graduating from Appalachian State University, Boone, North Carolina, in 2012, she has developed programs for adult patrons at her county library and is the secretary of the board of directors of the Friends of the Watauga County Public Library in Boone. She is employed by the regional magazine *Carolina Mountain Life* as an editor and feature writer.

Vanessa Neblett has worked for the Orange County Library System in Orlando, Florida, for the past ten years as a librarian, digital access architect, and is currently the assistant manager in the reference central department. Vanessa coordinates and has interviewed a number of Orange County residents for the Orlando Memory project. She earned an MLIS from the University of South Florida, an MA in history from the Claremont Graduate University, and a BA in history from the University of Dallas.

Padma Polepeddi is the coordinator and supervisor of outreach services at the Arapahoe Library District in Colorado. She coordinates implementation of decisions in the areas of outreach to special populations, language, literacy through foreign language collections, and ESL classes partnerships. She supervises mobile library services to residents who lack easy access to libraries as well as outreach to seniors. She was named 2008 *Library Journal* Mover and Shaker for her passion about diversity. She has an MA in English from University of Hyderabad, India, and is currently pursuing her doctorate at Emporia State University, Kansas.

Brian A. Reynolds, library director at San Luis Obispo County Library, San Luis Obispo, California, obtained his MLS from the University of California, Los Angeles, and his master in public administration from California State University, Chico. Brian's memberships include the California Library Association and American Library Association. For the past six years, he has served as adjunct faculty at San Jose State University's School of Library and Information Science. Brian's professional interests focus on the primacy of people and their relationships, using and supporting libraries for the common good.

Nancy Richey is a reference librarian, Warren County Public Library in Bowling Green, Kentucky, and image librarian at the Special Collections Library at Western Kentucky University. She has an MLS from the University of Kentucky and is interested in local history and genealogical research. She recently appeared in *Library Journal* and has made presentations to the National Genealogical Society and the Joint Conference of Librarians of Color (JCLC), which brought together a diverse group of public and academic librarians with community participants to explore issues of diversity in libraries and how they affect the ethnic communities.

April Ritchie is the adult services coordinator of the Erlanger Branch of the Kenton County Public Library, Erlanger, Kentucky. She has worked as a librarian and as a department head in Arkansas, Indiana, and Kentucky since obtaining her MSLS from the University of Kentucky. She is the statewide coordinator for the Kentucky Sister Library Project, an endeavor of the Kentucky Public Library Association. Her feature article on sister libraries was published in *American Libraries*. She was selected as one of *Library Journal*'s Movers and Shakers for 2012.

David Robinson, adult service librarian with the Shenandoah County Library in Edinburg, Virginia, received his MLIS from the Catholic University of America in Washington, DC. He has worked at the Library of Congress and the DC Public Library. Prior to becoming a librarian, he studied and taught English literature at Purdue University in West Lafayette, Indiana, where he received his PhD. He has also taught English and composition studies at Wayne State University in Detroit, Michigan.

Shane Roopnarine has worked as a librarian in the public library field for the past five years. Prior to joining the Orange County Library System in Orlando, Florida, he worked for Florida State University Libraries while enrolled in graduate school. Shane is involved with several projects that focus on digital preservation of local history, including Orlando Memory and EPOCH (Electronically Preserving Obituaries as Cultural Heritage). He attended the Florida State University, where he earned an MLIS, and the University of Central Florida.

Johnna Schultz, adult services manager, joined the Helen Matthes Library, Effingham, Illinois, in 2003. She has held a variety of positions, including circulation manager and operations director. Johnna holds a BA in English with middle and high school teaching certifications from Eastern Illinois University. She presented at the Illinois Library Association Annual Conference in 2013. Johnna has a strong desire to promote literacy and lifelong learning at the Helen Matthes Library and within the larger Effingham community.

Diana Stirling has been a rural public library director for more than seven years, most recently at the Mammoth Public Library in Mammoth, Arizona. Diana is passionate about the vital role of libraries in supporting and enlivening rural communities. She is a member of the Association for Rural and Small Libraries and has presented at the Arizona Library Association conference, LibTech, and the ARSL annual conference. She holds a master's degree in education and has published internationally on education topics.

Linda Burkey Wade, an elected trustee of the Brown County Public Library in Mt. Sterling, Illinois, began her career in this small town public library. She obtained her MLIS from Dominican University and MS in instructional design from Western Illinois University. Wade is in *Pre- and Post-Retirement Tips for Librarians* (2011) and *Jump-Start Your Career as a Digital Librarian: LITA Guide* (2012). She is the head of digitization at the WIU Libraries in Macomb, Illinois. She received the 2010 Distinguished Service Award for innovation and dedication and the 2012 Community Service Award.

Shawn D. Walsh is the emerging services and technologies librarian for Madison Public Library in Madison, Ohio. Working in libraries since 1997, he was most recently a senior technology analyst for the Northeast Ohio Regional Library System. Shawn has a BS/AS in computer information systems from Youngstown State University. Shawn is also responsible for maintaining Madison Public Library's technology infrastructure and oversees computer and technology instruction to patrons and staff. Within the community, Shawn is best known for school visits and the loud, messy elementary, tween, and teen programs he runs.

Amy White has been the director of the Lisbon Public Library in Lisbon, Iowa since 1989. Originally from Virginia, Amy received her BA in English from the University of North Carolina at Greensboro and her MFA in creative writing from the University of Virginia. She is a certified public librarian through the State Library of Iowa certification program. Besides her job, her passions include theater, thrift shopping, and knitting. She belongs to one playwriting group and two book discussion groups. Amy also serves on her local community theatre board and is active in their productions.

Judith Wines is the director of (and only librarian at) the Altamont Free Library in Altamont, New York. She is an active member of the New York Library Association, where she has served on the board of the New Members Round Table and presented on topics including Leadership for New Librarians and Thematic Arrangement of Picture Books. Prior to joining the Altamont Library in 2005, Judith was a Peace Corps volunteer in Jordan. Judith holds an MSIS from the University at Albany (SUNY) and a BA in classical languages from Williams College in Williamstown, Massachusetts.

Joy Worland is the director of the Joslin Memorial Library in Waitsfield, Vermont. She is co-chair of the Amelia Bloomer Project, an ALA committee that recommends feminist books for youth. She has published in *Children & Libraries: The Journal of the Association for Library Service to Children*, writes a biweekly column about books and library activities for *The Valley Reporter* in Waitsfield, and has contributed book reviews to other Vermont publications. She has an MLS from the University of North Texas, and has presented at ALA and Vermont Library Association conferences.